FEMINIST CIRCULATIONS

LAUER SERIES IN RHETORIC AND COMPOSITION
Editors: Thomas Rickert and Jennifer Bay

The Lauer Series in Rhetoric and Composition honors the contributions Janice Lauer has made to the emergence of Rhetoric and Composition as a disciplinary study. It publishes scholarship that carries on Professor Lauer's varied work in the history of written rhetoric, disciplinarity in composition studies, contemporary pedagogical theory, and written literacy theory and research.

BOOKS IN THE SERIES

FEMINIST CIRCULATIONS

Rhetorical Explorations across
Space and Time

Edited by Jessica Enoch,
Danielle Griffin, and Karen Nelson

Parlor Press
Anderson, South Carolina
www.parlorpress.com

Parlor Press LLC, Anderson, South Carolina, USA

Printed in the United States of America
S A N: 2 5 4 - 8 8 7 9

Library of Congress Cataloging-in-Publication Data on File

978-1-64317-242-2 (paperback)
978-1-64317-243-9 (hardcover)
978-1-64317-244-6 (pdf)
978-1-64317-245-3 (epub)

1 2 3 4 5

Lauer Series in Rhetoric and Composition
Editors: Thomas Rickert and Jennifer Bay

Cover design by Karen Nelson.

Printed on acid-free paper.

Parlor Press, LLC is an independent publisher of scholarly and trade titles
in print and multimedia formats. This book is available in paper, cloth and
eBook formats from Parlor Press on the World Wide Web at http://www.
parlorpress.com or through online and brick-and-mortar bookstores. For
submission information or to find out about Parlor Press publications, write
to Parlor Press, 3015 Brackenberry Drive, Anderson, South Carolina, 29621,
or email editor@parlorpress.com.

Contents

III Connections through Circulation   *171*

Feminist Circulations

1 CIRCULATING FEMINIST RHETORICS: AN INTRODUCTION

Jessica Enoch, Danielle Griffin, and Karen Nelson

Circulation. This rhetorical concept animates and distinguishes the feminist scholarship within this collection. At base, one way to define circulation from a rhetorical perspective is to see it as the suasive consequentiality of movement. Or as Laurie Gries writes, and as we elaborate on below, circulation prompts scholars to attend to the "rhetorical process" that enables "people, ideas, images, and discourse [to] become persuasive as they move through the world and enter various associations" (12). Speaking in unison, the chapters herein demonstrate the potential for this concept to enhance understandings of what women's rhetorics can do and how feminist rhetorical studies can operate. To articulate the overarching project of *Feminist Circulations* in this introduction, we consider the intellectual history of circulation within feminist rhetorical studies, define the term and its attending methodology, and assert the importance of circulation as a guiding principle for our summative work. As we establish the theme for the volume, we also use this introduction to identify the related contributions the chapters make in terms of feminist recovery and rhetorical theory as well as research methods and methodologies.

Before delving deeply into the tenets of feminist circulation studies that drive this collection, we want to mark the specific rhetorical context that inspired this collection and enabled these ideas to circulate to our readers. The seeds of this collection were planted in spring 2017, when we gathered in College Park, Maryland, to celebrate the careers of Jane Donawerth and Shirley Wilson Logan at a conference titled *Women, Rhetoric, Writing*. The implicit exigence was for presenters to show how these two exemplary scholar-teacher-mentors had inspired the presenters' research and writing.[1] The conference itself brought to life the networks and connections Donawerth and Logan had made throughout their fantastic careers; conveners' contributions served as evidence of the ways their ideas had inspired those across the academy. Indeed, the conference made clear how Donawerth's and Logan's ideas have circulated through fields from rhetoric and composition studies to women's studies and from early modern literary studies to African American literature and rhetoric. When we decided to collect work for this volume, then, the theme of circulation became a distinct connective tissue among the chapters, and with this theme, we once again recognize Donawerth's and Logan's abiding influence on a generation of scholarship.

In 1999, Shirley Wilson Logan anticipated this discussion regarding circulation of argument in her text *"We Are Coming": The Persuasive Discourse of Nineteenth-Century Black Women*. Here, she turns readers' attention to the ways arguments carry and echo across time and circumstance. In her study of rhetors such as Sojourner Truth and Fannie Barrier Williams, Logan uses the term *recurrence* to describe the argumentative repetitions she traced across African American women's rhetorical traditions. As Logan explains, Black women's arguments and strategies have at times repeated because they have "arisen from similar but not identical rhetorical situations" (xiv). Logan argues that they do so because they are "common practices that were molded and constrained by prevailing conventions and traditions" (xiv). Arguments recur because exigencies recur, and one way to understand and discern a tradition within African American women's rhetoric, as Logan models, is by tracking rhetorics that circulate and recirculate due to exigencies and situations.

Donawerth, too, sharpens feminist rhetorical attention to circulation through her 2012 work *Conversational Rhetoric: The Rise and Fall of a Women's Tradition, 1600–1900*. Attuned to the workings of circulation, it is clear that ideas flow and move through conversation. Donawerth's study, however, "develops a history of women's rhetorical theory based on conversation as a model of discourse" (9). That is, her research reveals how women crafted theories of conversation geared towards "small group communication, from any private, informal verbal communication, to artful verbal dialogue used in informative leisure and social activities" (11). Indeed, the theories Donawerth excavates and studies are significant because they counterbalance masculinist ideas about rhetorical practice: conversational rhetoric "privilege[s] consensus, collaboration, and collectivity over competition" (12). Donawerth thus paves the way for feminist scholars invested in circulation to consider how women rhetorical theorists have taught readers to effectively engage in conversation so that their thoughts, ideas, and arguments could not only travel but also change shape through collaborative interchange.

The contributors to this volume build on Logan's and Donawerth's work as well as over twenty-five years of feminist rhetorical scholarship that has wrestled with circulation, taking root in practices and methods that emphasize mapping, mobility, and movement. Cheryl Glenn helped to initiate this discussion with her landmark monograph *Rhetoric Retold*, in which she called feminist scholars to remap the rhetorical tradition so that through their recovery work they would move off the "Heritage Turnpike" of rhetorical history to find women rhetors in unchartered territory (4). The remapping Glenn called for aimed to take scholars to "more places, introducing us to more people, complicating our understanding in more ways than did the traditional map" (4). It has. This idea that feminist scholars need to plot new figures on the map of rhetorical history and be more conscious of how they take up this mapping process from a methodological perspective has invigorated feminist research, with scholars such as Tarez Samra Graban, Barbara L'Eplattenier, Eileen Schell and K. J. Rawson, Cristina D. Ramírez, Don Unger and Fernando Sanchez, Sarah Noble Frank, Jacqueline Jones Royster ("Disciplinary"), and David Gold adding depth and complexity to these cartographic conversations.

As feminist scholars have mapped and remapped the rhetorical terrain, they have also turned this metaphor of mapping kaleidoscopically, to borrow a term from Royster, to concentrate on the relationship between rhetoric and mobility (*Traces* 277). That is, as scholars have reflected on their own historiographic movements off the "Heritage Turnpike," they have also considered the spaces their subjects could or could not occupy, where they could or could not go, and how this movement (or lack thereof) inflected their rhetorical production. To be sure, women throughout history have been constrained in terms of their mobility, and this is especially true in terms of how they have been barred from esteemed rhetorical spaces of the platform, podium, and pulpit. Scholars such as Nan Johnson, Roxanne Mountford, Lisa Shaver (*Beyond*), Lindal Buchanan, Shirley Wilson Logan (*Liberating*), and Sarah Moseley have explored the ways women negotiated this constraint to move into and create new rhetorical territories that would cultivate their rhetorical production. Taking this conversation in still other fruitful directions, scholars such as Sarah Hallenbeck, Jessica Enoch, Alyssa A. Samek, Tiffany Lewis, Shaver ("No cross"), and Carly Woods have considered the rhetorical conditions that shape women's actual, physical mobility; how travel has enabled women's rhetorical production; and the ways women's movements can be seen as rhetorics in and of themselves.

This feminist investment in mapping, movement, and mobility culminates, in our eyes, as the prime rhetorical concern for this volume: circulation. As Gries writes in her introduction to the edited collection *Circulation, Writing, Rhetoric,* circulation has become an "emergent threshold concept" in rhetorical studies due to the way circulation can "deepen our understanding of rhetoric and writing in motion" (6). Seeing this term as one especially important for feminist scholars, Jacqueline Jones Royster and Gesa Kirsch name social circulation as a key feminist rhetorical practice that invites a research methodology in which scholars track "rhetorical interactions across space and time" (98)—an idea we echo in the title of this collection. For Royster and Kirsch, social circulation enables scholars to

> reimagine the dynamic functioning of women's work in domains of discourse, re-envision cultural flow in specific localities, and link analyses of these phenomena in an informative and compelling way in support of amplifying and magnifying the impacts and consequences of women's rhetoric as we forward an enlarged view of rhetoric as a human enterprise. (98)

The methodology of social circulation could thus be seen to encompass the feminist investments in mapping, mobility, and movement as well as recurrence and conversation. Circulation offers scholars an analytic that discerns women's rhetorical significance in new ways. Here the goal is to track how, why, and for what purpose women and their rhetorics have moved; to explore the ways these rhetorics have been taken up, recast, and mobilized in various rhetorical situations and for particular ends.

The *feminist* impulse in this collection, however, amplifies how gender and power animate rhetorical circulation. Specifically, the work is to consider how power inflects rhetorical opportunities for women's rhetorics and how possibilities for circulation open up or close down (speed up or slow down) due to the positionality of the rhetor. Furthermore, applying a feminist analytic to circulation also foregrounds the intersectional nature of women's rhetorical productions. This means that women's rhetorics and the ways they circulate are affected by the rhetor's gender identifications as well as by their raced, classed, cultured, religious, national/transnational, and temporal experiences. Indeed, among the central characters studied in this collection are early modern laborers, letter writers, petitioners, and embroiderers; African American elocutionists, freedom singers, and bloggers; Muslim religious leaders; Quaker suffragists; South African filmmakers; nineteenth-century conduct book writers; and twenty-first-century pop stars. Their many and overlapping identifications condition how these women's rhetorics took shape and how they and their rhetorics were able to move. One outcome of the feminist analysis that we find compelling is that circulation prompts a concern not only for the movement from one place or one time to another, but also to the connections that occur at the nexus of these meetings. Attending to these connections reveals how rhetors take advantage of still more opportunities to craft different kinds of feminist practices.

Building on this final point, as editors, we see that rhetorical circulations create possibilities for rhetorical listening, deep reflection, coalition building, and allyship. Indeed, feminist rhetoricians, from the start, have meditated on and attempted to make sense of what it means to cross borders intellectually, culturally, politically, and physically, bringing different scholarly perspectives, identity positions, political imperatives, and cultural realities into conversation (see for instance, Lisa Ede, Cheryl Glenn, and Andrea Lunsford's "Border Crossing"). This investment within feminist rhetorical studies is further evidenced by the excellent work of Lisa Flores, Adela Licona and Karma Chávez, Stacey Waite, and Patricia Bizzell and K. J. Rawson, and the vibrancy of this discussion reveals a deep feminist commitment to speaking across difference and meditating on the complexities of what Krista Ratcliffe and Royster have called "cross-cultural conduct."[2] We see the chapters in *Feminist Circulations* not only participating in and underscoring the critical importance of this conversation and feminist rhetorical practice, but also offering the field new strategies for how connection and coalition building can take place.

As we celebrate these connective possibilities that circulation may create, we also hesitate. The enterprise behind this collection also highlights a more fraught aspect of circulation: disjunctions and disruptions, the *lack* of tradition on which to build, the many moments when women's places within patriarchal systems short-circuit the transmission of ideas or arguments or efforts to move within the structures that circumscribe their lives and voices. That is, just as women's rhetorics have moved and circulated, just as there have been conversations and recurrences, there have also been disconnections, interruptions, divergences, immobilities, isolations, and silences that have prevented women and their rhetorics from circulating. We hope our readers see this volume as an invitation to mine the constraints that attend circulation in all its forms.

EARLY MODERN CONTRIBUTIONS

A major strength of this volume is its investment in bringing early modern women's rhetorics and writing into the conversation about feminist circulation. Chapters by Karen Nelson, Erin Sadlack, Danielle Griffin, and Michelle Osherow center attention on women's rhetorical contributions from the sixteenth through eighteenth centuries—moments in women's history not often studied with rhetorical scholarship. In line with our discussion of the specific practices circulation prompts, however, the work of the contributors is not simply to draw attention to this scholarly lacunae, but instead to consider how early modern to eighteenth-century women's rhetorics have circulated within and connected to other temporalities. By widening the historical trajectory of feminist scholarship and creating new circulations, this volume enables readers to learn more about pre-modern women's rhetorics and see them in relation to their nineteenth-, twentieth-, and twenty-first-century counterparts.

By creating this emphasis within *Feminist Circulations*, this volume also engages and builds on long-developed historiography and analysis in early modern women's studies, and we hope the bridge we help build here is one that creates more interaction with rhetorical studies. In recent decades, recovery of women's writings in sixteenth and seventeenth century European literature has flourished, and scholars have incorporated women's writings into the literary canon and classroom.[3] Indeed, Patricia Phillippy's recent volume on early modern women writers offers a particularly fruitful overview of the field as it currently operates. Focusing particularly on questions of circulation, early modern scholars such as Frances E. Dolan, Margaret Ferguson, Kim F. Hall, Ann Rosalind Jones, and Mihoko Suzuki trace women's places in culture and literature via methods related to the history of ideas. Here, representations of women are at the core, and scholarly analyses consider the conceptual categories associated with women and then assess the transmission of these ideas in England, France, Italy, and Spain; across Europe; in the

Mediterranean region; or in the trans-Atlantic context to evaluate how these gendered topoi function in the cultures concerned.

Adding even more depth to this discussion is the early modern scholarship that assesses the materiality of texts and the actual social and news networks of the period. Here, scholars examine all sorts of social practices such as reading, literacy, letter-writing, and book production to discover women's influence and its association with the propagation of ideas. Endeavors by scholars such as Ruth Ahnert, James Daybell, Heidi Brayman Hackel, Elizabeth Mazzola, Catherine Medici, Kate Narveson, Montserrat Piera, Erin Sadlack, Elisabeth Salter, Helen Smith, Edith Snook, Joad Raymond, and Noah Moxham reveal the shared affinities between circulation studies in rhetoric and those in early modern studies. *Feminist Circulations* strengthens these connections by taking a rhetorical focus, but it also points to the work that could still be done to consider how early modern women's rhetorics have circulated within and beyond these temporal moments.

CONTRIBUTIONS OF METHOD AND METHODOLOGY

The collection is marked by the variety in contributors' research and analytical choices that signal the depth of possibility for feminist circulation studies. To generate their claims, contributors draw from and make use of a breadth of archival and primary documents: music videos, tweets, petitions, letters, embroidery work, speeches, memoirs, diaries, and made-for-television movies. Authors read these "texts" with scrutiny and imagination, adding distinction to their chapters' arguments about circulation by zeroing in on specific rhetorical concepts. Chapters focus, for example, on their subjects' rhetorical agency, cultivation of ethos, development of rhetorical education, capacities for social networking, collective and collaborative authorship, and kairotic interventions. Making use of a robust array of theoretical lenses, contributors sharpen their analyses of archival/primary texts by leveraging such concepts as Carolyn Miller's *genre theory*, Joan Wallach Scott's *fantasy echo*, Matthew Kendrick's *laboring subjectivity*, and Gérard Genette's *paratexts*. Contributors also define and divine their own rhetorical theories, concepts, and genres—*rhetorical solidarity, embodied remembering,* and *conduct biography,* for example—to distinguish the circulation work under study. Highlighting yet another component of the circulation at work in this volume, individual chapters not only intervene in conversations with rhetorical and early modern studies but also speak to Islamic studies, Biblical scholarship, religious rhetorics, Reformation history, South African studies, media studies, civil rights rhetorics, whiteness studies, and intersectional social justice efforts in our contemporary moment.

CHAPTER DESCRIPTIONS

Feminist Circulations is organized into three sections that emphasize different types of circulation. The first, "Tracking Arguments," explores ways that women's rhetorical contributions travel across geographical space and highlights themes of mobility, movement, and migration. In her chapter, Jane Donawerth examines Hallie Quinn Brown's journals as a way to highlight and explore nineteenth-century African American women's literacy. In doing so, Donawerth especially notices the role of mobility, both in the literal sense reflective of Brown's "travelling career" as well as an "expansion of rhetorical literacy for women." Karen Nelson underscores the role of movement in "The Rhetoric of Reform: The Maydens of London, Liberty, and Marriage in 1567." Studying a pamphlet by a group of early modern maidservants, Nelson shows how their arguments about women's work mirrored debates about the marriage of Elizabeth I and religious politics, thereby demonstrating how localized arguments about women circulated in national and international debates. In the final chapter of this section, Nabila Hijazi expands visions of women's rhetoric outside of the West by analyzing the rhetoric of Zainab Al-Ghazali, a mid-twentieth century Islamic activist who argued against the circulation of Western feminism to her region. Though born in Egypt, Al-Ghazali's work addressing Muslim women's activism and religious rhetoric was influential across the Middle East. Hijazi focuses on texts such as Al-Ghazali's memoir to argue against the circulation of Western feminism to her region and discern her own ideas regarding Muslim women's gender roles. Together, these three chapters explore how women's rhetorics and literacies circulate geographically across a variety of local, national, and international boundaries.

The next section, "Circulating Genres," continues this theme of movement but shifts its focus to genre. The four contributors in this section analyze a variety of genres authored by or focused on women—petitions, conduct books, song, and film—exploring how these genres have moved and taken new shape. Erin Sadlack examines petitions of Elizabethan women, texts that "represent an archive of ordinary women's voices." Sadlack highlights the ways women negotiated and remade the genre conventions of the petition, enabling them to craft their own ethos and participate in Elizabethan politics. Lisa Zimmerelli considers how early modern conduct literature is remade in the nineteenth-century U.S. context through the genre of the conduct biography. Examining this genre, Zimmerelli explores the ways child readers learned gendered and raced constructions of girlhood and boyhood. Elizabeth Ellis Miller, too, highlights genre change over time as a key point of analysis in "Listening to Remember: Bernice Johnson Reagon and Embodied Memories of Civil Rights." Studying Reagon's use and representation of the freedom song, Miller reads "genre blending and appropriation" as central to Reagon's role as an African American activist who made and remade the genre of the freedom song throughout the civil rights movement and beyond. Lastly, Adele Seeff examines how the genre of film mediates themes of gender by examining a South African adaptation of Shakespeare's *Macbeth*. Seeff argues that the South African adaptation *Death of a Queen* "consistently revises Shakespeare's text to give women agency," and she explores the filmic affordances of the adaptation to showcase how deployments of Shakespeare circulate on an international stage. For the chapters in this section, studies of genre reveal much about how women's arguments and arguments about women circulate in a variety of sociohistorical moments.

The final section of this collection, "Connections through Circulation," examines feminist circulation from the perspective of time, with authors specifically asking: what happens at the moment of temporal connection? Danielle Griffin examines two petitions by working women in the early modern period addressing maidservants' working conditions. Although separated by over a hundred years, the petitions share many rhetorical strategies, and they are particularly marked by their similar deployment of collectivism and demonstration of class consciousness. Michele Osherow also engages the rhetorical work of early modern women but instead examines their embroidery practices. Osherow focuses on seventeenth-century women's embroidering of biblical characters and how the needleworkers exercised agency in their textiles through their engagements with biblical themes and their specific representations of Susanna. In "Just (Shut Up and) Listen: A Black Feminist Tradition of Teaching Rhetorical Solidarity," Ruth Osorio uses Shirley Wilson Logan's concept of *recurrence* to track Black women's efforts to teach rhetorical solidarity to white women. Focusing on the rhetorical connections between figures like nineteenth-century novelist and rhetor Harriet Jacobs and blogger Mia McKenzie two centuries later, Osorio explores concerns of allyship and solidarity. In the final chapter of this section, Jessica Enoch employs the concept of Joan Wallach Scott's *fantasy echo* to examine the "historiographic fantasies" that link twentieth-century suffragist Alice Paul with twenty-first century pop star Lady Gaga in a 2012 video entitled "Bad Romance: Women's Suffrage." In making such connections between women across time, Enoch considers what we remember and forget about various women as we seek to make historical connections. Shirley Logan offers an afterword to the collection, meditating on how recurrences—often across time and space—contribute to studies of women's rhetorical history and feminist rhetorical practice. Bringing her own mother's letters into circulation with the figures studied in this volume, Logan prompts us to think more deeply and capaciously about circulation's rhetorical power and promise.

NOTES

1. Complete program details are available at https://english.umd.edu/research-innovation/center-literary-and-comparative-studies/conferences/women-rhetoric-writing-2017.

2. See Ratcliffe, *Rhetorical Listening,* and Royster, "When."

3. See Pamela Joseph Benson and Victoria Kirkham, editors; Danielle Clarke; Lynn Enterline; Anne M. Haselkorn and Betty S. Travitsky, editors; Elizabeth Mazzola; Lynette McGrath; Patricia Pender and Rosalind Smith, editors; Jennifer Richards and Alison Thorne, editors; Paul Salzman; Betty S. Travitsky.

WORKS CITED

Ahnert, Ruth. "Maps versus Networks." *News Networks in Early Modern Europe,* edited by Joad Raymond and Noah Moxham, Brill, 2016, pp. 130–57.

Ahnert, Ruth, and Sebastian E. Ahnert. "Protestant Letter Networks in the Reign of Mary I: A Quantitative Approach." *ELH,* vol. 82, no. 1, 2015, pp. 1–33.

Benson, Pamela Joseph, and Victoria Kirkham, editors. *Strong Voices, Weak History: Early Women Writers & Canons in England, France, & Italy.* U of Michigan P, 2005.

Bizzell, Patricia, and K. J. Rawson. "Coalition of Who? Regendering Scholarly Community in the History of Rhetoric." *Peitho*, vol. 18, no. 1, 2015, pp. 110–24.

Buchanan, Lindal. *Regendering Delivery: The Fifth Canon and Antebellum Women Rhetors.* Southern Illinois UP, 2005.

Carrillo Rowe, Aimee, and Adela C. Licona. "Moving Locations: The Politics of Identities in Motion." *NWSA Journal: National Women's Studies Association Journal*, vol. 17, no. 2, 2005, pp. 11–14.

Chávez, Karma R. *Queer Migration Politics: Activist Rhetoric and Coalitional Possibilities.* U of Illinois P, 2017.

Clarke, Danielle. *The Politics of Early Modern Women's Writing.* Longman, 2001.

Daybell, James. *The Material Letter in Early Modern England: Manuscript Letters and the Culture and Practices of Letter-Writing, 1512–1635.* Palgrave Macmillan, 2012.

Dolan, Frances E. *Dangerous Familiars: Representations of Domestic Crime in England, 1550–1700.* Cornell UP, 1994.

—. *Whores of Babylon: Catholicism, Gender, and Seventeenth-Century Print Culture.* Cornell UP, 1999.

Donawerth, Jane. *Conversational Rhetoric: The Rise and Fall of a Women's Tradition, 1600–1900.* Southern Illinois UP, 2013.

Ede, Lisa, Cheryl Glenn, and Andrea Lunsford. "Border Crossings: Intersections of Rhetoric and Feminism." *Rhetorica*, vol. 13, no. 4, 1995, pp. 401–41.

Enoch, Jessica. *Domestic Occupations: Spatial Rhetorics and Women's Work.* Southern Illinois UP, 2019.

Enterline, Lynn. *Shakespeare's Schoolroom: Rhetoric, Discipline, Emotion.* U of Pennsylvania P, 2012.

Ferguson, Margaret W. *Dido's Daughters: Literacy, Gender, and Empire in Early Modern England and France.* U of Chicago P, 2003.

Flores, Lisa A. "Creating Discursive Space through a Rhetoric of Difference: Chicana Feminists Craft a Homeland." *The Routledge Reader in Rhetorical Criticism*, edited by Brian L. Ott and Greg Dickinson, Routledge, 2013, pp. 746–60.

Frank, Sarah Noble. "Feminist Historiography As If: Performativity and Representation in Feminist Histories of Rhetoric." *Rhetoric Review*, vol. 36, no. 3, 2017, pp. 187–99.

Genette, Gérard. *Paratexts: Thresholds of Interpretation.* Cambridge UP, 1977.

Glenn, Cheryl. *Rhetoric Retold: Regendering the Tradition from Antiquity through the Renaissance.* Southern Illinois UP, 1997.

Gold, David. "Remapping Revisionist Historiography." *College Composition and Communication,* vol. 64, no. 1, Sept. 2012, pp. 15–34.

Graban, Tarez Samra. *Women's Irony: Rewriting Feminist Rhetorical Histories.* Southern Illinois UP, 2015.

Gries, Laurie E. "Circulation as an Emerging Threshold Concept." *Circulation, Writing, and Rhetoric,* edited by Gries and Collin Gifford Brooke, Utah State UP, 2018, pp. 3–26.

Hall, Kim F. *Things of Darkness: Economies of Race and Gender in Early Modern England.* Cornell UP, 1995.

Hallenbeck, Sarah. *Claiming the Bicycle: Women, Rhetoric, and Technology in Nineteenth-Century America.* Southern Illinois UP, 2016.

Haselkorn, Anne M. and Betty S. Travitsky, editors. *The Renaissance Englishwoman in Print: Counterbalancing the Canon.* U of Massachusetts P, 1990.

Johnson, Nan. *Gender and Rhetorical Space in American Life, 1866–1910.* Southern Illinois UP, 2002.

Jones, Ann Rosalind. *The Currency of Eros: Women's Love Lyric in Europe, 1540–1620.* Indiana UP, 1990.

Kendrick, Matthew. *At Work in the Early Modern English Theater: Valuing Labor.* Fairleigh Dickinson UP, 2015.

L'Eplattenier, Barbara E. "Opinion: An Argument for Archival Research Methods: Thinking Beyond Methodology." *College English,* vol. 72, no. 1, Sep 2009, pp. 67–79.

Lesser, Zachary and Benedict S. Robinson, editors. *Textual Conversations in the Renaissance: Ethics, Authors, Technologies.* Ashgate, 2006.

Lewis, Tiffany. "Mediating Political Mobility as Stunt-Girl Entertainment: Newspaper Coverage of New York's Suffrage Hike to Albany." *American Journalism,* vol. 36, no. 1, 2019, pp. 99–123.

Licona, Adela C. *Zines in Third Space: Radical Cooperation and Borderlands Rhetoric.* State U of New York P, 2012.

Licona, Adela C, and Karma R Chávez. "Relational Literacies and Their Coalitional Possibilities." *Peitho,* vol. 18, no. 1, 2015, pp. 96–107.

Logan, Shirley Wilson. *Liberating Language: Sites of Rhetorical Education in Nineteenth-Century Black America.* Southern Illinois UP, 2008.

—. *"We are coming": The Persuasive Discourse of Nineteenth-Century Black Women.* Southern Illinois UP, 1999.

Mack, Peter. *A History of Renaissance Rhetoric.* Oxford UP, 2011.

Mazzola, Elizabeth. *Learning and Literacy in Female Hands, 1520–1698.* Ashgate, 2013.

McGrath, Lynette. *Subjectivity and Women's Poetry in Early Modern England: Why on the ridge should she desire to go?* Ashgate, 2002.

Medici, Catherine. "Using Network Analysis to Understand Early Modern Women." *Early Modern Women: An Interdisciplinary Journal,* vol. 13, no. 1, Fall 2018, pp. 153–63.

Miller, Carolyn R, and Amy J Devitt, editors. *Landmark Essays on Rhetorical Genre Studies.* Routledge, 2019.

Miller, Carolyn R, and Ashley R Kelly, editors. *Emerging Genres in New Media Environments.* Palgrave Macmillan, 2017.

Moseley, Sarah. "'A Strong Leadership That Does Not Show': Ladies Auxiliaries as Women's First Entrance Points into the Fire Department." *Rhetoric Review,* vol. 36, no. 4, 2017, pp. 348–62.

Mountford, Roxanne. *The Gendered Pulpit: Preaching in American Protestant Spaces.* Southern Illinois UP, 2003.

Narveson, Kate. *Bible Readers and Lay Writers in Early Modern England: Gender and Self-Definition in an Emergent Writing Culture.* Ashgate, 2012.

Pender, Patricia, and Rosalind Smith, editors. *Material Cultures of Early Modern Women's Writing.* Palgrave Macmillan, 2014.

Phillippy, Patricia, editor. *A History of Early Modern Women's Writing.* Cambridge UP, 2018.

Piera, Montserrat. *Women Readers and Writers in Medieval Iberia: Spinning the Text.* Brill, 2019.

Ramírez, Cristina D. *Occupying Our Space: The Mestiza Rhetorics of Mexican Women Journalists and Activists, 1875–1942.* U of Arizona P, 2015.

Ratcliffe, Krista. *Rhetorical Listening: Identification, Gender, Whiteness.* Southern Illinois UP, 2005.

Richards, Jennifer, and Alison Thorne, editors. *Rhetoric, Women, and Politics in Early Modern England.* Routledge, 2007.

Royster, Jacqueline Jones. "Disciplinary Landscaping, or Contemporary Challenges in the History of Rhetoric." *Philosophy & Rhetoric,* vol. 36, no. 2, 2003, pp. 148–67.

—. *Traces of a Stream: Literacy and Social Change among African American Women.* U of Pittsburgh P, 2000.

—. "When the First Voice You Hear Is Not Your Own." *College Composition and Communication,* vol. 47, no. 1, 1996, pp. 29–40.

Royster, Jacqueline Jones, and Gesa E. Kirsch. *Feminist Rhetorical Practices: New Horizons for Rhetoric, Composition, and Literacy Studies.* Southern Illinois UP, 2012.

Sadlack, Erin A. *The French Queen's Letters: Mary Tudor Brandon and the Politics of Marriage in Sixteenth-Century Europe.* Palgrave Macmillan, 2011.

Salter, Elisabeth. *Popular Reading in English c. 1400–1600.* Manchester UP, 2012.

Salzman, Paul. *Reading Early Modern Women's Writing.* Oxford UP, 2006.

Samek, Alyssa A. "Mobility, Citizenship, and 'American Women on the move' in the 1977 International Women's Year Torch Relay." *Quarterly Journal of Speech*, vol. 103, no. 3, 2017, pp. 207–29.

Schell, Eileen E, and K J Rawson. *Rhetorica in Motion: Feminist Rhetorical Methods and Methodologies.* U of Pittsburgh P, 2010.

Scott, Joan Wallach. *The Fantasy of Feminist History.* Duke UP, 2012.

Shaver, Lisa. *Beyond the Pulpit: Women's Rhetorical Roles in the Antebellum Religious Press.* U of Pittsburgh P, 2012.

—. "'No Cross, No Crown': An Ethos of Presence in Margaret Prior's Walks of Usefulness." *College English*, vol. 75, no. 1, Sept. 2012, pp. 61–78.

Smith, Helen. *"Grossly Material Things": Women and Book Production in Early Modern England.* Oxford UP, 2012.

Snook, Edith. *Women, Reading, and the Cultural Politics of Early Modern England.* Ashgate, 2005.

Suzuki, Mihoko. *Metamorphoses of Helen: Authority, Difference, and the Epic.* Cornell UP, 1989.

Travitsky, Betty, editor and compiler. *The Paradise of Women: Writings by Englishwomen of the Renaissance.* Greenwood, 1981.

Unger, Don, and Fernando Sánchez, "Locating Queer Rhetorics: Mapping as an Inventional Method." *Computers and Composition*, vol. 38, part A, December 2015, pp. 96–112.

Vickers, Brian. *In Defence of Rhetoric.* Oxford UP, 1988.

Waite, Stacey. *Teaching Queer: Radical Possibilities for Writing and Knowing.* U of Pittsburgh P, 2017.

Woods, Carly S. *Debating Women: Gender, Education, and Spaces for Argument, 1835–1945.* Michigan State UP, 2018.

I TRACKING ARGUMENTS

2 Hallie Quinn Brown's Journals and Nineteenth-Century African American Women's Literacy

Jane Donawerth

I n her earliest remaining journal, Hallie Quinn Brown begins with this inscription:

> In which will be found the odds and ends of a travelling career, begun March 16th in the year of our Lord 1881, by a girl who has an idea that she is not a cipher nor a figure head, and who here will write the humble name of Hallie Q. Brown of Wilberforce, O[hio]–Green Co[unty].

Brown's journals, intermittent from 1881 to 1923 and preserved in the library at Central State University in Ohio (earlier part of Wilberforce College) where she taught,[1] offer us a record of parts of her own "travelling career" as an elocutionist and African American activist, as well as glimpses of the circulation of literacies in the culture of the nineteenth-century African American middle class.

In this chapter, I consider what Brown's journals further tell us about African American women's rhetorical literacy, especially its connection to mobility. Brown's literacies enabled her mobility and her mobility enabled her to add to her literacies and to read not only texts but even her society more critically and capaciously. Brown's diaries record that nineteenth-century middle-class African Americans—including women—practiced continuing home schooling; studied elocution as Black activist rhetoric; benefitted from the migrating literacy of American democracy;

foraged in multiple literacy sites; and shared rhetorical literacy through both travel and texts with others in local, national, and international communities. One of my aims in this chapter, then, is to respond to Nan Johnson's call in "History" to widen our sense of what constitutes rhetorical performance and where it might occur. As historians, however, we have to keep in mind Cheryl Glenn's caution: "We write history knowing that we cannot tell the 'truth.' . . . knowing, for a fact, that our historical narratives are neither stable nor necessarily coherent" (35). Such a history is important because it helps us to understand the continuing migration, circulation, and expansion of rhetorical literacy for women, not only in political figures but also in our own research.

This analysis of Brown's rhetorical literacy allows us to acknowledge that the migration, circulation, and expansion of rhetorical literacy for women has continued. Rediscovering Brown's work—and the history of women in general—is the result of a general feminist movement that emphasized teaching and research as activism; the interdisciplinary nature of the fields of women's studies and of rhetoric and composition; collaboration among teachers, students, and family support; and the continuing expansion of rhetorical literacy for women.[2]

HALLIE QUINN BROWN, ELOCUTIONIST

Hallie Quinn Brown (1849–1949) was the daughter of freed slaves Frances Jane Scroggins and Thomas Arthur Brown. She was born in Pennsylvania into a middle-class family: her father worked as a porter, conductor, and steward, and so her dedication to an education and a career that involved travel was a family legacy. Her family's home was a center for the African Methodist Episcopal (AME) Church and the Underground Railroad. The family moved to Canada at the outbreak of the Civil War, and afterwards to Ohio, so that Brown and her brother could attend Wilberforce College, one of the two oldest Black colleges in the United States.[3]

Brown was extremely well educated and was herself an educator. She was taught elocution by Bishop Daniel Payne at Wilberforce College and gave her first public speech as salutatorian. After college she taught at plantation schools in Mississippi and South Carolina. Between 1874 and 1878, she further studied with Professor Peter Robertson in Dayton, Ohio, where she was teaching, and she graduated from the Chautauqua Lecture School, a summer program, in 1886. From 1885 to 1887 Brown was a dean of Allen University in Columbia, South Carolina, and from 1892 to 1893 she taught at Tuskegee Institute in Alabama under Booker T. Washington. In between, from 1887 to 1891, Brown taught public school again in Dayton, and at the same time ran a night school for African American migrants from the South. During the 1880s, Brown also toured with the Lyceum as an elocutionist, and in 1882 joined the Wilberforce Concert Company, an entertainment troupe that combined singers of spirituals with elocutionists to raise money for the college and traveled all over the United States. Brown also taught through her publications, privately printing and distributing her elocution handbooks: *Bits and Odds: A Choice Selection of Recitations* (c. 1884) and *Elocution and Physical Culture: Training for Students, Teacher, Readers, Public Speakers* (1910). [4]

As we can see from this survey of her life, Brown's journals are important for understanding nineteenth-century African American women's literacy because she traveled widely, was educated in both Black and integrated educational programs, attended and taught at a Black college, and was an elocutionist performer. She was involved in many of the political issues important to the Black middle class. She was a feminist, converted by Susan B. Anthony, whom she heard speak at Wilberforce. She was an acquaintance of Frederick Douglass and a colleague of Booker T. Washington. Loyal to the Republican Party, she campaigned for Warren Harding and Herbert Hoover, and she used her influence to promote an anti-lynching bill. She was an activist—a founder of the National Association of Colored Women's Clubs, and from 1920 to 1924, president of the National Association of Colored Women. Brown is representative of nineteenth-century African American women's literacy, then, because she traveled so widely and participated in so many of the educational institutions and practices of nineteenth-century African American culture. Her journals survey recurring literacy practices in the North, South, East, and West, as well as in parlor, in church, in classes, and in entertainments. As an elocutionist, Brown was purveying one of the most popular forms of dispensing cultural capital of that time. [5]

RHETORICAL LITERACY, ELOCUTION, AND AFRICAN AMERICANS

Before we turn to Brown's journals, we need to define literacy and elocution. Historians of rhetoric used to think of literacy as acquisition of the alphabet and a move from oral to print culture, with a resulting transformation from communal to private instruction. Recently, Deborah Brandt's studies, along with many others, have required us to rethink this conception. For Brandt, literacy is not simply "the . . . ability to deal with texts, but the broad ability to deal with other people as a writer or reader" (*Literacy as Involvement* 14). "Literacy is the broader term," Shirley Wilson Logan explains, "the ground upon which rhetorical education develops" (*Sites of Rhetorical Education* 4). In Brandt's theory of literacy, the skills of reading and writing are imparted not only by means of formal education, but also by mentors in informal or workplace settings; moreover, she has shown how dominant forms of literacy migrate in the modern United States through mentoring ("Sponsors," esp. 183). Brown's journals offer us a test case, allowing us to see the myriad ways in which the Black middle class and especially African American women helped themselves to literacy to make an argument for their rights as citizens.

This chapter is also concerned with what Jacqueline Jones Royster has described as "rhetorical competence" and "rhetorical literacy" (44–45, 47, 58). Achieving advanced skills in writing and speaking as well as rhetorical competence was more difficult for Black than for white Americans in the nineteenth century, as it is now, and especially difficult for women. Colleges were almost all segregated, and far fewer colleges for African Americans existed than for white citizens. However, we are beginning to recognize how important composition and rhetoric was to the constitution of African American identity as citizens after the Civil War. Where did African Americans, especially women, acquire advanced literacy and rhetorical competence? What sorts of rhetorical education were open to them? In *Liberating Language*, Logan has provided us with a map of the sites of African American acquisition of literacy, foregrounding self-education, literary societies and lyceums, the Black press, and other temporary sites of rhetorical education. Logan defines "rhetorical education" as "various combinations of experiences influencing how people understand and practice effective communication" (3). Brown's journals suggest that rhetorical competence for the Black middle class depended not only on Black colleges like Wilberforce, but also on a combination of self-education and practice in writing and speaking; travel; communal rhetorical entertainments; and attendance at racially integrated Chautauqua, the temporary summer camps that spread arts, culture, and history throughout the United States. Such rhetorical literacy is a classical ideal, one advanced by Quintilian and other classical rhetoricians, the education that lasts a lifetime (Quintilian XII. xi; 4:495–515.)

We also need to understand the nature of Brown's rhetorical education and deployment of persuasion, and so we need a definition of elocution. In *Conversational Rhetoric: The Rise and Fall of a Women's Tradition, 1600–1900*, I define elocution as "the performance of emotion through voice and body" (Donawerth 105; cf. Elizabeth Ellis Miller's analysis of "embodied Memory" in her study in this volume of Berenice Johnson Reagon's civil rights movement song-leading). Elocution was the art of reading, or of dramatically performing a piece of literature, an extension of the classical art of delivery.[6] During the nineteenth century, it was the most popular form of Anglo-American rhetoric. Elocution was studied by actors, teachers, and elementary school children, and dramatic reading entertained the middle class in parlors and on stages, in schools and in churches (Nan Johnson, *Gender and Rhetorical Space in American Life, 1866–1910*, esp. 21, 27, 32, and 70). Women as well as men studied elocution, took private lessons, and even established schools.[7] For Brown and other nineteenth-century women, elocution permitted expression of self and public performance because it seemed neither self-expressive nor public: it was reading others' words; it was women's caring, private parlor reading for family and friends staged for a larger audience.[8]

As we shall see from the study of her journals, Brown developed her rhetorical competence beyond college in a continuous education program that depended on migration of literacy from elite to less privileged groups and on the generosity of mentors within the Black community.

MIDDLE-CLASS AFRICAN AMERICAN LITERACY IN BROWN'S JOURNALS

Hallie Quinn Brown, the Black singers and elocutionists she traveled with, and the Black citizens she met on her journeys developed multiple literacies and advanced rhetorical competencies. Great effort was spent by middle-class Black citizens to acquire languages, starting with Standard English. In Brown's diary entry on 12 January 1883, she treats Black English as a different language, a comic performance: "Saw an old lady who walked and talked Aunt Jemima." But she also puts this dialect to political use. In *Bits and Odds*, a collection of pieces for recitation, she uses dialect humor—Black English, Irish English, and German

English.[9] In the last quarter of the century, members of the Black middle class were intent on racial uplift, proving to the United States' white population that they deserved full citizenship. Acquiring white English was seen as one means to that end. But in making fun of immigrants, and including African Americans among them, Brown is claiming that any inferiority attributed to them is temporary not ingrained, and that education rectifies it. She is contesting the essentialized stereotypes that white culture promoted about African Americans. Brown is also suggesting that performing ethnicity is not necessarily disrespectful.[10] Brown's ventriloquizing African American dialect reflects her own unstable political position.[11]

Besides taking lessons herself in elocution, which she did at Wilberforce College, at Dayton, Ohio, and throughout her travels, Brown helped other African Americans, through elocution lessons, to what I will call "spoken literacy," artful reading aloud. Literacy has often been thought of as a road away from orality, although historians of rhetoric have for half a century studied the intertwining of orality and literacy. Indeed, for Brown and many other feminist or African American activists, literacy and particularly training in rhetoric and elocution, were means to more engaging oral performance. Learning how artfully to read aloud and how to write and give a speech were significant aspects of nineteenth-century citizenship.[12] Brown's journals narrating her travels with the Wilberforce Concert Company include accounts of her giving elocution lessons on January 10, 1884, in Jefferson, Iowa, and on January 12, 1884, in Adel, Iowa. These were like the modern-day "master classes" for voice and dance students, when a visiting professional critiques the performance of a local class. On December 29, 1883, in Shelby, Iowa, for example, Brown wrote, "had a splendid rehearsal I can tell you in elocution. Class did finely."[13] Members of the Wilberforce Concert Company also had lessons, in Colfax, Iowa, for example, on December 27, 1883. Elocution, especially for women, allowed African Americans to claim expertise and demonstrate intellectual accomplishment publicly.[14] As in the case of learning languages, the travels of Brown's troupe enabled the troupe members to learn from each other and from other performers encountered in their travels, and the troupe members were also themselves teachers, promoting education in elocution through the expertise of visiting professionals.

Besides the glamour of listening to and performing memorized readings in elocutionary style, the members of Brown's traveling troupe read aloud to each other. Before radio and TV, this was a favorite entertainment, one of the activities of parlor entertainment, and suggests the collaborative nature of African American literacy.[15] In April 1882, Brown recorded in her journal reading aloud to a sick friend "from *Eminent Women of This Age* . . . , sketches of the lives of Mrs. Paston (Fanny Fern), Rosa Bonheur–the greatest female artist–Ristori–the Italian actress. Julia N. Howe–the poetess and now actress, and Eli[zabeth] Stanton–the champion for women's suffrage." In an 1884 diary, Brown cites another shared reading: "Found the book 'Cameron Pride' [by Mary Jane Holmes] and read it till tea time to the other ladies of the Com[pany]." Later Brown adds, "Lola completed the book. It was then 3 a.m." Brown also noted that she read aloud in local schools; in Falls City, Iowa, in 1884, Brown "Went to High School and sang and Read for them."

As in the centuries stretching back to the late Middle Ages and the Renaissance in England and Europe, when middle-class and aristocratic women gathered in a social circle to sew, gossip, and often, to be read aloud to, Brown combined handwork and reading.[16] In her journal, she lists embroidering her own dress, making Christmas presents for friends, crewel work, and beaded lace. In Marengo, Iowa, on December 22, 1883, Brown records, "Had some stamping done and did some work on Xmas presents." On January 12, 1884, Brown "Heard class recited; did some work"—which suggests Brown double-tasked, sewing or knitting while doing something else.[17] On January 19, 1884, Brown wrote in her diary that she "Had breakfast, then took lesson [at the time she was studying elocution, French, and the violin], embroidered till dinner." Just as Brown's literacy was a resistance tactic, a claim to status and political power, so Brown's sewing, especially the embroidery and beaded work, would have been a claim to middle-class status through clothing.[18] Moreover, when the women of the troupe gathered to hear a book read aloud, many of them must have been working on their hand-sewing at the same time.

In addition, Brown's diaries show her reading silently to herself, taking advantage, in an age in which books were expensive, of any she came across in the parlors of boarding houses the troupe visited. Here again Brown's mobility enabled her literacy. We might think of this practice as "scavenging," gathering up the bits and pieces of culture that became accessible. On January 2, 1884, in Oakland, Iowa, she was especially fortunate: "I found *Jane Eyre* among the number of books on the table and after hearing the class in elocution I read till tea time. . . . [After the concert] Home and read till nearly 1 a.m." The next day Brown continued: "read till dinner. Afterward finished J.E. and am perfectly enthused over C.B.'s works." In Concordia, Kansas, on February 3, 1883, Brown notes that she read Mary Denison's *A Lover's Trial or a Tale of the Revolutionary Times* "by the fire." On February 8, 1884, in Oskaloosa, Kansas, Brown read the *History of Kansas*.

The African Americans of Brown's journals fed their appetite for learning by foraging in multiple sites of literacy. As the many nine-teenth-century travel books demonstrate, visiting historical sites was a passion for nineteenth-century Americans, and middle-class African Americans shared this form of literacy, as well. Indeed, Brown treats "reading" monuments as political activism. In March 1883, in Osawat-omie, Kansas, Brown records in her diary that she visited a monument to the abolitionist John Brown, who helped win Kansas as a free state and later attempted an armed take-over of Harper's Ferry, Maryland, in the interest of an anti-slavery group. Then, on December 18, 1883, at La Harpe, Illinois, Brown records that she walked across the Mississippi River. The river's freezing was more common before industrial warming. Was this also reading political history, that of slaves who escaped across the Ohio and Mississippi Rivers, fictionalized in Harriet Beecher Stowe's abolitionist novel, *Uncle Tom's Cabin*?

In addition to the political history acquired through tours to historic places, Brown participated in other communal literate activities, which were tallied in her journals. In March 1882, when reflecting on the death of Longfellow, the American poet most revered by Brown's gener-ation, Brown mentions that she once saw the poet in his garden. Perhaps the troupe regularly toured local literary sites, walking past Longfellow's house the way we now visit the Mark Twain house. The company also at-tended plays, on December 19, 1883, in Iowa, for example, visiting "the O[pera] H[ouse] where "Romany Rye' [based on a novel by George Bor-row] was playing." Such acquisition of literate knowledge through com-munal interaction extended to science. In Augusta, Wisconsin, in 1884, Brown met Dr. Spencer, who "has about 40 bee hives and has made quite a number of scientific discoveries regarding the[ir] habits, etc."

Brown's journals reveal that literacies among the Black middle class were not only multiple but also migrating. The travels narrated in her journals indicate such literacy, since the Wilberforce Concert Troupe, encompassing both elocutionists and a gospel choir, toured all during the 1880s and all over the United States, from Connecticut to Minnesota, reaching a wide variety of audiences. Logan terms such activities "literacy events," in which "printed texts are produced or interpreted" (11). In addition, Brown herself spoke at colleges, performing at the University of the Pacific on November 14, 1892, and at the College of Notre Dame on November 15, 1892, both in California. Elocution brought the written text to a large audience orally; reading for many African Americans, indeed, for most Americans, often seems to have been a community activity. In 1882 in Caldwell, Kansas, Brown describes an audience of "principaly cowboys" wearing leather belts, six-shooters, and long dirk knives. At Fort Riley, Kansas, on March 16, 1883, Brown records giving an "entertainment for colored soldiers (4 Com[panies] . . . . About 250 in all)." In several entries Brown assesses the integration of the troupe's audience: on February 19, 1883, for example, in Kansas City, Brown comments, "A good audience, more colo'd [colored] than whites present"; and on February 4, 1884, in Highland, Colorado, she writes, "A large audience greeted us at the college chapel. Quite a number of Col'd [Colored] people out." Other troupes were also touring, and the Wilberforce Concert Company crossed paths during the years 1882 to 1884 with the Jubilee Singers, the New Orleans Troupe, Donovan's Company, and The Merrie Makers. Brown's *Bits and Odds*, which almost certainly represents the company's repertoire, suggests that variety is key to understanding how literacy traveled through the Black middle class: there are excerpts from Mark Twain and William Dean Howells, but also Frances Harper's poem, "The Dying Bondman."[19] Writings by both whites and Blacks were presented in the richly educated voice of the elocutionist as "culture." Although her race at times relegated her to the margins, Brown found an opportunity in elocution to enact her politics through performing others' words.[20]

Anne Ruggles Gere documents another important way that literacy migrated from woman to woman in the nineteenth century: salon conversation, organizational meetings, and clubs. On February 19, 1883 in her journal, Brown records speaking to a YMCA meeting in Wyandotte, Kansas, and noted that she "Met . . . Mr. Donavin Asst. Editor of 'The Enterprise.'" On June 10, 1883, Brown mentions hearing a lecture by Ms. Helen Gougar, "editress of 'Our Herald' a paper devoted to Tem. [perance] & 'Woman's Rights,' and then was introduced to her."[21] On March 2, 1908, near St. Louis, she "organized Woman's Club (32) at Du Quoin." By that time Brown was involved in the National Association of Colored Women, so perhaps she was the star speaker at an inaugural local meeting.

Throughout the journals concerning the Wilberforce Concert Company, Brown recounts visits to local Black families and especially ministers and church folk; these were often evening parlor entertainments, including piano-playing and singing, as well as conversation.[22] In November 1886, in Milwaukee, Wisconsin, for instance, she met a conductor on the train, a friend of her father who had been a porter; at his sister's they enjoyed "a long talk of Canada," where Brown had spent part of the Civil War. In Kansas, in February 1883, she writes, "After dinner had quite a chat with Mr. Badger (Prof.) who is a scientist, and a follower of Huxley." In Exira, Iowa, on January 5, 1884, Brown observes that "Miss Crowell the actress recited 'The Bobolink' very finely" in the parlor. Such salons included not just entertainment and culture, but also circulation of news about African American issues. In Hamilton, Illinois, on December 17, 1883, Brown commented that "The landlord has been a great underground R. R. Man." In Eureka, Kansas, on February 21, 1884, Brown learned that "There are several col'd [colored] men who are well to do owning property and shares in the fine hotel which will open on tomorrow."

Brown's journals provide further evidence of migrating literacy in documenting the movements of Black youth. Young northern Black women carried literacy to freed slaves, a reversal of the Southern migration northward after the Civil War. Brown herself had taught in a plantation school in Yazoo City, Mississippi. In May 1882, she mentions that she knows many women from the North who have gone south to teach freedmen, and on January 26, 1883, in Ellsworth, Kansas, she meets a fellow teacher from the days at Yazoo City. This north-to-south migration of literacy was modeled on church missionary work and established a network that remained in place for sharing news. On January 11, 1884, in Panora, Iowa, Brown reports, "I heard the terrible news of the brutal murder of a Miss[issippi] friend, Mr. Foote." On Sunday, January 13, after dinner, she "wrote several letters, one to poor Ms. Foote of Yazoo." On February 25, 1884, the reply from Ms. Foote in Yazoo caught up to Brown in Winfield, Kansas. One effect of growing Black literacy, then, was political cohesion—they did not have to take the word, or the silence, of the white press.

This network linked not only the North and South in the United States, but also the continent with Africa and Europe. The Black middle class was also sending young people to Africa as ministers, teachers, and purveyors of higher order literacies. In 1881, Brown mentions one friend going to Liberia to take a chair as Professor of Belles Lettres, History, and Language, another to Africa as a missionary. Brown herself toured and performed readings in England and Scotland in 1897 and performed elocutionary pieces and gave temperance speeches in England in 1899. On her way to London, on November 6, 1894, she comments wryly to her diary, "Recited on board. All took me for a Spanish lady."

Moreover, in her journals Brown gives detailed descriptions of her participation in two Chautauqua. These summer tent cities, bringing education as entertainment to many corners of the United States, were integrated. Brown and other members of the Black middle class could pay their fees and hear lectures, take music and elocution lessons, and participate in discussion groups at an advanced level in Chautauqua. This was continuing education in a very American form. It is also literacy as Thomas Laqueur defines it: "a consumption good" (45).

Brown notes participation in a Chautauqua at Rome City, Indiana, from July 10 to July 21 in her 1883 journal. She took Professor Pinkley's elocution class, and attended lectures on Elizabeth I, Shakespeare, and Protestant martyr John Huss. She heard Rabbi Joseph Krause R'oph of Cincinnati discuss the "Position of Women in Hebrew Literature." She went to talks on "Brain & Muscle," "Fossil Man," Palestine, and electrical storms. On Temperance Day she heard a woman lecturer, trained, perhaps, by the WCTU (the Women's Christian Temperance Union, the largest nineteenth-century political organization next to the political parties), to which Brown belonged.

From July 24 to August 6, 1883, she and her troupe moved to another Chautauqua, in Madison, Wisconsin, around Lake Mendota. Here Brown again taught elocution. Over the course of two weeks, she listed in her journal taking a "Chorus class," and on August 3 and 4, performing with the chorus the whole of the "oratorio," "Athalie."[23] Brown also visited the state capitol a few blocks away, and heard lectures on Leonardo da Vinci, Michaelangelo, "Heroic Boyhoods," and the customs of India. On the final day, August 6, they stayed up late to participate in astronomical observations.[24]

Finally, we may see Brown's journals themselves as a literacy practice. Her diary of 1894, for example, contains mainly notes on sermons. In an earlier journal, we can see how her religious reading and listening carry over into her diary writing; on December 15, 1883, Brown's description echoes the Psalms: "A most beautiful snow fall last night–and lays like a mantle over the dark earth–So has He promised to shield us and hide our sins" (as in Psalms 3:3, 18:35, 33:20, 91:4, 115:9–11, and 144:2). Summarizing sermons in journals was popularized among early Puritans and was practiced by Europeans and Americans up to the twentieth century. The entry of February 10, 1884, written in Osage, Kansas, recounts a sermon on missionary work in China, while an entire undated diary with "HQB" on the front contains notes on talks about global missionary work. Some entries extend into commentary. On one Sunday in Kansas in 1884, Brown notes, "The min[ister] spoke beautifully from the text 'And the end is better than the beginning thereof.' . . . He brought in the way of the wicked man and his end. . . . Of the Civil War and its end said that Appomattox was better than Bull Run better than Fort Sumpter. That Christianity was better in its end than beginning, that Wilberforce was better now than at first. Spoke glowingly of the temperance cause." Here Brown approves a providential view of history that sees God's order in very particular, political ways.[25] And Brown's God is firmly an Abolitionist.

Brown treated her journal as confidante, working out her judgments and feelings. She even personifies her diary: "Good night little book & friends." In the space of her journal, she battles racism, sorting out her own responses. In Vandalia, Illinois, on December 6, 1883, she comments, "Nice rooms but not fair treatment by the employees." In Mitchelville, Iowa, on November 13, 1882, Brown records, "At this hotel there is a very poor ignorant white southern woman who thinks it 'awful' that the landlord took us to board and asked him if he intended to bring niggers in his house." Brown is triumphant when "He replied that he did. . . . Well she . . . thinks we are human now. . . . we are glad when we can so bring them down." On May 8, 1882, in Illinois, the landlady refuses them entrance when she sees they are Blacks. Brown is relieved on May 16, a week later, when she reaches Sparta, "sympathetic soil": "a strong anti-Slavery town and a chief depot for the Underground railroad." In Elk City, Kansas, on January 16, 1883, Brown describes a nearly violent episode when the troupe enters the parlor, the landlord cursing and threatening troupe members, but Mr. Stewart refusing to ask them to leave. The parlors of the boardinghouses they stayed at seemed particularly fraught spaces. In Mt. Sterling, Illinois, on December 13, 1883, Brown judges the landlady: "Have a veritable <u>ogre</u> to deal with–Hurried us off post-haste to our rooms not allowing us to keep in the parlor."

As Jessica Enoch suggests in her essay on archival methods, we are not able to find the history of "resistant rhetorical education" (48) by and for women unless we expand our research to include the importance of multiple language literacy, geographical as well as social and cultural contexts, and small and community archives as well as those of major universities. Brown is an ideal example for this kind of research, since she herself studied multiple languages (including dialects), lived in both the Northern and Southern United States as well as Canada, and can be researched in only three small archives, all in Wilberforce, Ohio (Central State and Wilberforce Universities and Carnegie Library of the National Afro-American Museum and Cultural Center). Brown's diaries list the ways that Brown and her acquaintances continued their education through reading aloud with friends, through parlor entertainments, through private lessons, through sermons and church functions, through public entertainment, and through participation in frequent Chautauqua. Finally, the journals themselves become tools of literacy, for Brown took notes on lessons and sermons, practiced writing, noted elements of others' performances, and in writing sorted out her problems. This literacy program tallies with her theories of rhetoric as a means of moral and spiritual development, a route to self-mastery. Brown's diaries record the many community self-help programs in the Black middle class, and the ingenuity with which a newly-freed people pursued, circulated, and promoted multiple, migrating literacies. Brown's journals thus reinforce Shirley Logan's conclusions: "African Americans who found themselves in environments that limited their ability to develop English literacy created their own opportunities" (11).

NOTES

1. Brown taught at Wilberforce College, which split, during 1941–1949, into a state university named Central State University (where Brown chose to stay) and a private Wilberforce University; the institutions moved to separate campuses in 1976. I am grateful that I was able to travel to Central State University to research in the Hallie Q. Brown Library there in the 1990s: on this experience, and the support of my parents by caring for my children, see the dialogue essay on archival research that I coauthored with Lisa Zimmerelli and published in *Peitho*. In November 2019, I returned and did research on Brown at Wilberforce University and the Carnegie Library of the National Afro-American Mu-

seum and Cultural Center. My gratitude to librarians at all three archives, and especially to Sheila Darrow of the Hallie Quinn Brown Library at Central State University, who granted me the university's permission to quote from Brown's diaries.

2. As Carole Levin and Patricia A. Sullivan claim, a multidisciplinary approach is necessary for the study of women's rhetoric "because . . . a meshing, an interweaving, of different disciplines enriches our own subject matter" and allows us to "use the term political rhetoric in the broadest sense" (5). Especially important for my work was adapting what I learned in one area of expertise to another: in this essay, I suggest some of those connections, especially concerning the migration of women's literacy, women's adaptation of genres to their own purposes, the necessity of continued archival research and editing projects on women because women's writings are still not sufficiently available in contemporary editions and anthologies.

3. For more on Brown's biography, see the anonymous "A Sketch of the Life of Miss Hallie Quinn Brown" (my thanks to Shirley Logan for this reference); Mollie Dunlap's "A Biographical Sketch of Hallie Quinn Brown" from the 1963 *Wilberforce College Alumni Journal*; Annjennette S. McFarlin's dissertation and her article, both titled "Hallie Quinn Brown"; Susan Kates's "The Embodied Rhetoric of Hallie Quinn Brown," and *Activist Rhetorics* 53–74; Claire Strom; and Amy Hobbs Harris. Professor Harris's article is an example of the serendipity that is a part of collaborative feminist research. Decades ago, I taught Amy in a course on composition pedagogy, and when she published her article on Brown, she kindly sent me a copy.

4. Some biographical notes refer to a text by Brown titled *First Lessons in Public Speaking* (1920), which I have not located. Either it is a different title for *Elocution and Physical Culture*, or perhaps all copies were lost when a tornado destroyed the Hallie Q. Brown Library at Central State University in 1974. Some scholars assume that an untitled and unpublished manuscript in the Hallie Quinn Brown collection at Central State University (beginning "For centuries the attention of earnest thinkers has been attracted to the study of Human Expression.") is a draft for this text, but there seems no evidence for this assumption in the short essay or speech.

5. Brown's traveling literacies suggest that her gender was both limit and benefit, and that the Black middle class saw women as both "Other" (separate associations for colored women and colored men) and "Same"

(college education, elocutionary training, paid speaker). For considerations of these categories and applications to ancient culture, see Judith P. Hallet, "Women as *Same* and *Other* in Classical Roman Elite," esp. p. 62 on women and public speaking.

6. In the eighteenth century, as the focus of rhetoric changed from emphasis on the training of public orators to emphasis on the development of taste in the audience (see Barbara Warnicke), delivery was separated off from rhetoric as a specialized art of oral reading or recitation. The history of elocution remains to be written. Brenda Gabious Brown provides a brief survey; Eugene Bahn and Margaret Bahn's *A History of Oral Interpretation* summarizes development from classical delivery to later elocution with little analysis; Lindal Buchanan defines delivery as "socially situated public performance" (*Regendering Delivery* 4), a definition that also applies to elocution. But the connection to emotion or sentiment that my definition highlights was especially important to nineteenth-century women and helps to explain their frequent participation in this art form. Here we see a connection between the expansion of rhetorical literacy for women in the nineteenth century and in our time. As Patricia Bizzell comments, "We can now find feminist researchers in rhetoric openly discussing their feelings, both positive and negative, about their subjects of study" (12). Bizzell further argues the importance of "the acknowledgment of the multiple functions of emotions and experiences in defining one's relationship to one's research" (13).

7. On women in the elocution movement, see Karl R. Wallace, ed., *History of Speech Education*; and David Gold and Catherine L. Hobbs, eds., *Rhetoric, History, and Women's Oratorical Education.*

8. Cf. Catherine Field's essay on early modern women's recipe books as writing the self, esp. 49–50, and 54–55 (on multiple authorship).

9. On Brown's performance of Paul Laurence Dunbar's dialect poetry, see Amy Hobbs Harris.

10. On *Bits and Odds* as a "celebration of African American vernacular English," see Kates, *Activist Rhetorics*, 62–64. In an article on Aphra Behn's portrayal of Native Americans in her play *The Widow Ranter*, Rebecca Lush points out the dangers of the colonizer reshaping "political histories by shifting the focus . . . [and] blur[ring] the distinction between personal and cultural memories" (223). Lush's comment reminds me that we cannot attribute to Brown the same motivation for dialect comedy that we can attribute to white minstrelsy of the period.

11. Cf. Linda L. Dove on Lady Mary Wroth: "Wroth must negoti-

ate . . . intellectual and political games . . . [so that the] speaker [of the sonnets] reflects Wroth's own unstable position in the political world of early modern England" (142). Cf. also Ana Kothe on Sor Juana's use of epistolary rhetoric to disguise her political purpose.

12. See, for example, *The Memphis Diary of Ida B. Wells* 30, 34, 38, 52: Wells took elocution lessons from Mrs. Fannie Thompson on January 24, January 30, and March 1, 1886. See also Royster 194: Wells took elocution courses at LeMoyne-Owen College and Fisk University, and Selena Sloan Butler studied at Emerson School of Oratory.

13. Here "rehearsal" means not practice, but repetition of their memorized speeches.

14. Cf. Karen Nelson on seventeenth-century women's translation of religious texts: "Women . . . used the process of translation to confer upon themselves expertise in areas of divinity. . . ." (159).

15. Cf. Sadlack 236: in early modern England, women who could read often could not write, but could still achieve some rhetorical independence through collaborating with a scribe, thus demonstrating "a woman's ability to craft a delicate rhetorical position. . . ." Cf. Danielle Griffin's study in this volume of early modern working women's "supportive collaboration" with other women and with scribes to enable publication of their arguments.

16. On the relationship between early modern women, writing, reading, and embroidery, see Michele Osherow, "Mary Sidney's Embroidered Psalms," esp. 651–52, and 655. See also Osherow's essay in this volume on early modern women's embroidery and the biblical story of Susanna.

17. In many cases in the journals, Brown refers to the "work" she or other women were doing, and it took me a while to realize that these were references to sewing; women sewed continually before sewing machines and manufactured items, doing "plain" sewing to keep themselves in underclothes or the household in sheets and towels, and embroidering to make personalized gifts, like handkerchiefs.

18. On early modern sumptuary legislation, which established codes for clothing connected to class status, and resistance in literature, see, for example, Margaret Rose Jaster.

19. In Brown's performance of Harper's poem the audience might have experienced the "collapse of aesthetic distance" that Adele Seeff and others have found in a Black man's performance of *Othello* (377); and Brown's use of canonical writings might well have been similar to later use of Othello for activist political protest (Seeff 380).

20. Cf. Margaret Hannay: "Although relegated to the margins of discourse by her sex," and "barred by her sex from political councils and from the battlefield, [the countess of Pembroke] will use her pen. . . ." (156).

21. On Gougar, see Tarez Graban 93–142.

22. Cf. *The Memphis Diary of Ida B. Wells*, 33: Wells met weekly with a club called the Lyceum for recitations, debates, music, and news reading.

23. From her brief description, it is not clear whether Brown meant Racine's play *Athalie* with incidental music by Mendelssohn, or Handel's oratorio, "*Athalia*." Perhaps the first week the chorus class studied Mendelssohn and the second week prepared and performed Handel's oratorio.

24. Atop the highest hill of the University of Wisconsin in Madison stands Washburn Observatory, finished in 1881. Brown further mentions attending "Antioch Chautauqua" on June 22, 1908.

25. Brown's use of scripture to support the right of African Americans to education at Wilberforce College seems similar to Nabila Hijazi's reading in this volume of Al-Ghazali's use of the Quran to support the necessity of Muslim women's education.

Works Cited

Anon. "A Sketch of the Life of Miss Hallie Quinn Brown." *The AME Church Review*, 1889–1890, pp. 256–61.

Bahn, Eugene, and Margaret Bahn. *A History of Oral Interpretation.* Burgess Publishing, 1970.

Bizzell, Patricia. "Feminist Methods of Research in the History of Rhetoric: What Difference Do They Make." *Rhetoric Society Quarterly*, vol. 30, no.4, Fall 2000, pp. 5–17.

Brandt, Deborah. *Literacy as Involvement: The Acts of Writers, Readers, and Texts.* Southern Illinois UP, 1990.

—. "Sponsors of Literacy." *College Composition and Communication*, vol. 49, no. 2, May 1998, pp. 165–85.

Brown, Brenda Gabioud. "Elocution." *Encyclopedia of Rhetoric and Composition Communication from Ancient Times to the Information Age*, edited by Theresa Enos, Garland Publishing, 1996, pp. 211–14.

Brown, Hallie Quinn. *Bits and Odds: A Choice Selection of Recitations, for School, Lyceum and Parlor Entertainments Rendered by Miss Hallie*

Q. Brown. Introduction and sketches by Faustin S. Delaney, 1884. Chew Press, 1910.

—. Diaries.1881–1923. Manuscripts housed at Hallie Quinn Brown Library at Central State University, Wilberforce, Ohio.

—. *Elocution and Physical Culture, Training for Students, Teachers, Readers, Public Speakers*. Wilberforce, Ohio, Homewood Cottage [Brown's home], c. 1908.

—. Untitled speech on elocution, 1920? Typescript housed at Hallie Quinn Brown Library at Central State University, Wilberforce, Ohio. Rpt. as Appendix D, "Sample Manuscript of Text." In Annjennette S. McFarlin, "Hallie Quinn Brown–Black Woman Elocutionist: 1845(?)–1949," PhD diss., Washington State University, 1975.

Buchanan, Lindal. *Regendering Delivery: The Fifth Canon and Antebellum Women Rhetors*. Southern Illinois UP, 2005.

Donawerth, Jane. *Conversational Rhetoric: The Rise and Fall of a Women's Tradition, 1600–1900*. Southern Illinois UP, 2012.

Donawerth, Jane, and Lisa Zimmerelli. "Dialoguing with *Rhetorica*." *Peitho: Newsletter of the Coalition of Women Scholars in the History of Rhetoric and Composition*, vol. 8, no.1, Fall 2003, pp. 4–6.

Dove, Linda L. "Mary Wroth and the Politics of the Household in 'Pamphilia to Amphilanthus.'" In *Women, Writing, and the Reproduction of Culture in Tudor and Stuart Britain*, edited by Mary E. Burke, Jane Donawerth, Linda L. Dove, and Karen Nelson, Syracuse UP, 2000, pp. 141–56.

Dunlap, Mollie E. "A Biographical Sketch of Hallie Quinn Brown." Archival reprint from *Wilberforce Alumni Journal*, June 1, 1963. Carnegie Library of the National Afro-American Museum and Cultural Center, Wilberforce, Ohio.

Enoch, Jessica. "Changing Research Methods, Changing History: A Reflection on Language, Location, and Archive." *Composition Studies*, vol. 38, no.2, 2010, pp. 47–73.

Field, Catherine. "'Many Hands Hands': Writing the Self in Early Modern Women's Recipe Books." In *Genre and the Development of Women's Life Writing in Early Modern England*, edited by Michelle Dowd and Julie Eckerle, Ashgate, 2007, pp. 49–63.

Glenn, Cheryl. "Rereading Aspasia: The Palimpsest of Her Thoughts." In *Rhetoric, Cultural Studies, and Literacy: Selected Papers from the 1994 Conference of the Rhetoric Society of America*, edited by John Frederick Reynolds, Lawrence Erlbaum Associates, 1995, pp. 35–43.

Gold, David, and Catherine L. Hobbs, editors. *Rhetoric, History, and Women's Oratorical Education: American Women Learn to Speak.* Routledge, 2013.

Graban, Tarez Samra. *Women's Irony: Rewriting Feminist Rhetorical Histories.* Southern Illinois UP, 2015.

Hallett, Judith P. "Women as Same and Other in Classical Roman Elite." *Helios*, vol. 16, no.1, 1989, pp. 59–78.

Hannay, Margaret P. "'Doo What Men May Sing': Mary Sidney and the Tradition of Admonitory Dedication." *Silent But for the Word: Tudor Women as Patrons, Translators, and Writers of Religious Works*, edited by Margaret P. Hannay, Kent State UP, 1985, pp. 149–65.

Harris, Amy Hobbs. "'The Sole Province of the Public Reader': Elocutionist Hallie Quinn Brown's Performances of the Poetry of Paul Laurence Dunbar." *Reception: Texts, Readers, Audience, History*, vol. 9, 2017, pp. 36–55.

Jaster, Margaret Rose. "Of Bonnets and Breeches: Sumptuary Codes in Elizabethan Popular Literature." *Proceedings of the PMR Conference*, vol. 16/17, 1992–1993, pp. 205–11.

Johnson, Nan. *Gender and Rhetorical Space in American Life, 1866–1910.* Southern Illinois UP, 2002.

—. "History." *Peitho*, vol. 18, no.1, Fall/Winter 2015, pp. 15–18.

Kates, Susan. *Activist Rhetorics and American Higher Education, 1885–1937.* Southern Illinois UP, 2001.

—. "The Embodied Rhetoric of Hallie Quinn Brown." *College English*, vol. 59, 1997, pp. 59–71.

Kothe, Ana. "Whose Letter Is It, Anyway? Print, Authority, and Gender in the Publication of Sor Juana's 'Carta Atenagórica.'" *Women's Studies*, vol. 25, 1996, pp. 351–59.

Laqueur, Thomas W. "Toward a Cultural Ecology of Literacy in England, 1600–1850." *Literacy in Historical Perspective*, edited by Daniel P. Resnick, Library of Congress, 1983, pp. 44–57.

Levin, Carole, and Patricia A. Sullivan. "Politics, Women's Voices, and the Renaissance: Questions and Context." *Political Rhetoric, Power, and Renaissance Women*, edited by Carole Levin and Patricia A. Sullivan, State U of New York P, 1995, pp. 1–13.

Logan, Shirley Wilson. *Liberating Language: Sites of Rhetorical Education in Nineteenth-Century Black America.* Southern Illinois UP, 2008.

Lush, Rebecca. "The Memory of Romance: Love and War in Aphra Behn's Colonial Virginia." *Early Modern Women: An Interdisciplinary Journal*, vol. 6, 2011, pp. 223–30.

McFarlin, Annjennette S. "Hallie Quinn Brown: Black Woman Elocutionist." PhD diss., Washington State University, 1975.

—. "Hallie Quinn Brown: Black Woman Elocutionist." *Southern Speech Communication Journal*, vol. 46, 1980, pp. 72–82.

Nelson, Karen L. "'To Informe Thee Aright': Translating Du Perron for English Religious Debates." *The Literary Career and Legacy of Elizabeth Cary, 1613–1680*, edited by Heather Wolfe, Palgrave MacMillan, 2007, pp. 147–63.

Osherow, Michele. "Mary Sidney's Embroidered Psalms." *Renaissance Studies*, vol. 29, no.4, 2015, pp. 650–70.

Quintilian. *Institutio Oratoria. The Institutio Oratoria of Quintilian*, translated by H. E. Butler, 4 vols., Harvard UP, 1922, rpt. 1961.

Royster, Jacqueline Jones. *Traces of a Stream: Literacy and Social Change among African American Women*. U of Pittsburgh P, 2000.

Sadlack, Erin A. "Petitioning Power: The Rhetorical Fashioning of Elizabethan Women's Letters." *New Ways of Looking at Old Texts*, Vol. 4, Papers of the Renaissance English Text Society, 2002–2006, edited by Michael Denbo, ACMRS (Arizona Center for Medieval and Renaissance Studies), 2008, pp. 229–37.

Seeff, Adele. "Othello at the Market Theatre." *Shakespeare Bulletin*, vol. 27 no.3, 2009, pp. 377–98.

Strom, Claire. "Hallie Quinn Brown." *American National Biography*, edited by John A. Garraty and Mark C. Casranes, Oxford UP, 1999, vol. 3, pp. 676–77.

Wallace, Karl R., editor. *History of Speech Education in America: Background Studies*. Appleton-Century-Crofts, 1954.

Warnicke, Barbara. *The Sixth Canon: Belletristic Rhetorical Theory and Its French Antecedents*. U of South Carolina P, 1993.

Wells, Ida B. *The Memphis Diary of Ida B. Wells*, edited by Miriam DeCosta-Willis, Beacon Press, 1994.

3 The Rhetoric of Reform: The Maydens of London, Liberty, and Marriage in 1567

Karen Nelson

Feminist scholars have long noted the anachronism of seeking feminist politics or positions in early modern texts. Yet they have also long valued the genre of the "Querelle des Femmes" (literally, "dispute of women" or "woman question," more commonly, "defense of women")[1] as a site for tracing the sorts of issues associated with attacks on and defenses of women.[2] Many of these lines of arguments overlap with definitions that Kate Manne articulates in *Down Girl: The Logic of Misogyny*, especially of misogyny as a means to police and enforce gendered hierarchies and power structures, and shaming behavior as a mechanism of enforcement. These debates about the woman question flared up with repeated consistency in the fourteenth and fifteenth centuries, across Europe, in Latin and in vernaculars, and deployed fairly standardized rhetorical strategies. One particularly compelling outlier emerges from the discourses of the early reign of Elizabeth I in sixteenth-century England.

Printed in 1567, *A Letter sent by the Maydens of London, to the vertuous Matrones & Mistresses of the Same, in the defense of their lawfull Libertie, Answering the 'Mery Meeting' by us: Rose, Jane, Rachell, Sara, Philumias, and Dorothy* is a twenty-three page pamphlet defending serving-women's honor. *A Letter* makes use of the generic conventions of the debates on women, but its lines of argument diverge in ways that speak specifically to potential allies to be found amongst upper class women. As Erin Sadlack and Danielle Griffin note elsewhere in this volume, that strategy of seeking patronage from those with power operated throughout sixteenth- and seventeenth-century codes of acceptable behavior. In this paper, I assess how the Maydens construct arguments so that their positions converge with those of Elizabeth I, particularly in terms that resonate with national and international debates that surrounded her marriage, her legacy, and the religious fortunes of the realm. While, in the post-Victorian period, readers tend to code issues associated with marriage and religion as "private," "domestic," or "womanly," for sixteenth-century audiences, all were central to power politics and the public sphere. They thus needed to be encoded, in this case, as the words of lowly serving women, since Elizabeth I forbade critique of her marital alliances (and lack thereof) first by suspending Parliament and then by proclamation. The Maydens' divergences from standard lines of argument available from the genre of the "Querelle des Femmes" within *A Letter* actually converge in support of positions associated with Elizabeth I and the national and international debates that surrounded her marriage, her legacy, and the religious fortunes of the realm. Those appeals themselves bring this text into conversation with others in this volume, such as those examined by Nabila Hijazi and Michele Osherow, that consider ways in which women appropriate form to enter wider networks of discourse to make political interventions, and by Ruth Osorio and Elizabeth Miller, who consider the power of collective voices and the technologies of popular distribution, here associated with "cheap print" and pamphlet wars, to amplify women's politicized messages.

The Maydens use their positions as serving women and as a collectivity to fabricate a shared ethos, authority, and responsibility, and to deflect individual risk. They deploy particular arguments available from the "Querelle des Femmes," and also offer telling variations from the generic conventions that allow them to align themselves, as women subjected to social critiques, directly with Queen Elizabeth, which enabled them to appropriate power and strengthen their stance. These variations also permitted them to suggest and support positions that ran counter to those promoted by Parliament, again, as women speaking to the Queen. When *A Letter* is placed against the backdrop of the events surrounding religious reform and counter-reform in England, Scotland, and the European continent in the late 1560s, specifically as entangled in the marital politics of Elizabeth I of England and Mary Queen of Scots, its power to intervene in international controversies surrounding religion and politics emerges and belies its claims to be merely the work of serving women.

In this chapter, after I briefly summarize *A Letter*, I offer an overview of the texts and scholarship surrounding the "Querelle des Femmes" tradition to outline the mechanisms that "defenses of women," as a genre, offer to the Maydens. I turn then to a quick sketch of the scene in England in the late 1560s to delineate some of the narratives associated with religious politics and the concerns, fears, and anxieties circulating at the time, to consider why rhetors might choose to construct a collective, female ethos at this moment. One central issue was the English succession. While Elizabeth I ascended the throne in 1558, her rule was questioned by Roman Catholics, who dominated European courts and who viewed her as illegitimate. Her own English citizens feared civic uncertainty devolving from her lack of a husband or successor, concerns specifically tied in political discourse to her position as a young, unmarried, female, Protestant ruler. As I will develop more fully below, at the time of the publication of *A Letter*, Elizabeth I had disbanded Parliament because of its insistence that she select either a husband or name an heir (or both). Furthermore, she had banned the discussion of these related issues.[3] My argument in this chapter is that *A Letter* makes use of the collective ethos by unimportant, inconsequential serving women writing in an inconsequential, commonplace discourse, a defense of women, to offer critiques and suggestions to the Queen. Too, these comments were otherwise unsayable and unprintable and engaged with the politics at work in England and on the Continent in ways that were dangerous to circulate, especially in print.

In the third section of this chapter, I explicate two aspects of *A Letter* to explore how and why it functions as it does, given this particular context. The first of these are the lines of argument concerning liberty. Within the "Querelle" tradition, a common topic is women's liberty to choose their husbands. In *A Letter*, that component assumes added weight and prominence by its dominance within the text. It becomes a central concern in ways that are telling at a moment when the English Parliament and the bishops made repeated calls for Elizabeth to promise to marry and identify her successor. While that stance seems practical, it also carried significance in terms of religious politics, since it attempted to foster or preclude opportunities for foreign, especially Catholic, intervention in English governance. *A Letter* runs counter to those politics and is in sympathy with Elizabeth, whose stated intent was to preserve her individual authority and remain unwed, even if the succession remained unclear. The authors of *A Letter* therefore align themselves with her, as a woman, and enlist sympathy for her and for her refusal to commit.

A *LETTER* IN SUM AND IN THE CONTEXT OF "DEBATES ON WOMEN"

While scholars of contemporary rhetoric might view the defense of women as a topic, for writers from the medieval and early modern periods texts within the "Querelles des Femmes" tradition constituted a stand-alone genre. These texts might serve as the prompt for a debate or a display of oratory in an educational context; they recurred as treatises in their own right, with such models as Giovanni Boccaccio (*On Famous Women*, Italy, Latin, ca. 1362), Christine de Pizan (*City of Ladies*, France, French, 1405), Baldassare Castiglione ("The Court Lady," *The Courtier*, Italy, Italian, 1528), and Heinrich Agrippa, (*Declamation on the Nobility and Preeminence of the Female Sex*, Germany, Latin, 1529) developing works of varying length attacking or defending women. As even this short list demonstrates, these treatises spanned centuries and recurred throughout Europe and straddled both the universalizing international scholarly language of Latin and the varying local, vernacular discourses emergent and vying for prestige throughout these four hundred years. The rhetorical training associated with humanist education in the sixteenth century prompted an international European resurgence of these debates in the 1540s, 1550s, and 1560s, and again in the early seventeenth century.[4] Defenses of women often respond to misogyny from such writers as Aristotle, the apostle Paul, or myriad others who articulate women's inferiority, couched in terms of their inability to speak, reason, or learn.[5]

As the title suggests, *A Letter* defends the honor of its writers from an attack made upon them in the now-lost *Merry Meeting of Maydens* in London, entered into the Stationer's Register in 1566–67 by Edward Hake, a lawyer, translator, and controversialist who flourished in the 1560s and 1570s.[6] The Maydens address this appeal primarily to their mistresses, and then offer a rebuttal of Hake's detractions, which seemingly include charges that they are silly (which carried many more signifiers than now, "weak," "vulnerable," "trifling," "humble or insignificant," "lacking in judgment," or "empty-headed" are among those the OED lists[7]) girls who waste their mistresses' time and money and who take advantage of their liberty around London to frivol away their time with wanton pursuits. The Maydens note that, whereas their mistresses comprehend the scope of their duties, Hake really doesn't know much about the sorts of work they do. A particular point of contention is their use of time on Sundays; their response to Hake suggests he has charged the Maydens with lewd and idle thoughts, when their time would be better spent in church, or, when in church, focusing upon the sermons and not gazing about. The Maydens rebut the claim that they misspend their time and their mistresses' resources. The phrase that recurs is "liberty," which for this period encompasses freedom from spiritual ties and sin in addition to the more modern usage of the ability to act without constraint or physical bondage, and also carries the implication of "privileges."[8] *A Letter* works through the charges that Hake presumably made against such humble women as the Maydens, noting the errors in his logic, the sort of service and support they offer to their mistresses, and servants' rights to enjoy their lives when they have discharged their obligations. The Maydens castigate Hake for his incendiary rhetoric, for his false claims, and, in general, for what would now be categorized as trolling behavior. In its every aspect, this pamphlet proclaims its local engagement, its alignment with issues and debates in London, and its origins amongst women who warrant only a first-name designator. In every particular, it asserts the humble, collective, feminine ethos of its authors.

A Letter deviates from "Querelle" conventions in insisting upon the particularities for six individual servants in London, rather than offering generic defenses of "all women." Its lines of argument align with Roman Catholic efforts to justify individual control in matters of conscience. It diminishes its controversial stance by placing these positions in the mouths of a collective of first-name-only serving women. I assess the Maydens here not in terms of biography, but instead via the rhetorical category of ethos. While I suggest that this collective ethos allows the speakers to enter the lists of religious (and therefore political, as I explain later in this chapter) debates, I do not suggest these women operated along a spiritual or confessional register.[9] The characteristics that speakers ascribe to and appropriate for themselves, both implicitly and explicitly, allow these women to occupy a protected space within the religious-political ecosystem of 1567, in England and in the wider context of English-Scottish and English-Continental relations, necessarily inflected through alliances with International Calvinists and Roman Catholics coalesced under competing spheres of influence dominated by the Spanish Hapsburgs and the French.

In *A Letter sent by the Maydens of London*, disenfranchised serving women articulate positions that contradict those advanced by Parliamentary and episcopal leaders. These young, working-class women are themselves, as speakers, inversions of those entitled-class men and invert the power dynamics. The proposals they outline in *A Letter* resonate differently with Queen Elizabeth because of their place within social hierarchies; they have the potential to shift her receptiveness to "Liberties," to safeguards for those on the margins of government positions in 1567, Roman Catholics and nonconformists, especially Roman Catholics, in ways that those with more authority were unable to access.[10]

POLITICS, RELIGION, POWER, AND THE MAYDENS IN 1560S ENGLAND

While scholars in the twenty-first century remain interested in *A Letter* primarily because of its attribution to women writers, its preservation indicates a different sort of context within which to consider it: that of the power politics surrounding English religion and governance. *A Letter* exists in one copy, bound as part of the collection of the conformist prelate Archbishop Richard Bancroft, whose power was especially evident in the 1590s and early seventeenth century until his death in 1610.[11] It is bound along with six other anonymous or pseudonymous "letters," petitions, and treatises of social commentary that range in length from twenty-eight to a hundred and forty pages and is held in the Lambeth Palace Library.[13] *A Letter* has been more widely circulated than its companions because of the enormous efforts of scholars in the 1980s and 1990s, especially, to recover writings by women for modern readers. R. J. Fehrenbach transcribed and edited *A Letter* and published it in *English Literary Renaissance* in 1988.[12] Because it was coded as a women's text then, it garners scholarly interest and attention now in ways that its fellows too might warrant. Most offer social commentary and social critique and suggest that their collector compiled them in part because of their potentially fraught engagement with the politics of their day.

While Fehrenbach helpfully offered the generic category that gave *A Letter* exigence within that larger feminist textual recovery project as he placed it within the "Querelle des Femmes" tradition, he simultaneously displaced it from that canon. He called out its divergences from the genre, noted its aberrant legal references, and dismissed the possibility that six actual serving women could have written such an epistle.

Scholars quickly rebutted his claims,[14] but since biography continues to animate literary history (and herstory), and the 1560s themselves fall outside of "Shakespeare and His Contemporaries" rubrics,[15] *A Letter* remains on the peripheries of narratives of early modern women's writing and early modern literature surveys. Nonetheless, it is useful to consider its place in Bancroft's holdings and in the landscape of the religious and political controversies of the late 1560s to articulate some of the ways in which creating a collective women's ethos, one from the lower classes, provided a space for entry into prohibited discourses and served to empower the writers.

Removing *A Letter* from its generic contexts within the "Querelle des Femmes," locating it in its 1567 origins, and focusing on its rhetorical strategies, allows a different set of textual considerations to come forward. Its modern editor Fehrenbach notes that many of its lines of arguments deviate from the standard points delineated in women's defenses.[16] These variants align with a different set of debates, those that surrounded Mary Stewart, Queen of Scots, and Elizabeth Tudor, Queen of England. At issue, in particular, are the queens' alliances through marriage, their liberties, and the relationship of those coded issues to the fraught religious-political situation as it emerged in the late 1560s.

England and Scotland, in 1567, shared a precarious relationship to the largely Roman Catholic continent, although the specifics for each kingdom differed. The religious situation in Europe in 1560 was rife with complexities, a lack of hegemonies, and an enormously dynamic and transitional set of religious alliances with very local variations. In addition, outward confession served as an unreliable identifier. The difficulties of knowing what people's religious practices reveal about their religious beliefs and affiliations were complicated by differing levels of local and state enforcement.[17] Nonetheless, from a territorial standpoint, the "Conformist" region of the English national church is quite small. Its status as an "English" church is also relatively recent. Elizabeth and her counselors broke with the Roman Catholic church in 1558, after she ascended to the throne. Her sister Mary Tudor had spent her brief reign from 1553–1558 attempting to recover England's Catholic traditions. As part of that project, in 1554 she married Philip II of Spain (crowned in 1556), a member of the Hapsburg family. The parameters of the English church remained contested in the 1560s, and one of the reasons Richard Bancroft, the collector of this pamphlet, is important to the story is that he outlined the "outliers" in a text entitled *Dangerous Positions* published in 1593.

Scotland, until 1603 its own nation, was Calvinist. For it, the complicating factor was that its ruler, Mary Stewart, vehemently Roman Catholic, disagreed with many of the feudal lords and their people, whose inclinations were Calvinist. Mary Stewart, daughter of the Catholic Mary of Guise, raised at the French court and married to the French prince-then-king in her youth, only returned to rule Scotland in 1561. Some of the Roman Catholic feudal lords in England and powers in Ireland and on the continent, along with the Pope, were actively working to have Mary Stewart assume the throne in England.[18] The Pope issued his Bull against Elizabeth in 1571, four years hence. However, versions circulated earlier among the Catholic nobility in part to foster this change.[19] Indeed, the Revolt of the Northern Lords occurred in 1569, one indicator of the dangers Elizabeth faced. Thus, while *A Letter* is framed explicitly with a localized argument—the Maydens of London, to their Mistresses—the debates concerning religion, and religious politics, assumed international proportions and significance.

Even with this brief background, it is quite evident that these rulers were shaky in their relationships to state churches, to their efforts to rule these churches, and to bring them into compliance with their own doctrines.[20] The larger continental context only underlines the volatility of these situations. The first rumblings of the Eighty Years War placed Margaret of Parma, Philip II's governor of the Hapsburg Netherlands, in a similarly perilous position.[21] Roughly four hundred nobles petitioned her to stop the Inquisition in the region in April 1566, and the Dutch nobility and Spanish rulers began to amass polyglot armies at this stage. Ireland, an ally of Hapsburgs, was part of that effort, as its forces and their families moved to the continent as part of that mobilization.[22] England perceived itself as a country surrounded; William Cecil, Elizabeth's Secretary of State, received reports in 1567 from his spies on the continent of a "secret contract and confederation or league, made between the pope, the [Hapsburg] emperor, the kinge of Spaine, the kinge of Portingall, the duke of Bavier, the duke of Savoye, and other their confederats, and companions, or consorts: into the which contract or leage they have sought meanes to drawe in the French king, which hath allreadye consented, anno 1567" (Strype 243–4). This intelligence included an item specifying the plans for Elizabeth's territory: "Callis [Calais], and other places lately belonging to the crowne of Englande [thus, Elizabeth 1], shalbe delivered to the kinge of Spaine: and he shall helpe and assist the quene of Scotland; and restore her to her kingdome, in chasinge awaie the quene of Englande; and helpe to destroye all suche as be affectioned or make claime to the same kindom" (Strype 245). Elizabeth's concern was well-founded. And, too, both Scotland and England chafed at women's rule, in part because the state's stability required them to marry and bear heirs, but those alliances were themselves potentially politically destabilizing.

Two cases that underlined this instability in 1567 were Elizabeth Tudor's at-risk reign and Mary Stewart's disintegrating situation. In 1566, the English lords held up Mary as an example to Elizabeth. They noted that Mary had been allied to the French court in her first marriage to King Francis II and, widowed in 1560, had married a Scottish Lord, her cousin Henry Stewart Lord Darnley, in 1565; she maintained the potential for an heir, and better still, kept her allegiance contained within Scotland. Mary had then born an heir—her son James, in May 1566. James became James 6 of Scotland and eventually would be crowned James 1 of England; the crucial point in 1566 was that Mary had secured the succession.[23] The English Parliament noted that Elizabeth should follow suit; even though she had, in 1566, declared this topic off-limits, Parliament still encouraged her to make a match and reminded her of the necessity to resolve the succession. Here, for example, is Bishop of Salisbury John Jewel's report on the situation, from a letter to Swiss reformer Henry Bullinger dated 24 February 1567:

> We have assembled within these few months the parliament of the whole kingdom. . . . Laws have been enacted concerning religion, by which the obstinate malice and insolence of the papists may be kept within due bounds. The question respecting the succession was likewise brought forward; that is, to what family belongs the right of sovereignty, in case anything, which we should much regret, should happen to queen Elizabeth. This question occupied the minds of all parties for a month or two: for the queen was unwilling that any discussion should take place upon the subject; while every one else was exceedingly anxious about it; and the contest was carried on with great earnestness and zeal on both sides. What next? after all nothing could be done; for the queen, who is a wise and cautious woman, suspects that, when her successor is once determined upon, there may hence arise some danger to herself. For you

know the saying, that there are more worshippers of the rising than of the setting sun.

At issue, then, was the succession. Elizabeth's caution was known, and her reasons for preserving her rule and her position as a single, singular female ruler, were unambiguous. Too, her concern that naming an heir would lead to her own demise was genuine and well founded. Even without an heir in place, the Northern Earls attempted to secure her throne and the kingdom two years later.

However, in February 1567, the momentum shifted away from Mary Queen of Scots as exemplar. Mary developed affinities with James Hepburn, Fourth Earl of Bothwell, who eventually murdered her husband, carried Mary to his castle, and kept her there, thereby enacting the full sixteenth-century meaning of rapine. Mary's "casket sonnets" to Bothwell were used against her in her trial and helped her lose her throne in July 1567. These sonnets are sometimes taught as examples of women's writing. Here, though, as with *A Letter*, the authorship is suspect, since her defenders claimed much of this evidence—the sonnets themselves—was engineered.

LINES OF ARGUMENT

I relate this historiography to the Maydens of London because flash points from these controversies intersect directly with the lines of argument to which Fehrenbach points as anomalies in the debates on women, namely, who dictates whom a maiden might marry, a point which Elizabeth Tudor debated with her lords, as did Mary Stewart; what sorts of liberties a serving woman has in respect to the matrons and mistresses of London; and where the obligations lie—and end. These debates all resonated with advice to both queens, which in turn stemmed from anxieties about the religious configuration of each state, and the jurisdiction of local authorities vs. a more regional authority (such as a queen, or, even more tellingly, a pope) and also vs. an individual or collection of individuals. All of these issues emerged in the religious-political debates of the day; all concerned the queens; all, more explicitly expressed, were dangerous to their authors.

Most "Querelle" texts defend women in a general way against misogynist attacks but don't disambiguate beyond "women." *A Letter* states the very specific concerns of individual women in this moment and this geographically specific place of London in 1567, especially regarding their autonomy on how to decide how they will use their "Liberty" on Sundays. This set of arguments aligns with debates about how to reform the Elizabethan church and who has jurisdiction once these reforms are enacted. While many in Parliament and a subset of "gospellers" (one preferred name chosen by nonconformists) advocated for more centralized, government control of religious practices, *A Letter* advocates for localized, individualized governmental control in ways that especially the more radical nonconformists and most Roman Catholics urged.

One could pursue many trajectories through *A Letter*, but two stand out as most in line with religious reform and counter-reform. They also diverge from standard aspects of "Querelle" texts.[24] Liberty is the refrain, and it emerges in the letter in regard to the arguments for maidens and servants, to pursue their own rights in marriage, not to answer parents or other outside influences, to control their use of their own time and money on Sundays, and more.

These two examples provide the tenor of the tract. First, after defending the practice of attending plays and interludes, which they claim edify as do the sermons their mistresses attend, the authors claim that the general charges against the women, of excess and waste, are, first, too general to defend against and, second, implausible. The Maydens complain that the critiques are generic: "Our great costs and charges in good chere and banketting objected by him against us, sith he hath named no great deynties, nor any great shot or reckoning, he hath but sayd a thing that he hath not proved, and so we have the lesse to say therein: and so much the rather sith he him selfe against his will, or more than he remembereth, hath sayd metely well for us in that behalf" (301/sig. B3). But still, the women will tackle this charge and demonstrate its hyperbole:

> For when ROSE would have sent for wyne, JANE wold not suffer hir, and so had they but bare beere alone that we hard of. Now at that feast or rather a bare beere banket, there were but they alone, the day was halfe spent and more, for it was well in the after none. And they are no such quaffers but that a quart would serve them well when they had well drunken before at their dynner. Also a quart of the best beere may be bought or a penny, so that they two that daye spent ech of them a halfepenny. Summa Totalis of all that was spent that daie between them two at the costely banket, was a penny. (301-302/sig. B3-B3^v)

In this passage, the wit emerges, as does the care of the argument's crafting. Too, individual women help disprove the general accusation against all women, as does articulating a particular example and its budget. At the heart of the debate, though, remains these women's freedom to spend their limited resources as they wish.

Similarly, after expounding at length on the potential ills that arise in the course of arranged marriage—"inheriting" a household of young children along with a widower as a husband or landing an ugly and old but wealthy partner, the benefits of matching for love, and more—the women exclaim, "Blame us not if we wold avoid so great inconveniences in the choyce of them who we must serve all our lyfe tyme, when no wise wench willingly wold be hyred of any for a yeare, without a proofe of time of liking" (301/sig B2ᵛ). These are women experienced in contracting their services and working under supervision. They know already the peril of committing to an unknown, or to an awful or abhorrent master, as they demonstrate repeatedly in the course of their discussion. Here too, their plea is for liberty to determine their own fates.

These two lines of argument can be read against Parliament's efforts, in 1566, to exact a promise from the queen to marry and to declare her successor, and to regulate and reform the nation's religious practices along the lines that eventually became the 39 Articles. These pressures were among the reasons Elizabeth dissolved Parliament in 1566; she did not convene it again until 1571.[25] In aligning these particular arguments, the Maydens make a claim that these issues—of the liberty to choose one's mate, and the liberty to self-regulate one's Sunday practices—belong to individuals, not the State, and not Parliament. While these things are not in and of themselves related, eliding the two into a discussion of "liberty" ultimately places jurisdiction with the individual. In essence, the queen's probable sympathy for the first promotes her accord with the second and conjoins the two.[26]

The ethos of the Maydens serves to buffer them from any possible perils of arguing against those regulating these practices. The Maydens of London construct a pairing that becomes an argument for religious liberty in ways that would resonate with the queen and that run counter to the efforts of some of the most strident reformist elements of Parliament, and also counter to those who carried the most institutional power in England's bishopric in 1566 and 1567. The authors create an ethos as a collective of women, of non-threatening maidservants beyond the margins of all of these centers of power; garner added sympathy and empathy; and make use of the particularities as servants and subjects to advance their arguments to the queen and within these debates surrounding the internationally inflected politics of England's religion.[27]

Indeed, the arguments they offer are coded with words such as "blast" and "liberty" that mark their discussion as one entered into the lists of religious reform and counter-reform. Those particular phrases placed in the mouths of women add to the complexity of the coding. The Maydens open their discourse within this disputation:

> We were in a very evill case, and right good cause had we to dread and to dispaire of oure well doings, (most woorthie Matrones & Mistresses) wer it not that we knew ye to be such as are not moved wyth every wynde, nor such as hang upon the blastes of every mans mouth: for else what great mischief and trouble those fond and malicious Dialogues of *The Mery meting of Maydens in London*, might have bred us siely girls, what disquietnesse of mind and body also to you myghte thereby have growne (if ye wer as light of credite, as the Author is of Judgement) your wisedomes well wote, and we are noy to learne. (293–4/Sig. A3)

Their phrasing is telling. John Knox, a Calvinist reformer, printed *The First Blast of the Trumpet Against the Monstrous Regiment of Women* in 1558, and controversialists plucked up the image of the blast throughout the 1560s, with such polemics as Ninian Winzet, *The Last Blast of the Trompet of Godis vvorde aganis the vsurpit auctoritie of Iohne Knox and his Caluiniane brether intrudit prechouris &c.* (Edinburgh: [J. Scot], 1562); and Thomas Stapleton, Robert Horne, and Nicholas Harpsfield, *A Counterblast to M. Hornes vayne blaste against M. Fekenham, . . . touching the Othe of Supremacy* (Louvain: Apud Ionannem Foulerum, 1567). While these invectives diverge in the actual issues they debate, their authors link them via the construction of their titles. The repurposing of the terms serves as a reminder that assigning anything the Maydens say to a particular confession, either Catholic, conforming, or reforming, is tricky, since all of the groups recycled and appropriated one another's arguments as they refuted and reframed them. Suffice it to say, the Maydens root themselves within these conversations with their opening statement, and align themselves with their astutely wise, female, readers.

The Maydens' invocations of legal language locate them at home in the Inns of Court, a zone Peter Ackroyd and others identify as a place of refuge for those, both Catholic and non-conformist, unwilling or unable to conform or swear uniformity. Here again, this placement muddies their position within religious controversies, and indeed as Patrick Collinson describes "The Protestant Underworld," London in 1567 saw the conviction of a cell of reformers associated with hiring a hall, ostensibly for a wedding but really to hold nonconformist services. Collinson notes the central role women played to promote reform. Others have observed the crucial role of women for preserving Roman Catholic culture in England, especially because they were less likely to be prosecuted, and if they were convicted, the family was less likely to lose its property holdings.[28] Nevertheless, all of the groups operating outside of the state church hierarchies made use of women of all classes to move forward their agendas in various ways.

The arguments they offer that link them most explicitly to church politics emerge once the authors establish the need for liberty and align their mistresses with their case. The Maydens note their objections to Hake's claim that they "mispend [s.i.c.] our time in the Church in gazing and looking about us, and that our coming thither is not to pray" (296/ sig. A3). They observe a central issue for themselves, one that resonates directly with polemics of the period:

> And for our thoughtes, sith they are so privie, that were he as cunning as the Divell, yet coulde he not knowe them, sithe God alone hathe that priveledge of all others, to know the thoughts of men, wemen, children, and of every living creature, so that he may as well lie, as say true herein, as it is more likely that he doth: therefore ye may credite him as ye shal see cause: we dare take it upon our consciences that if ye believe it not all, it shal be nothing at al prejudicial to you, nor your lacke of beleefe therein shall any thing hinder your salvation. (296/sig. A6-A6v)

This claim—the right to one's conscience, and the privacy of one's thoughts—comes directly from Elizabeth's justifications of her policies, and plays into Roman Catholic strategies for accommodation, especially those espoused by church Papists, those who outwardly conformed to the national church but maintained their own liberties in matters of conscience.[29] Indeed, the Maydens continue in this regard as they close this portion of their defense: "And thus this being well tried & examined, we have not past two houres at the most upon the Holy day for our talkes, meetings, drinkings, going to playes and sporting, &c" (296/Sig. A6v).

The "trial" and "examination" stems both from their defense, here, and also from their case more generally; they are prepared to withstand any trial, including verbal debate, both in *A Letter* and on any larger stage, even if it becomes catechismic or inquisitorial.

A Letter diverges from many tracts defending women in its recognition of the Maydens' individuality in ways that more generic defenses of women do not attempt to offer. Here, it overlaps with the descriptive realism emergent in the art of Erhard Schoen in his "Lament of the Three Poor House Maids," and other artists of the period. The particularities of the speakers themselves are called out from the title page: Rose, Jane, Rachell, Sara, Philumias [Philomena?], and Dorothy.

These women, as various critics have suggested, are rhetorically astute; in the examples I pointed to earlier, the figurative language and erudition is evident. They include extensive citations of Latin maxims, proverbs in circulation in England and on the continent, catch-phrases from ballads, and more. Just a few examples demonstrate the method, as well as the erudition; they are cited here along with the translations, so crucial to a modern audience, that Fehrenbach offered. One early on, after the emphatic sounding of the note of "liberty," underlines the theme: "and such as are Citizens borne, should repaire also to the country, or to other Cities where they might be free, than to abide as slaves and bondewomen in London, *Libertas namque potior metallis* [for indeed, freedom is preferable to money]" (294/sig. A4). As they argue for their earned right of time of leisure, they aggregate their proverbial proofs to intensify the impact: "Would you not thinke him mad that would every day in the yeare journey his horsse? or that would course with his greyhound whilest his tayle will hang on? (as the Proverbe is) or overflye his Hauke?" (295/sig. A5). As their attack upon Hake builds, so too do the proverbs intensify; the section specifically questioning his prowess as orator includes three Latin proverbs and three Latin legal terms in the space of the verso and recto sequence of signatures (297/A7v and A8). These samples are just a few of the proverbs that lard the text and substantiate the women's claims; they demonstrate the range at work in the text.

Whether the voices of the Maydens are ventriloquized or real is only of nominal importance. Their collective, female, working-class ethos is crucial to their argument. These women existed in this rhetorically constructed London of 1567, and they mounted their defense for reasons that Bancroft and others recognized as noteworthy, worth saving and binding and keeping in a collection. Work remains, to discover with more nuances the function of this ephemeral object, its preservation, and its compilation. These pamphlets performed and continue to perform work that we need to understand more fully. This "letter" in this bound volume is only the beginning; R. J. Fehrenbach has spent the last thirty years (or more) documenting the collections and catalogues of early modern books. He recently announced the publication of the ninth volume in the *Private Libraries in Renaissance England*, and in the process of canvassing these libraries, he has discovered many more texts. They too belong to deepen our understanding of rhetoric, of persuasion, of early modern writers, readers, and audiences, how the debates of the sixteenth century echo and inform the debates of the twenty-first century.

NOTES

1. Joan Kelly articulates some of the key figures in this genre and its general importance to those defending women against misogynistic attacks. Linda Woodbridge offers essential information for England. See also Patricia Demers, 37–46; Blumenfeld-Kosinksi and Brownlee; Forhan; and Miller, Platter, and Gold.

2. With gratitude to Jane Donawerth for suggesting this inquiry, to Adele Seeff for reading early drafts, to audiences at the "Women, Rhetoric, and Writing" conference held April, 2017, at the University of Maryland and at the Sixteenth Century Studies Conference held October 2017 in Milwaukee, Wisconsin, and to my co-editors Danielle Griffin and Jessica Enoch for their questions, comments, and suggestions. Errors and omissions remain mine.

3. Deborah Shuger in "Civility and Censorship" offers an informative discussion of some of the concerns at work for censors in sixteenth-century England. See also three volumes by Annabel Patterson for formative discussions in the field.

4. Jessica Winston observes, "The literary culture of the Inns [of Court, training-ground for lawyers in England] in the 1560s results from the fortuitous meeting of two trends: first, long-term developments in humanist education and, second, recent changes in the legal profession, namely the undersupply of legally trained men who could meet England's litigious and administrative needs," 50.

5. Cheryl Glenn's sweeping and magisterial narrative of women's rhetorical participation from the beginnings of western writing to the present notes these difficulties and necessarily plucks out Margaret Roper,

Anne Askew, and Elizabeth I for her section "Inscribed in the Margins: Renaissance Women and Rhetorical Culture," in 118–72.

6. Fehrenbach 285. See also Patricia Phillippy, especially 439–40. *A Letter* might rightly have a place in such anthologies as *English Women's Voices 1540–1700*, edited by Otten.

7. See "silly, adj., n., and adv." *OED Online*, Oxford UP, Dec. 2018, www.oed.com/view/Entry/179761. Accessed 14 January 2019.

8. See "liberty, n.1." *OED Online*, Oxford UP, Dec. 2018, www.oed.com/view/Entry/107898, and "liberty, v." *OED Online*, Oxford UP, December 2018, www.oed.com/view/Entry/107900, accessed 14 Jan. 2019.

9. For useful articulations of this sort of work, see Sarah Covington, Susannah Brietz Monta, Kimberly Anne Coles, and Micheline White.

10. For a discussion of the link between *A Letter* and Elizabeth I and marriage politics, see Ilona Bell, "Popular Debate." I extend here beyond Bell's focus on the English political situation to the implications of religious politics and the relationship of England to the continent, as well as Scotland and Ireland.

11. To learn more about Richard Bancroft and his involvement in Conformist politics, see especially two volumes by Patrick Collinson. See also Donna B. Hamilton, Peter Lake, Peter Marshall, and Michael C. Questier.

12. Fehrenbach asserts, "That a scullion or a laundress employed at one of the Inns might have picked up such knowledge is, however appealing, very unlikely. Private training in the law, such as the tutoring in the humane studies given the educationally fortunate Margaret More Ropers by their fathers or others, does not seem to have existed for anyone, man or woman. In the end, whether any woman in the 1560s would have had the range of legal knowledge revealed in *A Letter* is, I think, the matter on which the sex of the author must turn, and not the slightest evidence exists to suggest that any woman was likely to have such knowledge. The author was thus likely a man, one who was able to create the persona of domestic maidservants by successfully adopting certain class attitudes and by effectively demonstrating an acquaintance with the domestic world, both easier to come by second hand than English law" (288).

13. Most offer social commentary and descriptions of social systems. See *A knowledge for kings; A plaine description; The mirrour of madnes; A Letter sent by the maydens of London; A breefe discourse; A discouerie of the countries of Tartaria, Scithia, & Cataya;* and *A letter sent by I.B. Gentleman.* The volume is part of the holdings of the Lambeth Palace Library,

call number ZZ1576.5.

14. Among the earliest to do so were Phillippy and Ilona Bell, "In Defense of Their Lawful Liberty." Many scholars either overtly or implicitly acknowledge female authorship; see for example Ann Rosalind Jones, Laurie Ellinghausen, especially 3–5, Pamela Joseph Benson, and Maggie Ellen Ray, especially notes 47 and 48.

15. Aside from work on Isabella Whitney cited above, scholarship on service in the sixteenth century tends to focus on drama and on the end of the century. See, for example, Dowd and Korda, editors.; Rivlin; and Kendrick. Issues surrounding labor emerge as well in studies of the pastoral, but those necessarily look to rural concerns; see especially Little, *Transforming Work*. Some essential histories of working women include Gowing, *Domestic Dangers*, and Paula Humfrey, who focuses especially on court records 1667–1735.

16. For a more recent overview of scholarship in the field with details regarding Bancroft as a censor in the 1590s, see Keener. See also Benson.

17. See Alexandra Walsham's work. For an invaluable guide to the polemics, see Peter Milward. See also Brian Cummings; Norman Jones; and Deborah Shuger, *Sacred Rhetoric* and *Censorship and Cultural Sensibility*.

18. Peter Ackroyd.

19. See "John Jewel to Henry Bullinger, 7 Aug 1570."

20. See Alec Ryrie, especially chapters "Two Restorations: Mary and Elizabeth, 1553–60," "Reformations on the Battlefield: Scotland, 1542–73," and "Gaping Gulfs: Elizabethan England and the Politics of Fear."

21. *A Briefe request or declaracion*. Also held in Lambeth Palace Library, marked "R.B.," ZZ1584.13.10. A quick scan of this volume's fourteen pamphlets suggests they range from this early treatise with the rest from the 1570s through the compilation date of 1585 and focus largely on issues concerning the Low Countries' struggles around religion.

22. See David Parrott; Geoffrey Parker; and Grainne Henry.

23. John Strype, 234–56.

24. Kelly. Fehrenbach observes, "Suzanne Hull writes in *Chaste, Silent, and Obedient: English Books for Women* (San Marino, Cal., 1982), that 'Favorite subjects for the Elizabethan and Jacobean satirist were women's apparel and cosmetics, jealousy, greed and extravagance, pride, lust and infidelity, gossiping or sharp tongues, and women's attempts to dominate men' (111)" (288, n. 8). Fehrenbach provides a useful overview of many of the deviations in *A Letter* from the conventions of the

"Querelle," 288–93.

25. See Strype, *Annals of the Reformation Under Queen Elizabeth*, 1.2: 234.

26. Ackroyd, 316–17, notes that statutes included the 39 Articles, but also made efforts to regulate the poor, minimum wage, and more, including the workhouses, hospitals, and other social agencies formerly managed by ecclesiastical bodies such as monasteries as they were replaced with lay authorities. Penalties increased for noncompliance, deviance, and vagrancy.

27. For a useful assessment of female collectivity, see Margaret Ferguson, especially "Interlude," 173–79. See also Ann Rosalind Jones.

28. Collinson, *Elizabethan Puritan Movement*, 84–97.

29. The phrase points more strongly to issues surrounding Oaths of Supremacy and Obedience later in the Tudor period (see Hamilton 30–58), but the Roman Catholic Thomas Stapleton uses the phrase, "privie thoughts" in his *1567 Counterblast*. For an excellent study of equivocation in the seventeenth century, see Frances E. Dolan.

Works Cited

Ackroyd, Peter. "The Two Queens." *Tudors: The History of England from Henry VIII to Elizabeth I*. St. Martin's Press, 2012.

Bell, Ilona. "In Defense of Their Lawful Liberty: A Letter Sent by the Maydens of London." *Women, Writing, and the Reproduction of Culture in Tudor and Stuart Britain*, edited by Mary E. Burke et al., Syracuse UP, 2000, pp. 177–92

—. "Popular Debate and Courtly Dialogue: Always Her Own Free Woman." *Elizabeth I: The Voice of a Monarch*, Palgrave-Macmillan, 2010, pp. 116–45.

Benson, Pamela Joseph, editor. *Texts from the Querelle, 1521–1615*. Essential Works for the Study of Early Modern Women, Pt. 2, Vol. 1, Ashgate, 2008.

Boccaccio, Giovanni. *De mulieribus claris: English & Latin: Famous Women*. Edited by Virginia Brown, Harvard UP, 2001.

A breefe discourse, declaring and approuing the necessarie and inuiolable maintenance of the laudable customes of London namely, of that one, whereby a reasonable partition of the goods of husbands among their wiues and children is prouided: with an answer to such obiections and pretensed reasons, as are by persons vnaduised or euil persuaded, vsed against the same. London: Henrie Midleton for Rafe Newberie, 1584. STC 16747.

A Briefe request or declaracion presented vnto madame the Duchesse of Parma &c. regent of the Lowe Countrie of Flaunders, by the lordes and nobilitie of the same countrie with the answere and replie, and other writynges, englished by W.F. London: Jhon Kyngston for Thomas Humbel, 1566. STC 11028.

Coles, Kimberly Anne. *Religion, Reform, and Women's Writing in Early Modern England.* Cambridge UP, 2008.

Collinson, Patrick. *The Elizabethan Puritan Movement.* 1967. Clarendon Press, 1991.

—. *Richard Bancroft and Elizabethan Anti-Puritanism.* Cambridge UP, 2013.

Covington, Sarah. *The Trail of Martyrdom: Persecution and Resistance in Sixteenth-Century England.* U of Notre Dame P, 2004.

Cummings, Brian. *The Literary Culture of the Reformation: Grammar and Grace.* Oxford UP, 2002.

Demers, Patricia. *Women's Writing in English: Early Modern England.* U Toronto P, 2005.

Dolan, Frances E. *True Relations: Reading, Literature, and Evidence in Seventeenth-Century England.* U of Pennsylvania P, 2013.

Dowd, Michelle M., and Natasha Korda, editors. *Working Subjects in Early Modern English Drama.* Ashgate, 2011.

Ellinghausen, Laurie. "Literary Property and the Single Woman in Isabella Whitney's 'A Sweet Nosegay.'" *Studies in English Literature, 1500–1900,* vol. 45, no. 1, Winter 2005, pp. 1–22.

Fehrenbach, R. J. "A Letter sent by the Maydens of London (1567)." *English Literary Renaissance,* vol. 14, no. 3, Autumn 1984, pp. 285–304.

Fonte, Moderata (Modesto Pozzo). *The Merits of Women: Wherein is Revealed their Nobility and their Superiority to Men.* Edited and translated by Virginia Cox, U Chicago P, 2018.

Forhan, Kate Langdon. *The Political Theory of Christine de Pizan.* Ashgate, 2002.

Ferguson, Margaret. *Dido's Daughters: Literacy, Gender, and Empire in Early Modern England and France.* U Chicago P, 2003.

Frampton, John. *A discouerie of the countries of Tartaria, Scithia, & Cataya, by the northeast: with the maners, fashions, and orders which are vsed in those countries. Set foorth by Iohn Frampton merchaunt.* London: Thomas Dawson, 1580, STC 11255.

Glenn, Cheryl. *Rhetoric Retold: Regendering the Tradition from Antiquity through the Renaissance*. Southern Illinois UP, 1997.

Gowing, Laura. *Domestic Dangers: Women, Words, and Sex in Early Modern London*. Clarendon P, 1996.

Hamilton, Donna B. *Shakespeare and the Politics of Protestant England*. UP of Kentucky, 1992.

Henry, Grainne. *The Irish Military Community in Spanish Flanders, 1586–1621*. Irish Academic Press, 1991.

Humfrey, Paula, editor. *The Experience of Domestic Service for Women in Early Modern London*. Ashgate, 2011.

Jewel, John. *The Works of John Jewel, Bishop of Salisbury, The Fourth Portion, containing The Defence of the Apology, Parts IV-VI, the Epistle to Scipio, A View of the Seditious Bull, A Treatise on the Holy Scriptures, Letters, and Miscellaneous Pie*ces, edited and translated by John Ayre, Parker Society, vol. 26, Cambridge UP, 1850.

Jones, Ann Rosalind. "Maidservants of London: Sisterhoods of Kinship and Labor." *Maids and Mistresses, Cousins and Queens: Women's Alliances in Early Modern England*, edited by Susan Frye and Karen Robertson. Oxford UP, 1999, pp. 21–32.

Jones, Norman. *The English Reformation: Religion and Cultural Adaptation*. Wiley-Blackwell, 2002.

Keener, Andrew S. "Robert Tofte's Of Marriage and Wiuing and the Bishops Ban of 1599." *Studies in Philology*, vol. 110, no. 3, Summer 2013, pp. 506–32.

Kelly, Joan. "Early Feminist Theory and the *Querelle des Femmes*." *Signs*, vol. 8, no. 1, 1982, pp. 4–28.

Kendrick, Matthew. *At Work in the Early Modern English Theater: Valuing Labor*. Farleigh Dickinson UP, 2015.

Knox, John. *The First Blast of the Trumpet Against the Monstrous Regiment of Women*. Geneva, 1558.

A knowledge for kings, and a warning for subiects conteyning the moste excellent and worthy history of the Raellyans peruerted state, and gouernment of their common wealth: no lesse rare, then strange. First written in Latine, by Iames Glaucus a Germaine: and now translated into english by VVilliam Cleuer scholemaster. By speciall recorde, this monument was two thousande yeares of antiquity: and so dusked and forworne with age, that being in a plaine writte[n] letter, could scarce be read . . . I with my painefull indeuour haue now renewed it into fresh memorye. London: Richard Jhones, 1576. STC 11920.

Lake, Peter. *Anglicans and Puritans? Presbyterianism and English Conformist Thought from Whitgift to Hooker.* Unwin Hyman, 1988.

A letter sent by I.B. Gentleman vnto his very frende Maystet [sic] R.C. Esquire vvherin is conteined a large discourse of the peopling & inhabiting the cuntrie called the Ardes, and other adiacent in the north of Ireland, and taken in hand by Sir Thomas Smith one of the Queenes Maiesties priuie Counsel, and Thomas Smith Esquire, his sonne. [London: Henry Binneman for Anthonhson,] [1572]. STC 1048.

A Letter sent by the maydens of London, to the vertuous matrones & mistresses of the same in the defense of their lawfull libertie, answering The mery meeting / by us Rose, Iane, Rachell, Sara, Philumias and Dorothie. London: Henry Binneman for Thomas Hacket, 1567, STC 16754.5.

Little, Katherine C. *Transforming Work: Early Modern Pastoral and Late Medieval Poetry.* U of Notre Dame P, 2013.

Manne, Kate. *Down Girl: The Logic of Misogyny.* Oxford UP, 2018.

Marshall, Peter. *Heretics and Believers: A History of the English Reformation.* Yale UP, 2017.

Miller, Paul Allen, Charles Platter, and Barbara K. Gold, *Sex and Gender in Medieval and Renaissance Texts: The Latin Tradition.* SUNY P, 1997.

Milward, Peter. *Religious Controversies of the Elizabethan Age: A Survey of Printed Sources.* U of Nebraska P, 1977.

Monta, Susannah Brietz. *Martyrdom and Literature in Early Modern England.* Cambridge: Cambridge UP, 2005.

Otten, Charlotte F., editor. *English Women's Voices 1540–1700.* Florida International UP, 1992.

Parker, Geoffrey. *The Army of Flanders and the Spanish Road 1567–1659.* 1972. Cambridge UP, 2004.

Parrott, David. *The Business of War: Military Enterprise and Military Revolution in Early Modern Europe.* Cambridge UP, 2012.

Patterson, Annabel. *Censorship and Interpretation: The Conditions of Writing and Reading in Early Modern England.* U Wisconsin P, 1984.

—. *Pastoral and Ideology: Virgil to Valéry.* U California P, 1987.

—. *Reading between the Lines.* Madison: U Wisconsin P, 1993.

Pizan, Christine de. *The Book of the City of Ladies,* 1405, translated by Rosalind Brown-Grant, Penguin, 1999.

—. *The Selected Writings of Christine de Pizan: New Translations, Criticism,* edited by Renate Blumenfeld-Kosinski and Kevin Brownlee, Norton Critical Editions, 1997.

A plaine description of the auncient petigree of Dame Slaunder togither with hir coheires and fellowe members, lying, flattering, backebyting, (being the diuels deare darlinges) playnly and pithely described and set forth in their colours from their first descent, of what linage and kinred they came off. Eyther of them seuerally in his place set forth, as thou mayest reade hereafter. London: By [H. Middleton for] Iohn Harrison, 1573. STC 22630.

Phillippy, Patricia. "The Maid's Lawful Liberty: Service, the Household, and 'Mother B' in Isabella Whitney's 'A Sweet Nosegay,'" *Modern Philology*, vol. 95, no. 4, May 1998, pp. 439–62.

Questier, Michael C. *Catholicism and Community in Early Modern England: Politics, Aristocratic Patronage, and Religion, c. 1550–1640.* Cambridge UP, 2006.

Ray, Maggie Ellen. "'The simple fool doth trust / too much before he try': Isabella Whitney's Revisions of the Female Reader and Lover in The Copy of the Letter," in *Early Modern Women: An Interdisciplinary Journal*, vol. 6, 2011, pp. 127–58.

Rivlin, Elizabeth. *The Aesthetics of Service in Early Modern England.* Northwestern UP, 2012.

Ryrie, Alec. *The Age of Reformation: The Tudor and Stewart Realms 1485–1603.* 2008. Routledge, 2017.

[Sandford, James]. *The mirrour of madnes, or a paradoxe maintayning madnes to be most excellent: done out of French into English, by Ia. San. Gent.* London: Thomas Marshe, 1576, STC 17980.

Shuger, Deborah. *Censorship and Cultural Sensibility: The Regulation of Language in Tudor-Stuart England.* U of Pennsylvania P, 2006.

—. "Civility and Censorship in Early Modern England." *Censorship & Silencing: Practices of Cultural Regulation*, edited by Robert C. Post, The Getty Research Institute, 1998, pp. 89–110.

—. *Sacred Rhetoric: The Christian Grand Style in the English Renaissance.* Princeton UP, 1988.

Stapleton, Thomas, Robert Horne, and Nicholas Harpsfield. *A Counterblast to M. Horne's Vain Blast.* Louvain: Apud Ionannem Foulerum, 1567, 277/sig. aa. *Early English Books Online*, gateway.proquest.com/openurl?ctx_ver=Z39.88–2003&res_id=xri:eebo&rft_id=xri:eebo:image:18356:297. Accessed Mar. 9, 2018

Strype, John. *Annals of the Reformation and Establishment of Religion and Other Various Occurrences in the Church of England during Queen Elizabeth's Happy Reign*, vol. 1, part 2, 1824, Burt Franklin, 1968.

Walsham, Alexandra, *Charitable Hatred: Tolerance and Intolerance in England, 1500–1700.* Manchester UP, 2006.

—. *Church Papists: Catholicism, Conformity, and Confessional Polemic in Early Modern England.* Boydell Press, 1993.

—. "Dumb Preachers: Catholicism and the Culture of Print." *Catholic Reformation in Protestant Britain.* Ashgate, 2014, pp. 301–35.

White, Micheline, editor. *English Women, Religion, and Textual Production, 1500–1625.* Ashgate Press, 2011.

Winston, Jessica. *Lawyers at Play: Literature, Law, and Politics at the Early Modern Inns of Court, 1558–1581.* Oxford UP, 2016.

Winzet, Ninian. *The Last Blast of the Trompet of Godis vvorde aganis the vsurpit auctoritie of Iohne Knox and his Caluiniane brether intrudit prechouris &c.* Edinburgh: [J. Scot], 1562.

Woodbridge, Linda. *Women and the English Renaissance: Literature and the Nature of Womankind, 1540–1620.* 1984. U Chicago P, 1986.

4 Zainab Al-Ghazali: Transgression or Affirmation of Gender Roles

Nabila Hijazi

Feminist scholars of rhetoric posit that Western Christian women justified their violations of social norms prohibiting women's speech by claiming moral and spiritual positions from which to preach and educate children (Bizzell, Enoch, Minifee, Nardin, Shaver, Zimmerelli). In this chapter, I build upon this work and respond to calls for expansion of feminist rhetorical recovery and investigation to global spectrums (Hesford and Schell; Royster and Kirsch).[1] I evoke the theme of circulation, as I widen the lens to consider whether and how these methods travel, circulate to, and operate in the Middle Eastern, Islamic, twentieth-century context. I trace Muslim women's rhetorical tradition by tracking rhetorics that circulate and recirculate in the Middle East. The work of women such as Zainab Al-Ghazali offers the opportunity to think complexly about how rhetoric and religion circulate to a different context, temporality, and geographical location and relate to Muslim gendered identity and how Muslim women negotiate their roles. Especially as the religion of Islam calls for separate spheres and gender-specific roles for men and women, and specifically domestic roles for women, the methods Muslim women use should be of great interest to feminist rhetoricians.

Zainab Al-Ghazali was an Egyptian leader and a resilient and controversial female Muslim figure of the twentieth century. She started as an Islamic feminist, adopting the secular themes of the West that critique the notion of asymmetrical gender roles in favor of an egalitarian model of the family. However, Al-Ghazali changed her position later in life to argue against her earlier feminist arguments that leveraged nuanced interpretations of the Quran to solidify the Islamic feminist movement by grounding it within the Islamic faith. Scholars such as Mariam Cook and Valerie Hoffman have written essays on Al-Ghazali from a feminist or gendered perspective; however, few concentrate on her rhetoric. In this chapter, I focus on the rhetorical strategies that guided Al-Ghazali's socio-political activism and enabled her to call for a return back to Islam as a way of life. I show how her rhetoric enabled the mobility and circulation of her activism and preaching. I examine Al-Ghazali's publications, especially her multi-genre memoir, *Ayyām min ḥayātī (Days from My Life)*—a text first published in Arabic in 1989, translated into English by Mokrane Guezzou and published by the Islamic Foundation in 2006, under the title *Return of the Pharaoh: Memoir in Nasir's Prison*, allowing the mobility of her memoir to Western context and readers. Through my analysis, I demonstrate how she adopts an Islamic activist rhetoric and constructs a religious identity, defiant of the Nationalist political party of Egypt and fiercely resistant to Western feminist ideology that was embodied by the new wave of Islamic feminisms. I argue that Al-Ghazali uses religious rhetoric to forcefully establish her ethos and legitimize her call to revitalize the Islamic tradition and encourage women to adhere to its conservative gender role ideology—roles Al-Ghazali rhetorically and religiously transgresses to succeed in her activism and religious mission, Da'wah[2] movement, which gained momentum and traveled beyond Egypt to reach other Middle Eastern countries. In appropriating traditional religious rhetoric to her own ends through methodical selection of Quranic verses, emulation of the style of Islamic religious texts, and her own mystical visions of Prophet Mohammed, Al-Ghazali legitimizes different modes of resistance to the political authority that existed in Egypt in the 1960s and calls for reinstatement of Islamic laws as the only foundational support for women against an often predatory culture. She thus occupies an unequivocal rhetorical position that fortifies her advocacy for readopting the religion of Islam in all matters of life and to promote conservative, separate gender roles.

AL-GHAZALI: BIOGRAPHY AND POLITICAL TRAJECTORY

Zainab Al-Ghazali influenced millions of young Muslims, not only in Egypt but also in other Muslim countries. Her religious teachings and influence traveled through several mediums and to different geographical places to reach wider audiences and congregations. She was born in 1917 in modern-day Egypt into the household of a local religious leader, who instilled in her the importance of religion in everyday life. Influenced by her father who was a graduate of Al-Azhar, Egypt's oldest degree-granting university and "Sunni Islam's most prestigious university," she received her formal secondary education from Al-Azhar, where she studied and received certificates in hadith,[3] preaching, and Quranic exegesis (Hoffman 275–76). Al-Ghazali gained prominence in Egyptian society at a turbulent time for women and the country, when many Middle Eastern Muslim countries, including Egypt, were going through political transformation and figuring out their political stance as they became liberated from colonial powers that had exercised formal sovereignty over the lands of Arabia and the Middle East from the early sixteenth-century Ottoman Empire to the end of British protectorate in 1922. Egypt became a kingdom under the rule of Muhammad Ali's dynasty, which lasted until 1952 to be overthrown by Gamal Abd Al-Nasir, a controversial political leader, who led the 1952 coup. Nasir became the president of a new Egypt, the Republic of Egypt, and championed Arab nationalism, advocating pan-Arabism over pan-Islamic unity, an ideology Al-Ghazali strongly advocated for in her mission. She appealed to the masses that "Islam is the solution,"[4] by reverting back to Islam and re-adopting its practices in all walks of life, Egyptians can overcome the problems the country was facing internally and externally.

During the Egyptian nationalist and women's movement, Al-Ghazali became exposed to women's socio-political activism and witnessed first-hand Egyptian women's participation in public space. She invested herself in the movement of Egyptian women who opted for secularism, the ideology that calls for the separation of the state from religious Islamic institutions. She joined the Egyptian Feminist Union (EFU),[5] a non-profit, non-governmental organization, which promoted European social values and secular orientation, when she was no more than eighteen. She started as a feminist looking up to the West[6]—endorsing Western values and secularization of women's roles in society; however, Al-Ghazali shortly had a change of heart, vigorously critiquing and challenging EFU's feminist approach on the basis of its rejection of Islam's definition of women's roles in society. In 1936, she left the Egyptian Feminist Union and established Jamaat Al-Sayyidat-al-Muslimeen, or, the Muslim Ladies Association (MLA). The MLA was a female branch of Al-Ikhwan,[7] the Muslim Brotherhood, a transnational Sunni Islamic revivalist organization founded in Egypt, which calls for political activism in combination with Islamic charity work. Since its inception, the Brotherhood's stated goal has been to instill the Quran and the Sunnah[8] as the "sole reference point for ordering the life of the Muslim family, individual, community and state," a goal Al-Ghazali passionately and fully endorsed (Kull 167).

Joining a long history of religious women who attempted to use men's institutions to bolster their own authority while avoiding being consumed by them, Al-Ghazali maintained MLA's autonomy and independence while publicly stating her loyalty and affiliation to the Muslim Brotherhood (Abdel-Latif 3). MLA encouraged women to seek education and be active in the community. Most importantly, Al-Ghazali called them to embrace the religion of Islam as a means to personal agency, since, she claimed, it is religion that grants women full personhood and many rights, including the right of inheritance and owning and managing property. By the time the government dissolved it in 1964, MLA had millions of members throughout Egypt, according to Al-Ghazali. The organization's mission was not political per se; rather, it focused on social work projects, such as health clinics, orphanages, and schools for children (Baron 169; 186). MLA's vision was providing charitable services and educating women, especially in the field of Quranic exegesis, as a form of women's empowerment: to be active within the home as well as strengthen the community at large. MLA's strategies parallel many efforts by Christian women but shift because of the specific ways in which Islamic property law and charitable practices operate, granting Muslim women property rights and legal persona as a norm of their existence.[9]

Al-Ghazali modified her methods in response to the social upheavals that followed in the wake of the military coup of 1952, which was led by Gamal Abd Al-Nasir who assumed power and secured a secular-nationalist state. Considering the Muslim Brotherhood and its Islamic ideology as a threat to the newly secured power, Nasir and his government quelled the organization, accusing hundreds of Muslim Brothers[10] of sedition and either imprisoned or assassinated them. The Muslim Brotherhood was calling for "Islam Is the Solution" and aiming to establish a democratically introduced civic Islamic state, which would threaten Nasir's secular-nationalist government. Al-Ghazali was the first "Muslim Sister" who was publicly active, both socially and politically, during the Nasir years, when most Muslim Brother members were jailed by Nasir's regime (Abdel-Latif 4). Initially, she set out to offer assistance of food, medical care, and other forms of support to the families who were left behind to fend and provide for themselves, while their husbands, Muslim Brotherhood members, were in prison. However, it was necessary for Al-Ghazali not only to keep the organization's social work and vision alive but also to shift her focus from purely social work to political activism grounded in Islamic vision to save the Muslim Brotherhood from dissolution (Roded 258).

She vigorously worked to reconstitute the organization while conducting various seminars and preaching the Islamic message: seeking gradual (re)implementation of Islam at a political level and teaching it to the masses as the best solution to the recurring problems of the time. Insisting that Islam repudiates violence and torture, she maintained the educational intention and the pacific tone in her teachings and lectures. During that time, she was instrumental in maintaining the Muslim Brotherhood's political mission and presence, until she was incarcerated herself in 1965 (Lewis 24–25). Accused of conspiring to assassinate the president, Nasir, Al-Ghazali was locked up in a military prison before her transfer to Al-Qanatir, an all-women's prison. Before her transfer, she was tortured, facing some of the most inhumane practices, which she vividly describes in her memoir. She was later released in 1971 by Nasir's successor, Anwar Al-Sadat (Farag 228–29).

After her release from prison, she wrote her multi-genre memoir, *Ayyām min ḥayātī (Days from My Life)*, hoping it would become a living example that would inspire others to adopt the same religious and political path she had taken. Her memoir solidified her fame, which traveled beyond Egypt's borders as she became a popular Muslim activist utilizing different venues to preach her cause. She appeared numerous times on Egypt's national TV, either to be interviewed or for anchoring her lecture series in which she reflected on her imprisonment or advised women on social issues, including marriage and family life. After 1971, she reclaimed her position as the editor of the women's and children's section of the Muslim Brotherhood's magazine, *Al-Da'wah*, and became very active in Al-da'wah,[11] "the social movement whose participants seek Islam as a way of life, not merely a religion." As a Da'iya,[12] she devoted her life and energy to spread Islam to all sectors of Egyptian society. She gave weekly sermons to thousands of women at Ibn Tulun Mosque in Cairo. In 1981, she started writing a women's column for *Al-Da'wah Magazine*, publishing articles on the domestic nature of women and on the importance of motherhood and wifedom for Muslim women.

MEMOIR AS GENRE FOR ACTIVIST RHETORIC

Realizing that Islam is not about performance but a turning of the whole mind to God and a way of life, Al-Ghazali used the genre of the memoir to articulate her gendered activism within the realm of Islam. By doing so, she legitimized her piety and strengthened her argument against corrupt secular groups that called women to deviate from the Islamic path and instilled Western ideas—practices that, according to Al-Ghazali, would destroy Egyptian Muslim society.[13] Much like many Western women rhetors, such as Jarena Lee and Alice Thornton, Al-Ghazali leverages the genre of the memoir to preach her religious and activist message and to graphically and vividly narrate her prison experience, including the sufferings and the inhumane forms of gruesome torture she endured. In *Ayyām min ḥayātī*, which was retitled to *Return of the Pharaoh*, she is explicit about exalting her religious mission and status. After glorifying Allah,[14] Al-Ghazali presents herself as a devoutly religious woman who committed all of her life to a lofty cause: Al-da'wah; her leadership and struggle stand as an immortal example for many Muslims to adopt and follow. Continuously placing her trust in Allah, she received enormous support from her followers who felt her sincerity and were inspired to carry her mission forward. Her activism is recorded in her memoir, which she frames as a "pledge of allegiance [and a] fight in His sake [Allah's sake]" (35) and a "legend of unsurpassable cruelty and torture" (87). Her text is one that she hoped would ignite fellow Muslims, men and women, to resist the government's wrongdoings and join her activist and religious mission against tyrant, un-Islamic governments. [See Figures 4.1 and 4.2.][15]

Al-Ghazali establishes her religious ethos by methodically imitating the style of Islamic religious texts and meticulously quoting verses from the Quran, which became her sanctuary during her imprisonment. In both the introduction and on the cover page of her memoir (see Figure 4.1), she cites sacred scriptures and Quranic verses the way they would be presented in the holy Islamic book, the Quran:

> Do you suppose that you will enter Paradise untouched by the suffering endured by the men of faith who passed away before you? They were afflicted by misery and hardship and so convulsed that the Messenger and the believers with him cried out: 'When will Allah's help arrive?' They were assured that Allah's help was close by. (2:214)[16]

The verse, which is kept in the translated copy of the memoir in both Arabic and English (see Figure 4.2), rhetorically captures her struggle and religious mission regarding the multiple trials one should endure to establish the word of Allah on earth and seize His rewards in the hereafter. She acknowledges that in order to emerge from difficult times closer to Allah, she had to live through and respond to them. By situating herself and deriving her authority from the Quran, she constructs her religious authority and presents herself as a credible Islamic scholar who is morally and ethically fit to guide since her guidance is not based on human but heavenly authority. By connecting her word to the word of Allah, she places herself within the ultimate authority of Him, operating under His power. The choice to include this verse also sets the tone for the memoir: the text is not by any means entertaining; rather, it is inspirational and descriptive of the hardships and the struggles one should endure in order to re-establish the legacy of Islam and to enter paradise in the hereafter.

أَمْ حَسِبْتُمْ أَن تَدْخُلُوا الْجَنَّةَ وَلَمَّا
يَأْتِكُم مَّثَلُ الَّذِينَ خَلَوْا مِن قَبْلِكُم
مَّسَّتْهُمُ الْبَأْسَاءُ وَالضَّرَّاءُ وَزُلْزِلُوا حَتَّى
يَقُولَ الرَّسُولُ وَالَّذِينَ آمَنُوا مَعَهُ مَتَى
نَصْرُ اللَّهِ أَلَا إِنَّ نَصْرَ اللَّهِ قَرِيبٌ ﴿٢١٤﴾

Do you suppose that you will enter
Paradise untouched by the suffering
endured by the men of faith who
passed away before you? They were
afflicted by misery and hardship and
so convulsed that the Messenger
and the believers with him cried
out: 'When will Allah's help arrive?'
They were assured that Allah's help
was close by.

(Surah al-Baqarah, 214)

Return of
the Pharaoh
Memoir in Nasir's Prison

ZAINAB AL-GHAZALI

Translated by
Mokrane Guezzou

The Islamic Foundation

Figure 4.1: Cover Page, *The Return of the Pharoah*, translated by Mokrane Guezzou. Kube Publishing Ltd., © 2006. Used by permission.

Al-Ghazali further constructs her religious credentials in the introduction of her memoir by adding religious statements such as, "Bismillah al-Rahman al Raheem, Wassalatu Wassalamu Ala Sayidna Muhammad

Wa 'ala Aalihi Wasahbihi Ajma'een,"[17] which translates to "In the Name of Allah, the Merciful, the Compassionate. Peace and blessings be on our master Muhammad, his household and Companions" (1). Such an introductory statement is commonly used to preface religious Islamic tracts. Therefore, readers would expect a spiritual text that excites, energizes, and moves Muslim readers to take action in bringing back Islam to their lives and acting according to its teachings. By situating her memoir in a religious context, Al-Ghazali associates her experience with the experience of Prophet Mohammed and his companions, who endured countless episodes of physical, financial, and even emotional torture in order to spread the word of Allah and firmly establish Islam. Like them, Al-Ghazali, as a political, religious leader and survivor, struggled for the sake of others who are expected to carry the Islamic mission further. In other words, she suffered, following the Prophet's path, so that the legacy of Islam could be revived and others could enjoy living its fruitfulness and carry its mission forward.

IN THE NAME OF ALLAH,
THE MERCIFUL,
THE MERCY-GIVING

Figure 4.2: Detail, Cover Page, *The Return of the Pharoah*, translated by Mokrane Guezzou. Kube Publishing Ltd., © 2006. Used by permission.

In the memoir, Al-Ghazali also recalls mystical visions of Prophet Muhammad that she experienced during her sojourn in prison, and through this recollection she further confirms her special place as a guide whose enlightenment and strength stem from a higher prophetic source. She writes:

> I do not know how but I fell asleep while invoking Allah, and it was then that I experienced the first of four visions of the Prophet (peace be upon him) that I was to see during my stay in prison. There in front of me, praise be to Allah, was a vast desert and camels with hawdahs as if made of light. On each hawdah were four men, all with luminous faces. I found myself behind this huge train of camels in that vast, endless desert, and standing behind a great, reverent man. This man was holding a halter, which passed through the neck of each camel. I wondered silently: "Could this man be the Prophet (peace be upon him)? Silence has no safeguard with the Prophet," who replied: "Zaynab! You are following in the footsteps of Muhammad, Allah's Servant and Messenger." (53)

Such strong religious association with the Prophet Muhammed solidifies Al-Ghazali's call and validates her words. Rooted in solemn, reverent, and divine authority, the Prophet Muhammad who, through his da'wa and Islamic teachings, was able to change non-Islamic Arabia and spread Islam to the whole world. This tenacious understanding thus invigorates Al-Ghazali to maintain her position and stoutly adhere to her cause.

Al-Ghazali's dramatic and pathetic descriptions of the struggle and torture she went through in prison work to evoke emotions of pity, support, sympathy, and compassion from her readers. In her memoir, she vividly describes the scenes of breathless violence enacted on her body while in prison: "Within seconds [dogs] were upon me . . . two devouring my flesh, the other, Shams Badran, cursing me with his impudent tongue! Eventually, realizing the futility of all this he called off the dogs, demanding instead that I be flogged" (108–9). By describing the different types of torture she suffered in prison, she crafts a stalwart religious persona that is guided by and working for Islam and presents a stamina that exceeds any masculine endurance. Even though some members of the Muslim Brotherhood were arrested as well, Al-Ghazali endured more severe forms of torture and punishment. In fact, her special suffering surpassed what the men endured: "The psychological abuse I had suffered was becoming almost as intolerable and unbearable as their physical perversions" (83). Her refuge was in religion and in Allah who, according to Al-Ghazali, supplemented her with constant strength to stand against the evil and the hardship enacted on her body. She writes, "my only consolation being the following which I repeated continuously: 'Allah is Sufficient unto us, and He is the best Disposer of affairs! O Allah! Relieve me from evil with whatever You want and in whatever manner You want'" (109–10). "Allah is Sufficient unto us, and He is the best Disposer of affairs!"[18] is a famous du'a (prayer and invocation) that Muslims have used in the face of calamity and fearsome situations; it comes from the Quran (3:173).[19] Such du'as, along with her extensive use of Quranic verses, confirm Al-Ghazali's esteemed spiritual identity. Her rhetorical decisions in her memoir also emphasize that, even after her release from prison, she resumed her mission to inspire others to join in her cause, and she was sure to point out that all of her efforts—her commitment to justice as well as her strength and stamina—came only from Allah. As a result, Al-Ghazali's memoir reveals how her life stands as a testament to many Muslim victims, including men and women; by holding fast to the rope of Allah, she challenged her oppressors and showed true patience and extraordinary resilience.

Religious Rhetoric Legitimizing Gender Roles and Defying Islamic Feminism

Further analysis of Al-Ghazali's rhetoric reveals the gendered inflection to her activist work in which she praises domesticity and traditional gender roles. Along with her memoirs, Al-Ghazali's lectures and other writings emphasize her belief that Islam grants women the right to be active in public domains, as long as that does not interfere with their first and most sacred duty and domestic role: that of being a good wife and mother. She enunciates her rhetoric "with great vehemence in an array of articles, interviews, and polemics published in a variety of outlets, including the journal of the MLA, the Brotherhood's *Al-Da'wa*, and the Islamist magazine *Liwa al-Islam*" (Hoffman, *Princeton Readings*, 279). Extending her religious resilient role while adopting a profound role as a "murshida," a Muslim female guide and spiritual teacher, Al-Ghazali uses her publications to change the social inequality female Muslims face and to gain access to and achieve freedom in the public domain. However, her rhetorical claims are always situated within the framework of the tenets of Islamic faith. She does not believe that Muslim women need emancipation from Islam but rather from the political and despotic *interpretations* of Islam that Islamic feminism and the secular-nationalists political movement of Gamal Abd Al-Nasir called for. Through reliance on the teachings of Islam, Al-Ghazali relentlessly works to revitalize the rights that were robbed from Muslim women through various forms of oppression and practices that deviated from the core principles of Islam. She is quoted thusly in a 1981 interview:

> Islam has provided everything for both men and women. It gave women everything—freedom, economic rights, political rights, social rights, public and private rights. Islam gave women rights in the family granted by no other society. Women talk of liberation in Christian society, Jewish society, or pagan society, but in Islamic society it is a grave error to speak of the liberation of women. The Muslim woman must study Islam so she will know that it is Islam that has given her all her rights. (Hoffman, *Princeton Readings,* 284)

While guiding women back to Islam and reinstating the Islamic law as the ultimate law, Al-Ghazali underscores the liberatory nature of Islam for women. She explains how both women and men can function within their natural societal space without enacting any form of injustice on each other, and such an approach establishes the foundation for her rhetoric which legitimizes strict adherence to gender roles but presents women as both individually and socially powerful.

Al-Ghazali strongly rejects Islamic feminism that calls for new interpretations of classical Islamic sources of the Quran and the Sunnah, aimed at socio-political and economic equality with men. To be an Islamic feminist is "not to perform a fixed identity but to create a new, contingent subject position," in which commitment to Islam as well as women's activism and public agency is adopted (Cook, *Women,* 152). Al-Ghazali calls Islamic feminism preposterous and reproaches it, because according to her, it alters the tradition of Islam and questions religious laws in an attempt to provoke women to deviate from the assumed gender roles. Al-Ghazali thus attacks Islamic feminism on the basis of its adoption of new and Westernized gender roles, which can potentially shatter and threaten the kernel of Islamic society—the Muslim family. She explains her reasoning for leaving EFU and forming MLA:

I was working with Mrs. Huda al-Sharawi in the women's movement, which calls for the liberation of women. But I, with my Islamic upbringing, found that this was not the right way for Muslim women. Women had to be called to Islam, so I founded the Muslim Women's Association after I resigned from the Feminist Union. . . . Our goal was to acquaint the Muslim woman with her religion so she would be convinced by means of study that the women's liberation movement is a deviant innovation that occurred due to the Muslims' backwardness. We consider the Muslims to be backward; they must remove this backwardness from their shoulders and rise up as their religion commands, as it should be in Islamic lands. (Hoffman, *Women and Family*, 234)

Al-Ghazali argues that Islam does not marginalize women because they are considered as the fundamental building blocks of society as mothers and teachers of future Muslim generations.

Due to this immense responsibility, Muslim women need to be educated and religious to build a strong Muslim society. Al-Ghazali asserts this point in an interview, stating:

Women must be well educated, cultured, knowing the precepts of the Quran and the Sunnah, knowing world politics, why we are backward, why we don't have technology. The Muslim woman must study all these things, and then raise her son in the conviction that he must possess the scientific tools of the age, and at the same time he must understand Islam, politics, geography, and current events . . . Islam does not forbid women to actively participate in public life . . . as long as that does not interfere with her first duty as a mother. (Hoffman, *Princeton Readings*, 285–86)

Thus, education is needed because Muslim women are always in a position of responsibility and with responsibility comes power and autonomy.

It is a woman's first duty, according to Al-Ghazali and in adherence with Islamic rules, to be a wife and mother:

The family comes first. If an urgent need arises, then work in education until you marry; then work stops, except in absolute necessity. . . . Learn, and earn the highest degrees of learning. That is not too precious to be spent in raising a Quranic generation of which we are in the greatest need. Return, my dear, to the house. Stay in your home and obey your husband. You will be rewarded for your obedience to your Prophet and to him.[20]

Education enables women to take their rightful place in society, not necessarily to awaken or enlighten them in a deviant way to break from their gendered roles. Rather, education is the means to equip them with the tools that would facilitate and solidify their sacred jobs of wives and mothers.

Al-Ghazali clarifies that Muslim women can actively participate in public life and hold jobs; she insists, however, that a Muslim woman should focus first and foremost on her sacred roles of mother and wife, and that no other activity should interfere with these roles. If, thereafter, a Muslimah[21] has free time, she may take on different kinds of work; Islam does not forbid her. Al-Ghazali stresses, though, that men are financially responsible, and it would be a disgrace if women have to work to support their families: "What good comes to a nation in which a woman has to work to feed herself? That woman is a commodity, and the men suffer from it, and the children suffer even more."[22] While Islam, according to her, allows women's participation in public life, she, nevertheless, explicitly and vehemently pronounces that women's most important role is that of domestic caretaker—a rhetoric of domesticity that she keeps articulating and emphasizing in her teachings and tracts as well.

GENDER TRANSGRESSION OR ADHERENCE TO LOFTIER MORAL ROLE?

Since Al-Ghazali strongly advocated for adherence to Islamic laws and conservative gender roles, many attacked her, claiming that Al-Ghazali's public role and practices did not follow what she strongly preached. However, deeper rhetorical analysis of her religious and activist moves confirms her adherence to her Islamic mission. She asserts that Islam does not forbid women from actively participating in public life so long as this participation is not at the expense of their most sacred jobs of wifehood and motherhood. Al-Ghazali divorced her first husband, whom she felt hampered her da'wah activities and commitment to the MLA and the Muslim Brotherhood, and because of this divorce she was able to spread Islam to all sectors of society and relentlessly work for Al-da'wah. Though she remarried, Al-Ghazali never had children of her own, and as such, she had the opportunity for spreading her cause. Upon this second marriage, though, Al-Ghazali skillfully utilized the Islamic doctrine that grants women the freedom to craft their own clauses in marriage contracts; she insisted on including a prenuptial agreement in her marriage contract stipulating that her new husband could not prohibit or prevent her activism. She writes in her memoir:

> Let trust, she said, be full between us. A full trust between a man and a woman, a woman who, at the age of 18, gave her whole life to Allah and da'wah. In the event of any clash between the marriage contract's interest and that of da'wah, our marriage will end, but da'wah will always remain rooted in me. I know that it is your right to command me and that it is my duty to obey you, but God in our souls is greater than our souls, and His da'wah is dearer to us than ourselves. (Al-Ghazali ix)

Such actions manifest her commitment to the Islamic movement and full understanding of Islamic ruling on gendered roles and wives and women's personal agency and choice. While being childless and with a prenuptial agreement and a cooperative husband, Al-Ghazali fully committed herself to a life of public leadership at which she succeeded without transgressing the dictates of Islamic gendered roles. Al-Ghazali's religious rhetoric enabled her to craft a loftier moral role for herself: her life's work was dedicated to Allah and the teachings of Islam (Mahmood 180–82). She was sure to point out that it was Allah's "blessing" to not grant her children so that she could continue her da'wah mission.[23] She emphasizes women's agency in determining the precise balance between the duties of a wife and mother and their participation in public spaces, and suggests that a woman has a choice in determining whether she wishes to marry or to work (Karam 215). However, if a woman decides to get married and have children, her responsibility to her husband and children comes first. Al-Ghazali explains the mainstream Islamic Sunni ruling of gender roles in this way:

> Men's and women's roles in the Sharī'ah[24] are broadly defined— yet the Sharī'ah allows for flexibility and overlap if the need arises. While it is undeniable that men and women are spiritually equal, there are gender-specific roles that men and women have been assigned in Islam. With this in mind, we must also realize that there is a spectrum of permissibility that individu-

als, couples and society can agree on and that the religion allows. (Qadhi)

Throughout her life and in her writings, Al-Ghazali skillfully negotiated
these gendered regulations for the sake of Islam and da'wah movement.

NEGOTIATING THE PULPIT (MIMBAR)[25]

While Western Christian women used religion to negotiate their roles between private and public arenas, to access masculine religious spaces, and
to legitimize their speech (Mountford; Shaver), Al-Ghazali held firmly
to the rope of Islam, adhering to its practices in terms of strict gender
roles and spaces. Discerning Al-Ghazali's religious moves and Islamic religious stipulations adds nuance to our understanding of how one Muslim woman leveraged religious rhetorics for her own needs. Scholars such
as Shirley Logan, Roxanne Mountford, and Lisa Shaver have examined
how Western Christian women's mobility was restrained from esteemed
rhetorical spaces like the pulpit. I, on the contrary, demonstrate how
Al-Ghazali negotiated her mobility in accordance with Islamic rulings
to build her ethos and validate her preaching. Since Al-Ghazali endorsed
orthodox Sunni Islam, which forbids women from preaching from the
mimbar (pulpit) to mixed-gender congregations in the mosque, she did
not deliver Friday sermons, khutbah,[26] a patriarchal, masculine act.
Rather, she used the space of the mosque and the mimbar to preach to
women only. Al-Ghazali did utilize other venues outside the walls of the
mosque where preaching happens, though. Unlike many Islamic feminists who argue that Muslim women should be able to access the mimbar and preach to both genders, Al-Ghazali purposefully avoided the
mosque when preaching to mixed-gender audiences because that would
challenge her ethos and work against her gendered message. According
to conservative, orthodox Sunni Islam, which Al-Ghazali adhered to and
called for, while a woman can take the role of the Imam and lead other
women in prayer (salat), she cannot lead a mixed group, due to the nature of prayer; it is not proper for men to look at the woman whose body
is in front of them. Women can be scholars and preach Islam to both
genders but can lead only women in prayer. In fact, Muslim scholars and
preachers are considered of a higher status than Imams, and throughout
history, many Muslim woman scholars, starting with the Prophet Mohammed's wife, Aisha, existed and flourished. Al-Ghazali would never
preach to both genders in a mosque, since that would damage her reli-

gious ethos. As Erin Sadlack highlights the ways women negotiated the genre conventions of the petition to build their ethos and participate in Elizabethan politics, I argue that Al-Ghazali uses other spaces like the memoir, magazine articles, lectures, or television programs as a way to exercise all of her rights: instruct, teach, and guide. Through these spaces, her religious rhetoric and influence traveled across space and time to reach wider audiences and gauge support for her claims to go back to Islamic teachings.

CONCLUSION

Women around the world and across time have used religion as exigence to negotiate their gendered roles and to take an active position in public domains. Al-Ghazali's rhetoric touches on the issues of religion, activism, and domesticity, prompting us to think about how Muslim women make these negotiations. Through her activist rhetoric, Al-Ghazali impacted many people, especially women who have been involved in the contemporary da'wah movements. Many Muslims have felt rejuvenated by her lectures and writings, wanting to emulate her and do da'wah work (Hoffman, *Princeton Readings,* 275). Yet, even though Al-Ghazali advocates for religion as a way of life and promotes conservative, separate gender roles, it is a way of life she did not strictly abide by. Instead, she identified a higher mission for herself: instilling Allah's word. Even though Al-Ghazali preached about the importance of domesticity, she skillfully took advantage of her Islamic rights as a woman to take on a public role of political activism with the goal of rebuilding the Islamic state in Egypt. As part of her rhetorical strategy, she relies on the genre of memoir to advocate for her reform and to oppose the influence of the West and colonialism from circulating and recirculating in Middle Eastern countries, especially her country Egypt. Her writings and teachings instruct Muslim people on how to adhere to the orthodox practices of Islam and affirm their gender roles. For Al-Ghazali, Islam grants women equal rights and ascribes gender roles which keep the family, and society by extension, intact.

NOTES

1. See also Kathryn Fitzgerald, and Jacqueline Jones Royster and Jean C. Williams.

2. Call for Islamic activism.

3. A hadith is one of various reports describing the words, actions, or habits of the Islamic prophet, Muhammad, not in the Quran but accepted as guides for Muslim behavior.

4. See Meir Hatina.

5. The Egyptian Feminist Union (EFU) was founded in 1923 by the activist Huda Sha'rawi, who served as its first president until her death in 1947. EFU was affiliated with the International Woman Suffrage Alliance.

6. West: A socially constructed term derived from the assumption of a binary relationship between the "East" and "West." See Lila Abu-Lughod, *Remaking Women*. Princeton UP, 1998.

7. Brotherhood or Brothers refers to the Muslim Brotherhood Islamic Organization.

8. Sunnah: the words and actions of Prophet Muhammad written down by his early followers.

9. See Maya Shatzmiller.

10. Members of the Muslim Brotherhood Islamic Organization.

11. Islamic theology which invites people, Muslims and non-Muslims, to understand the worship of God, Allah, as expressed in the Quran and the sunnah of prophet Muhammad and to inform them about Muhammad.

12. Da'iya (singular) Da'iyat (plural): Female participant in Al-da'wah.

13. Al-Ghazali followed the example of Prophet Muhammad's third wife, Aisha, who was intelligent and brave. Aisha was a scholar in hadith (sayings of the Prophet), with the largest numbers of hadith recorded by her. She also became the first Muslim military commander to lead nine thousand soldiers against the fourth Caliph Ali bin Abu Talib in the Battle of Camels.

14. Allah is the Arabic word referring to God in Islam.

15. This page comes from the translated version of the memoir; it is a replica of the same page in the Arabic version of the memoir but with added translation in English.

16. Surah al-Baqarah, verse 214: أَمْ حَسِبْتُمْ أَنْ تَدْخُلُوا الْجَنَّةَ وَلَمَّا يَأْتِكُمْ مَثَلُ الَّذِينَ خَلَوْا مِنْ قَبْلِكُمْ مَسَّتْهُمُ الْبَأْسَاءُ وَالضَّرَّاءُ وَزُلْزِلُوا حَتَّى يَقُولَ الرَّسُولُ وَالَّذِينَ آمَنُوا مَعَهُ مَتَى نَصْرُ اللَّهِ أَلَا إِنَّ نَصْرَ اللَّهِ قَرِيبٌ.

17. An Islamic benediction often used to begin prayer or a public speech: بسم الله الرحمن الرحيم والصلاة والسلام على سيدنا محمد و على

آل و صبحاً أجمعين.

18. حسبنا الله ونعم الوكيل معن والمولى ونعم النصير.

19. Surat Āl Imrān, verse 173:الَّذِينَ قَالَ لَهُمُ النَّاسُ إِنَّ النَّاسَ قَدْ جَمَعُوا او
لَكُمْ خَافَ مُوْشَمُوْ إِفَازَدَاهُمْ وَقَاوَلاَ اولْ حَسْبُنَا اللَّهُ وَنِعْمَ الوَكِيلُ.

20. Al-Ghazali, "Al-Mara Al Muslima" p. 34.

21. Muslim is an Arabic word which refers to the one who believes in Islam. A female Muslim is called a Muslimah.

22. Al-Ghazali, "Al-Mara Al Muslima" p. 34.

23. Personal Interview with Zainab Al-Ghazali by Sherifa Zuhur, 13 September 1988.

25. Sharia law, or Islamic law (Arabic: شَرِيعَة) is a religious law forming part of the Islamic tradition. It is derived from the religious precepts of Islam, particularly the Quran and the Hadith.

26. The word minbar (Arabic: مِنبَر) is the Islamic pulpit in the mosque where the imam (prayer leader) stands to deliver sermons (خُطبَة, khutbah) or where the speaker sits and lectures the congregation.

27. Khutbah (Arabic: خُطبَة) serves as the primary formal occasion for public preaching in the Islamic tradition. Such sermons occur regularly. The Islamic tradition can be formally at the dhuhr (noon) congregation prayer on Friday.

WORKS CITED

Abdel-Latif, Omayma. "In the Shadow of the Brothers: The Women of the Egyptian Muslim Brotherhood." *Carnegie Papers*, vol. 13, 2008, pp. 1–32.

Abu-Lughod, Lila. *Remaking Women*. Princeton UP, 1998.

Ahmed, Leila. *Women and Gender in Islam*. Yale UP, 1992.

Al-Ghazali, Zainab. "al-Mara al-Muslima/The Muslim Woman." *al-Da'wah*, no. 57, Jan 1981.

Al-Ghazali, Zainab, *Return of the Pharaoh: Memoir in Nasir's Prison*. Translated by Mokrane Guezzou, The Islamic Foundation, 1994.

Badran, Margot. *Feminists, Islam, and Nation: Gender and the Making of Modern Egypt*. Princeton UP, 1995.

Badran, Margot. "Between Secular and Islamic Feminism/s: Reflections on the Middle East and Beyond." *Journal of Middle East Women's Studies*, vol. 1, no. 1, 2005, pp. 6–28.

Ballif, Michelle, et al. *Women's Ways of Making It in Rhetoric and Composition*. Routledge, 2008.

Baron, Beth. *The Women's Awakening in Egypt: Culture, Society and the Press.* Yale UP, 1994.

Bizzell, Patricia. "Frances Willard, Phoebe Palmer, and the Ethos of the Methodist Woman Preacher." *Rhetoric Society Quarterly,* vol. 36, no. 4, 2006, pp. 377–98.

Burton, Vicki Tolar. *Spiritual Literacy in John Wesley's Methodism: Reading, Writing, and Speaking to Believe.* Baylor UP, 2008.

Cooke, Miriam. "Zaynab Al-ghazālī: Saint or Subversive?" *Die Welt des Islams,* vol. 34, no. 1, 1994, pp. 1–20.

Cooke, Mariam. "Ayyam Min Hyati: The Prison Memoirs of a Muslim Sister." *Journal of Arabic Literature,* vol. 26, 1995, 147–63.

Cooke, Mariam. "Women, Religion, and the Postcolonial Arab World." *Cultural Critique,* vol. 45, 2000, pp. 150–84.

Donawerth, Jane. *Rhetorical Theory by Women Before 1900 An Anthology.* Rowman & Littlefield P, 2002.

Enoch, Jessica. *Refiguring Rhetorical Education: Women Teaching African American, Native American, and Chicano/a Students, 1865–1911.* Southern Illinois P, 2008.

Ezzaher, Lahcen E. "Alfarabi's Book of Rhetoric: An Arabic-English Translation of Alfarabi's Commentary on Aristotle's Rhetoric." *Rhetorica: A Journal of the History of Rhetoric,* vol. 26, no. 4, 2008, pp. 347–91.

Farag, Mona. "The Muslim Sisters and the January 25th Revolution." *Journal of International Women's Studies,* vol. 5, no. 13, 2012, pp. 228–37.

Fitzgerald, Kathryn. "The Platteville Papers: Inscribing Frontier Ideology and Culture in a Nineteenth-Century Writing Assignment." *College English,* vol. 64, no. 3, 2002, pp. 273–301.

"Ghazali, Zaynab Al- (1917-)." *Encyclopedia of Islam and the Muslim World.*

Hatina, Meir. *Identity Politics in the Middle East: Liberal Thought and Islamic Challenge in Egypt.* Tauris Academic Studies, 2007.

Hesford, Wendy S., and Eileen E. Schell. "Introduction: Configurations of Transnationality: Locating Feminist Rhetorics." *College English,* vol. 70, no. 5, 2008, pp. 461–70.

Hoffman, Valerie J. "An Islamic Activist: Zaynab al-Ghazali." *Princeton Readings in Islamist Thought: Texts and Contexts from al-Banna to Bin Laden,* edited by Roxanne L. Euben and Muhammad Qasim Zaman, Austin, 1985, pp. 275–301.

—. "An Islamic Activist: Zaynab al-Ghazali." *Women and the Family in the Middle East: New Voices of Change*, edited by Elizabeth Warnock Fernea, Austin: U of Texas P, 1985, pp. 233–54.

Karam, Azza. "Women, Islamisms, and State: Dynamics of Power and Contemporary Feminisms in Egypt." *Muslim Women and the Politics of Participation*, edited by Mahnaz Afkhami and Erika Friedl, Syracuse UP, 1997, pp. 18-28.

—. *Women, Islamisms, and the State: Contemporary Feminisms in Egypt*. St. Martin's Press, 1998.

Kull, Steven. *Feeling Betrayed: The Roots of Muslim Anger at America*. Brookings Institution P, 2011.

Lewis, Pauline. "Zainab al-Ghazali: Pioneer of Islamist Feminism." *Journal of History*, Winter 2007, pp. 1–47.

Logan, Shirley W. *With Pen and Voice: A Critical Anthology of Nineteenth-Century African-American Women*. Southern Illinois UP, 1995.

—. *Liberating Language: Sites of Rhetorical Education in Nineteenth-Century Black America*. Southern Illinois UP, 2008.

Nardin, Jane. "Hannah More and the Rhetoric of Educational Reform." *Women's History Review*, no. 10, 2001, pp. 211–27.

Mahmood, Saba. *Politics of Piety: The Islamic Revival and the Feminist Subject*. Princeton UP, 2005.

Minifee, Paul A. "'I Took Up the Hymn-Book': Rhetoric of Hymnody in Jarena Lee's Call to Preach." *Advances in the History of Rhetoric*, vol. 18, no. 1, 2015, pp. 1–28.

Mountford, Roxanne. *The Gendered Pulpit: Preaching in American Protestant Spaces*. Southern Illinois UP, 2002.

Qadhi, Yasir. "Gender Roles in Islam." *No Doubt: A New Online Experience Discussing God, Religion, and Politics in the Modern World. AlMaghrib Institute Online*, 2017.

The Quran. Translated by M.A.S. Abdel Haleem, Oxford UP, 2005.

Roded, Ruth. *Women in Islam and the Middle East: A Reader*. I.B. Tauris, 2008.

Royster, Jacqueline Jones, and Gesa Kirsch. *Feminist Rhetorical Practices: New Horizons for Rhetoric, Composition, and Literacy Studies*. Southern Illinois UP, 2012.

Royster, Jacqueline Jones, and Jean C. Williams. "History in the Spaces Left: African American Presence and Narratives of Composition Studies." *College Composition and Communication*, vol. 50, no. 4, 1999, pp. 563–84.

Sadlack, Erin. "Petitioning Power: The Rhetorical Fashioning of Elizabethan Women's Letters." In *New Ways of Looking at Old Texts*, vol. 4. Papers of the Renaissance English Text Society, 2002–2006, edited by Michael Denbo, Arizona Center for Medieval and Renaissance Studies, 2008, pp. 229–37.

Said, Edward. *Orientalism*. Vintage, 1979.

Shatzmiller, Maya. *Her Day in Court: Women's Property Rights in Fifteenth-Century Granada*. Harvard UP, 2007.

Shaver, Lisa J. *Beyond the Pulpit: Women's Rhetorical Roles in the Antebellum Religious Press*. U of Pittsburgh P, 2012.

Stowasser, Barbara. *Women in the Qur'an, Traditions, and Interpretation*. Oxford UP, 1994.

Uthman, Ibrahim Olatunde. "A Triadic Re-reading of Zaynab Al-ghazali and the Feminist Movement in Islam." *Islamic Studies*, vol. 49, no. 1, 2010, pp. 65–79.

Zimmerelli, Lisa. "'The Stereoscopic View of Truth': The Feminist Theological Rhetoric of Frances Willard's Woman in the Pulpit." *Rhetoric Society Quarterly*, vol. 42, no. 4, 2012, pp. 353–74.

Zuhur, Sherifa. *Revealing Reveiling: Islamist Gender Ideology in Contemporary Egypt*. Albany, NY, 1992. Chapter 5, "Construction of the Virtuous Woman," includes Zaynab al-Ghazali's perspectives, with portions of an interview conducted by Zuhur.

II Circulating Genres

5 "POOR AND DAILY ORATORS": THE RHETORIC OF ELIZABETHAN WOMEN'S PETITIONS"

Erin A. Sadlack

On December 17, 1849, Lucretia Coffin Mott gave a public lecture in Philadelphia, Pennsylvania, in which she argued that a woman "is deprived of almost every right in civil society, and is a cypher in the nation, except in the right of presenting a petition" (13).[1] Mott's words speak volumes to me, partly because I first heard about them when I started researching Elizabethan petitions, and Jane Donawerth, who was codirecting my dissertation, shared this allusion with me. As such, Mott's assertion attests to the value of collaboration and connections that arise in the course of feminist scholarship and illustrate Donawerth's own claims about the rhetorical value of conversation, showing how women's ideas spread by word of mouth, even sometimes over a century after they were first spoken aloud. It struck me even then as remarkable that the petitions I was studying were the very artifacts proving the truth of Mott's claim that through letter-writing, women became visible in the political realm. It feels all the more appropriate now to be able to honor these connections—both Jane's and mine, and Mott's to her predecessors—in a volume that explores feminist circulations across time and space.

When Mott delivered these words, she knew well that women actively engaged in petitioning on issues ranging from slavery to temperance; early in 1848, she had led a successful petition campaign that helped encourage the Pennsylvania legislature to grant married women some rights to property (McMillen 76). The conclusion of the Declaration of Sentiments and Resolutions adopted at the Seneca Falls Convention a year earlier specifically named petitioning for women's rights as one of the post-convention action steps.[2] Women took up that call across the country throughout the 1850s, organizing petition drives with volunteers covering neighborhoods street by street. Although many individual drives failed initially to sway state legislatures, further petition campaigns across decades continued to raise consciousness about the need for women's suffrage. Mott's observation that petitioning makes women visible in society thus rings true.

Yet, although today we tend to think of petitioning only in terms of its collective form—such as the petitions Danielle Griffin and Karen Nelson explore in other sections of this volume—historically, an individual woman's right to petition could also make a significant difference in the quality of her life. The right of the individual petitioner to address the government for redress of grievances in Anglo-American political tradition extends back to the late Middle Ages under the reign of Edward I and was eventually enshrined in the United States Constitution with the First Amendment.[3] Historical records preserved in both the UK National Archives and individual state archives demonstrate that hundreds of women in England and her colonies took advantage of this right at least as early as the sixteenth century.[4] These texts represent an archive of ordinary women's voices. Attending to them not only allows us to explore how everyday people practiced techniques of rhetorical argumentation but also to further our appreciation of the ways that women across various time periods employed a particular genre to increase their political agency and how the genre itself facilitated that endeavor.[5]

The petition genre shows in manifold ways how the personal is inherently political. Collective petitions such as Mott's eventually led to changes in society affecting the lives of every woman in the United States. At the same time, individual petitions often drove legislatures to draft new laws. Indeed, the very first act passed by the colony of Connecticut—an injunction against selling guns to Native Americans—was inspired by one man's petition complaining about his neighbor (Higginson 144). In the same way, women's petitions about domestic abuse helped to change child custody laws in England, as well as property and divorce laws in both countries.[6] Such petitions rely on the government's recognition of the woman subject as part of the state it rules. For this reason, Elizabethan petition letters are a particularly interesting case study because their writers rely on a shared understanding about the nature of the body politic in which the individual owes fealty and prayer to the monarch in return for justice and good governance. Examining their writing shows how women petitioners established the presence of women within the body politic and claimed the same rights to petition as male subjects, setting the foundation of the petition as women's first political right.

Elizabethan petitions also reveal new insights into the petition as a genre and the boundaries of its fluidity. On the one hand, by the sixteenth century, the petition letter was understood as a legal document, and the most formal petitions adhered rigidly to the prescribed layout and content. Ironically, these tended to be petitions by the lower classes, since these letters were usually penned by professional scribes. On the other hand, the reality of the act of petitioning was far less uniform; sometimes people were able to petition in person, their letters serving as an accompaniment that could be forwarded to other members of the court for processing or investigation. Sometimes the letter was all that would reach the audience. While most petitions from this period were made by individuals, there was a growing trend in group petitions, such as the inhabitants of a neighborhood protesting the building of a theatre nearby, or victims of a shared vandalism asking for help protecting their church.[7] All of these were recognized as acts of petition by the authorities.

Models of petition also abounded, each suggesting variations to the established form. In this culture, it was customary to share interesting letters or poems or speeches and hand copy them into personal commonplace books. Letter-writing manuals were popular, giving writers various samples to adapt to different occasions. In addition to written exemplars, playwrights often portrayed the act of petition to create drama. Aside from theatergoing audiences, petitioners may well also have seen acts of petition staged in real life by their monarchs, who sometimes answered petitions publicly while travelling across the realm on royal progress or on special occasions as proof of their good rule. Even at church or reading the Bible, would-be petitioners could heed the example of Esther begging Ahasuerus for the lives of the Jewish people or Joseph's brothers unwittingly asking their own brother for famine relief. Petitioners could take their cue from any of these sources, and as a result, petition letters ranged widely in tone, appearance, and content. Yet Elizabethan society recognized them all as petitions, providing further evidence for Carolyn Miller's assertion that genre is better understood by its aims, not its appearance or content (151). Nonetheless, despite these differences, there are a few conventions, particularly the closing prayer, that remain constant across the surviving records, suggesting that for the Elizabethan petitioner, some features of the genre were considered essential.

Even within the bounds of the most formal petitions, the conventions of the genre nonetheless encouraged creativity and personalization. As Risa Applegarth notes, "constraints built into genres are the foundation of the creativity that genres enable" (455). Because petitions are often made in epistolary format, they draw on dictaminal traditions that require the writer to fashion an ethos and tailor her plea to her specific audience. As such, the petitionary letter must conform to standards while presenting the writer's request in the most effective fashion. Petitioners therefore conformed to conventions but employed them creatively. For instance, writers often customized the contents of their prayers to link the audience's perceived desires to their own situations. Even more, they considered carefully which "self" to project to that audience, whether it would be more effective to petition as wife, daughter, mother, or subject, or even to inhabit multiple roles.

Petition letters thus provide a way to explore the sophistication of early modern women's rhetorical self-fashioning and their sense of *kairos*, their ability to tailor their arguments to seize the moment effectively through their delivery and careful presentation of the situation. Moreover, the specific circumstance of subject writing to ruler affects the rhetorical choices these women make as they humble themselves deeply before Elizabeth and her Council, emphasizing that they and their families will be "utterly undone" without help.[8] As Cristy Beemer observes, *kairos*, together with careful attention to propriety, is all the more essential when a subject addresses a monarch with power over the subject's life or death (76–77). Elizabeth's petitioners were right to do so, since the Queen once ordered William Fitzwilliam, the Lord Deputy of Ireland, to punish the petitioner Agnes Chamberlen if he found her case to be baseless. Elizabeth thought that too many people were using the excuse of petitioning to "coller their repaire hither to begge and live lewdelie being otherwise hable to worke for their livinges" (Dasent 78).[9] It is therefore worth examining the ways that petitioners carefully manipulate the epistolary genre to thread a path between causing offense and winning help.

In what follows, I concentrate on three aspects of Elizabethan petitioning: first, I consider how women encountered various iterations of the petition genre, particularly through the theatrical and literary portrayals of letter-writing and petitioning informing the sixteenth-century

Londoner's understanding of the power and role of petitioning in society. Second, I examine rhetorical strategies women commonly used in these petition letters, especially the ways they sought to infuse a sense of presence into their writing in order to occupy spaces otherwise closed to them and the ways they tailored petition conventions to the circumstances of their plea. Finally, I explore these writers' multi-faceted self-fashioning as they decide what "self" would project the best ethos to their audiences. Ultimately, these letters demonstrate the creativity and complexity of sixteenth-century women's epistolary negotiations as they engage as full subjects in the Elizabethan body politic. Every time a woman exercised her right to petition, she deepened women's claims to that right, thus opening up a rhetorical space congenial to women's voices and empowering generations of women after her to call for women's suffrage, education, and freedom via the petition letter.

THE PETITION AND THE BODY POLITIC

Early modern playwrights frequently stage the act of petitioning, partly because watching a character plead for help creates dramatic tension, but also because the response provides a code for understanding that ruler as either just or tyrannical. Even a short petition scene enables the playwright to establish tone, setting the stage for events to come. Consider the poignancy of Titus Andronicus kneeling before the Tribunes of Rome, begging for his sons' lives:

> O reverend Tribunes, O gentle, agèd men,
> Unbind my sons, reverse the doom of death,
> And let me say, that never wept before,
> My tears are now prevailing orators! (Shakespeare, *Titus Andronicus* 3.1.23–6).

Titus's ignored petition underscores the absence of justice in Rome, which has become "a wilderness of tigers" (3.1.53). Moreover, acts of petition were not limited to men. From Esther's impassioned plea on behalf of the Jewish people in the anonymous Tudor morality play *Godly Queene Hester* to Shakespeare's Duchess of York in *Richard II*, women petitioned power on stage throughout the early modern period.

No fewer than eight petition scenes highlight the contrast between different rulers in George Whetstone's 1578 *Historie of Promos and Cassandra*, a source of Shakespeare's *Measure for Measure*, in which the Angelo-prototype Promos fosters an environment of political corruption, bribery, and legalized extortion. When the king comes home, Whetstone signals the return of justice by staging the success of a poor man's honest petition; the man rejoices, saying that for two years he has had no help, "But God save his Grace, at fyrst dash, my Supplycation he tooke," and he blesses the king for his goodness (K.iii^i). In this fashion, Whetstone depicts the contract between the various components of the body politic. The king's duty is to protect his people and to treat them fairly; the subject's duty is to give the monarch fealty, love, and prayer.

The theatrical bargain of the body politic extended far beyond the walls of the Globe, the Rose, and their counterparts. Early modern monarchs regularly staged acts of petition to reinforce narratives of themselves as good rulers. For instance, John Stow records how Henry VIII and Cardinal Thomas Wolsey arranged an elaborate clemency spectacle for some four hundred apprentices found guilty of riot in the "Evil May Day" of 1517 (851). Catherine of Aragon, joined by Henry's sisters Mary, former queen of France, (who was seven months pregnant), and Margaret, queen of Scotland, all knelt to beg the king to show compassion on the prisoners, many of them just thirteen- and fourteen-year-old boys, as well as eleven women (Sadlack 143–44). Upon the queens' plea, Henry ordered the executions to stop, and then six days later, the prisoners, bearing ropes around their necks, were marched through the streets of London to Westminster, where they were brought before the king to beg and receive his mercy. Henry's spectacle projected the image of a benevolent king to his subjects, but also abroad, since observers from European courts reported home the popularity of the king's actions.[10]

Henry's daughter Elizabeth I understood the power of theatrical petitioning from the start. Richard Mulcaster notes that when the new queen entered London for her coronation, if the people "moved to her any suit, she most gently, to the common rejoicing of all . . . stayed her chariot and heard their requests. So that if a man should say well, he could not better term the City of London that time than a stage wherein was showed the wonderful spectacle of a noble-hearted princess toward her most loving people" (53). People from all classes of Elizabethan society responded to the queen's promise of justice through petition.

Despite the existence of the Court of Requests, which was formally established as an outlet for addressing the complaints of the poor in the reign of Henry VII, hundreds of Elizabethan petitioners hoping for redress of grievances or for legal or monetary assistance continued to send their pleas directly to the Queen or her Privy Council. Many factors influenced a petitioner's choice to bypass the legal avenue to the Court of Requests. Women petitioning for the release of a prisoner may have chosen to appeal to those who could immediately order a husband's pardon. Other petitioners cited poverty as their reason for making direct appeals. Tim Stretton notes that if a woman lacked funds to go to court:

> she could petition to gain entry *in forma pauperis* and have an attorney and other legal counsel supplied and her fees waived. Nevertheless, the ancillary costs of litigation, such as travel and accommodation, combined with women's ignorance of their legal opportunities, meant that the silent majority were not in a position to defend their customary interests in central courts such as Requests (185).[11]

Alternately, if a woman had a connection to someone who could influence the Queen or a member of the Council, she might feel it was more effective to contact that person directly.

At times, the sheer number of petitioners threatened to overwhelm the workings of the Queen's court. Yet whenever the Queen and Council attempted to steer petitioners elsewhere, they nonetheless continued to make exceptions for those with extraordinary circumstances, and in so doing, they encouraged suitors to think of addressing the Queen or her Council as a court of last resort. In her 1587 petition, the Countess of Shrewsbury calls the Privy Council the "Laste and principaleste relevers of the most distressed" (SP 12/207/17).[12] Such rhetoric suggests that Elizabeth's subjects saw the queen's willingness to hear petitions as part of her duty to protect them, making their ability to speak to the highest levels of government an essential component of the body politic. In this sense, as Applegarth notes, "genres frequently normalize and reproduce relations of power and stabilize the worldviews they imply" (473). In reinforcing existing power structures, petitions may enhance monarchical authority, but they also strengthen a vision of government that recognizes the political agency of ordinary people.

LEARNING THE CRAFT OF PETITIONING

Models of letter-writing in early modern England abounded in manuscript and in print, providing letter-writers guidance as to the appropriate way to craft their missives.[13] Angel Day's well-known treatise, *The*

English Secretorie, identifies the petition as its own sub-genre, the "Epistle Petitorie," and notes that any petition must be a "just, lawfull, and honest" request within the power of the recipient to grant (170). Day notes that a full petitionary letter would have an *exordium* flattering the recipient with reports of "his care & willingnesse to do good," a *narration* and *proposition* outlining the background of the situation, the *petition* itself, with reminders of how righteous it is to help the poor, and a *remuneration* at the end in which the petitioner offers to serve the recipient (173). Briefer petition letters might omit all but the *petition* and the *remuneration* (180). The heart of the petition letter therefore relies on the reciprocal covenant of the body politic: the subject's ability to receive protection and assistance from his monarch and his duty to provide services such as prayer and loyalty in return. Imagining the state as a body creates the possibility of an alliance between its members that stretches across boundaries of class. When the body is headed by a female monarch, that alliance even more clearly encourages women to engage in that rhetorical space.

Both Day and William Fulwood acknowledge the existence of women letter-writers and provide sample women's letters in their dictaminal treatises. Yet, as Diana Barnes observes, such acknowledgment is slight: less than five percent of the total letters in each manual were by women.[14] Moreover, both men include only familiar and love letters by women, not petitions (122). Yet despite the lack of printed exemplars, given the number of extant petitions in the National Archives and the hundreds of references to women petitioners in the Privy Council registers, it is clear that gender was no barrier to petitioning.

Nor was literacy. Provided a woman could pay to dictate her letter to a scribe, she effectively had access to the monarch. Documents penned by scribes tended to be much stricter in their format and content, following the pattern set by such books as *A newe boke of presidentes*, a 1543 printed collection of sample English legal documents and letters that went through some forty editions before 1641. As a result, petitioners typically identify and abase themselves rhetorically at the start, explain the request, and offer prayer at the end, as shown in the following exemplar from *A newe boke* of a scholar petitioning the king for financial support: "And your sayde oratour shal daylye praye to God for the preservacion of youre royall estate long to contynue in felicitye" (fol. 89ᵛ). In professionally scribed petitions, even the layout is standardized, with the document laid out in landscape orientation, the address line centered at the top, the first word of the letter starting with a majuscule, and the signature, if present, nearly always placed at the bottom right corner, providing a visual profession of humility. Petitions written by nonprofessionals or the petitioners themselves will vary much more in layout, although they tend to follow the same pattern of content.

In either circumstance, individual petitioners tailored the letter to their own specific situations. For instance, in 1585, Margaret Blackwell moved to a new home and was reported as a recusant for refusing to attend her new local church. She promptly petitioned the Privy Council, providing certificates from the church wardens at her former parish testifying that she continued to attend services there. Six days later, by the hand of another scribe altogether, she issued a nearly identical petition to Sir Francis Walsingham, supplying yet another set of certificates from the wardens.[15] Blackwell's petitions provide telling evidence of how much control a woman might retain over the wording. The relationship between petitioner and amanuensis varies across the spectrum, with some scribes providing more guidance in the wording, others less. Ultimately, however, the woman petitioner claims the words as her own speech when she delivers the petition.

PETITIONING AND THE VOCABULARY OF PRESENCE

Although theatrical and literary depictions of petitioning usually portrayed the supplicant physically begging the monarch for aid, it was not always financially possible for petitioners to plead their suits in person. Other barriers existed too: when the plague broke out in 1592 and 1593, Elizabeth issued proclamations forbidding suitors to come to court altogether (Dyson 312). Yet petitioners were permitted to send letters alone during such times.

In light of such difficulties, or for those petitioners who lacked the financial wherewithal to appear in person at court, the letter's ability to speak for its sender becomes particularly important. Absence of the petitioner's physical person could be an advantage, especially for women, since a letter would help act as a screen for her modesty, obscuring the female body speaking in public. The lack of such presence potentially renders a petition less immediate, less personal, less effective. Therefore, early modern petitioners employed an epistolary vocabulary that enables a letter to reproduce such presence figuratively. Examining the contents of these petition letters underscores how the letter straddles the boundaries of presence and absence, and how early modern women sought to take full rhetorical advantage of its liminal nature to infuse presence into their work and increase the urgency of their pleas.

Because these petitions were so often made in epistolary form, their writers can draw on literary precedents that help to establish that the epistolary genre is well suited to a woman's voice. As ancient as Cicero's correspondence is Ovid's *Heroides*, a collection of fictional epistles in which Ovid assumes the voices of classical heroines who send letters to their absent lovers.[16] Following Ovid's example, many canonical writers, including Chaucer, Gower, and Shakespeare, employ letters as devices to foster the illusion of a woman's authentic voice. These literary letters foreground the relationship between the writer and her creation, especially the letter's ability virtually to embody the sender and carry her voice where she is physically unable to go. Even as the letter protects the woman writer's modesty, literary representations establish the letter as a physical manifestation of the woman's voice that simultaneously creates a link between itself, its writer, and its reader.

Attending to literary traditions of letter-writing also demonstrates how the very genre of the letter facilitates the aura of presence. Works from the *Heroides* to Chaucer's *Legend of Good Women* and *Troilus and Criseyde* to Philip Sidney's *Countess of Pembroke's Arcadia*, Shakespeare's *Twelfth Night*, *Two Gentlemen of Verona*, *As You Like It*, and other early modern plays and poems portray an epistolary communion, wherein the letter so incorporates the voice and person of its sender, that through the paper and ink, the sender virtually appears as the letter is read. Consider how, in *The Merchant of Venice*, the horrified Bassanio explains Antonio's downfall to Portia by saying:

> Here is a letter, lady,
> The paper as the body of my friend,
> And every word in it a gaping wound
> Issuing life-blood. (3.4.261–4)

Bassanio might seem melodramatic, but he envisions no mere metaphor for Antonio. Moreover, only such a close connection between sender and letter could explain Julia's behavior in *The Two Gentlemen of Verona*, when she tears Proteus's love letter, then collects and kisses the pieces:

> Lo, here in one line is his name twice writ:
> "Poor forlorn Proteus," "passionate Proteus."

"To the sweet Julia."—That I'll tear away.
And yet I will not, sith so prettily
He couples it to his complaining names.
Thus will I fold them one upon another.
Now kiss, embrace, contend, do what you will. (1.2.104–30)

Julia's actions are comedic, yet that does not negate the close link between the letter and Proteus's person; indeed, the humor depends on it. In preserving the piece containing both names, Julia envisions the paper as her literal union with Proteus, sharing what pleasure they would. Julia is not alone in this; the very next scene has Proteus exclaiming over her response, "Sweet love, sweet lines, sweet life! / Here is her hand, the agent of her heart" (1.3.45–47). Offstage, real petitioners employ similar rhetoric of the body; in 1602, Ursula Walsingham imagines her petition as "ye beggar that hauntes most where hee findes best releef" and requests in a second letter that Thomas Windebank deliver her letter to Elizabeth's "sacred handes," the better to persuade the queen (SP 12/284/8 and SP 12/284/17). Both letters create vivid images of the bodies involved in epistolary transactions. As Michele Osherow observes in the final section of this volume, the objects women create become their representatives, conveying their voices where their bodies cannot physically reach.

Building on these literary traditions, petition writers employ a vocabulary that sustains a language of presence even in the petitioner's absence. Male petitioners refer to themselves as "orator," while women usually employ the feminine "oratrix" or "oratrice."[17] The *Oxford English Dictionary* notes that these words might denote "a petitioner or suppliant," yet the word itself strongly evokes the rhetorical situation of speaking eloquently aloud, pleading for a cause. A petition read aloud to the Queen or Council carries the woman's voice directly into the room. "Suppliant," another common self-referent in the petitions, evokes images of kneeling or begging to underscore the petitioner's humility.[18] For example, in 1582, when Jane Bolding begs aid after her husband was maimed fighting under Ralegh's command in Ireland, she makes explicit her obeisance, noting that she, her husband, and her children "*uppon our knees* wee, as wee are bounden, shall daylie pray unto thallmightie for the moste happie and prosperous preservacion of yor most royall highenes in healthe and Tranquyllitie longe to rule and reign over us" (SP 12/12/157, my emphasis). Bolding thus creates a powerful image of submission to close her petition.

Connections between a letter and its sender are strengthened all the more when a letter is marked with tears or blood, such as when Bel-Imperia uses her own blood as ink in *The Spanish Tragedy*. Through such conceits, these plays perpetuate the idea that the letter can incorporate the self. But where literary characters actually weep on the paper, petition writers use the imagery of tears instead to evoke a sense of presence. For example, when young Barnabe Actton's friend Thomas Appletree accidentally shot one of Elizabeth's bargemen in the arm while the Queen was sailing down the Thames, both young men were sent to the Marshalsea Prison. Barnabe's mother Annies wrote begging pardon, "In moste humble and [no less] Lamentable wise with wepping teears and bowinge knees beseching your honors, Annies Actton, wedow" (SP 12/131/50).[19] The imagery summons a vivid picture of a mother desperately afraid for her son. The same scribe writes Appletree's petition, using the identical phrase, "weeppinge teears and bowinge knees" (SP 12/131/51).[20] Unlike Margaret Blackwell's petition, the similarity in phrasing throughout the petition suggests a higher degree of collaboration between the petitioners and their scribe. However, the repetition does not lessen the power of the image; rather it suggests that the scribe and each petitioner, regardless of gender, considered the phrase an effective way to convey the appropriate level of grief. Conjuring presence through tears, each petitioner figuratively kneels before the Council.

Verbs similarly evoke presence. Margaret Androwes and her son, whose ship *The Gift of God* was sunk by Francis Drake, open their August, 1589 petition, "In most humble wise beseching *sheweth* unto your honors your poore and dailie orators" (SP 12/225/78, my emphasis). Margaret Aston similarly "exhibited" her proofs against John and Richard Daniel when she petitioned the Earl of Leicester about a land dispute in 1575 (SP 15/24/31).[21] Such diction encourages the audience to imagine the petitioners standing before them. Moreover, the phrase "daily orators" suggests the recurring nature of the plea. Sometimes the reiteration is literal; Mary Harte writes to William Cecil, Lord Burghley, twice in three days for a renewal of a commission, while Sir Francis Walsingham receives three letters about Mary Scott's inability to pay a fine for recusancy.[22] More usually the phrase is metaphorical—daily requesting assistance contributes to the immediacy a petition might convey. The letter preserves a petitioner's speech at one moment frozen in time. But every time the letter is re-read, she makes her request again.

The Economics of Prayer

In recompense for daily suits, petitioners typically promise daily prayers. For instance, the Androwes' petition states: "they shalbe bound daily to praie for the prosperitie of your honors." Margaret Overend ups the ante, promising to pray *hourly* for Walsingham if he will intervene in her lawsuit with Phillip Smith (SP 12/229/90). In an economy of prayer, repetition is a valuable currency. Moreover, repetition suggests an ongoing relationship between the supplicant and her audience.

Within Elizabethan society, such prayers commanded respect. Jane Donawerth includes prayer amongst the many offerings, such as poetry, clothing, food, and money, that Englishmen and women would offer each other in a gift-exchange system vital in building and maintaining community (3). For the poorer petitioner, prayer might be the only commodity possible that enables the writer to participate in the patronage culture and thus claim her place within the body politic. Offering prayers actually enhances the petitioner's ethos; not only does the prayer establish the person as godly, but it also shows that she understands her role within society, her duty to her sovereign, and her willingness to participate in the social exchange. That ethos is enhanced by the rhetoric of prayer in which the individual requests that God grant specific favors. Underlying the petitioner's promise is an assumption that God will grant the worthy petitioner's request. And in a parallel that could only flatter, the petitioner thus suggests that the Queen should follow God's precedent and similarly grant her wish.

Such prayers provide a formulaic closure to a petitionary letter. James Daybell points out that adherence to strict epistolary rules might fluctuate in ordinary correspondence, but not in formal letters such as petitions, where "deviation from established protocols would be impolitic or impolite" (*Material Letter* 73). This is perhaps most true of the opening and closing of the letter, where, he states, even everyday letters tended to conform most closely to dictaminal models. Examining Day's *English Secretorie*, Lynne Magnusson focuses particular attention on such forms of address and conclusion. Noting that Day identifies three general approaches—"humilitie and entreatie," "pleasure or courteu[si]e," and "supposall and assurance,"—Magnusson argues that by observing the choice of script, we may recognize a rhetorical choice that reflects the writer's self-perception and creativity (57). In a similar fashion, the petitioner's choice of prayer reflects the writer's individuality and ingenuity. Often the writers try to tailor their prayers to the category of request. For example, in 1581, Edith Bulman begs Elizabeth's aid in regaining the ownership of copyhold lands forcibly taken from her (SP 12/151/31). She vows, "your said Subject, accordinge to her most bounden dutie, shall daylie pray to god for the prosperous preservacion of your highnes' royall estate longe to reigne over us." Bulman's conclusion emphasizes her identity as Elizabeth's subject; by promising to pray for the Queen's long reign, she fulfils her communal responsibilities. Her final "us" further underscores that Bulman understands herself as part of the English state.

More than just a nicety, tailoring prayers in this fashion is a strategic rhetorical move that becomes vitally important to the petitioner's self-fashioning. This is especially the case when the petitioner is a recusant. Given the fears of Catholic plots against Elizabeth, a recusant's prayer for the Queen's long life and continued reign is inherently politically charged. In April 1586, mere months before the exposure of the Babington plot to assassinate the Queen, Elizabeth Beaumont petitioned the Justices of Leicestershire that she be remitted the financial penalty assessed for recusancy: "althoughe my hartye good will is with all dewty and humilytie to yeld unto her Majestie (yf I were able) as muche as anie poore subjecte her highness hath. . . . I do most humbly submitte myself to the princelye clemencye of her highenes, ffor whose longe and prosperowsse reigne over us, I do and will contynuallie praye" (SP 12/189/17II). Beaumont's humble submission and desire for Elizabeth's long reign distance her rhetorically from the enemies of the Queen. Instead, she allies herself with Elizabeth's loyal subjects, in the hopes that doing so may show that her failure to pay the fine is due only to her financial situation. Beaumont's example thus demonstrates the ways that women could shape rhetorical convention to position themselves effectively to their audiences.

The petition is therefore a genre whose conventions shape women's voices, yet which opens up new pathways for their creativity. The variety of ways women tailored the closing prayers show how their writers affirm their place in the body politic by adhering to its values yet simultaneously emphasizes their individual needs and agency. These handwritten, often single-authored petitions illustrate the invention of strategies of effective argumentation that women would continue to deploy even as the genre of petitioning evolved, especially as individuals banded together for the purposes of calling attention to issues of social justice. In other sections of this collection, Karen Nelson and Danielle Griffin each explore the petition genre after it moves to print publication and collective authorship. Together, we demonstrate that studying women's rhetoric through the lens of genre, we are better able to appreciate the ways that rhetoric reflects, shapes, and responds to changing social power dynamics.

WOMEN'S SELF-FASHIONING IN PETITION LETTERS

Not only did early modern petitioners exhibit rhetorical choices in their closing prayers, but they also did so in the self they chose to project in their petitions. Married women often petitioned in their own right, particularly on behalf of their families, perhaps because the family decided a woman might be seen as the more pitiable—and hence more persuasive—figure. Sometimes petitioners for inheritance rights might prefer to emphasize their status as daughters, or a woman might possess court connections her husband did not have. But there were also married women who petitioned in direct opposition to their husbands' wishes, exploiting the opportunity that arose in the conflict of their different roles as mothers, wives, daughters, sisters, and above all, subjects. All of these petitions nonetheless encapsulate a moment in which women are perceived as individuals separate from their husbands.

Barbara Harris notes that Elizabethan society encouraged wives to exercise authority, provided they did so to further their husbands' interests (61–87). This is borne out in extant petitions. Noting that most women petitioners were married, Daybell cites the example of Lady Anne Dacre, whose "use of the collective term 'we' to refer to herself and her husband indicates a strong degree of marital partnership" (*Women Letter-Writers* 238). A wife's voice could add elements of pathos that would be particularly effective. For example, in Shakespeare's *Henry VI*, Part III, the hapless Henry muses that his wife Margaret may influence the French king:

> a prince soon won with moving words.
> By this account, then, Margaret may win him—
> For she's a woman to be pitied much.
> Her sighs will make a batt'ry in his breast,
> Her tears will pierce into a marble heart. (3.1.34–42)

When Margaret speaks to Louis, she focuses on Henry and Edward's losses, not her own:

> Henry, sole possessor of my love,
> Is of a king become a banished man . . .

> This is the cause that I, poor Margaret,
> With this my son, Prince Edward, Henry's heir,
> Am come to crave thy just and lawful aid.
> An if thou fail us all our hope is done. (3.3.24–33)

She is there to be her husband's voice, with her claim on Louis grounded in her husband's royalty. Only when Warwick addresses her disrespectfully as "Injurious Margaret" does Margaret claim her title, indignantly exclaiming, "And why not 'Queen'?" (3.3.78). Up until the moment when her queenly authority is challenged, Margaret speaks for her husband; when her status is contested, she asserts her own right but abandons the rhetorical position of wifely concern. Such would indicate that her original choice of expression was a deliberate move intended to sway Louis. Making that choice in turn points to the authority that wifely status conferred on a woman, enabling her to assume her husband's mantle.

Shakespeare's play reflects the rhetorical positioning and emotional tactics historical women employed to speak, especially when their spouses were incapacitated because of incarceration, exile, or illness. In March, 1586, the wives of mariners from the ships the *Emanuel* and the *Julian* petitioned the Privy Council for help getting their husbands released from a Spanish prison and some financial relief for themselves in the meanwhile. Identifying themselves not by name but collectively as wives, these women emphasize their common circumstances, amplifying the rhetorical power of their plea. Their rhetoric moved the Council to investigate further, having the Lord Mayor of London, Wolfstan Dixie, take up the wives' cause with the owners.

Although the wives also face financial ruin, their petition centers mostly on the men, even to the fact that their only identity comes from their status as wives. In relating the situation, they emphasize their husbands' peaceful intent and desperate state: "they themselves for noe offence by them done or pretended are stayed, lying in prison almost starved, their shipps and goodes made confiscat and are spoyled to their great losse and utter ympoverishment" (SP 12/187/3).[23] They beg the Council to send money and find means to negotiate the "speedier release of their poore husbandes out of their extreame miserye."[24] Speaking for their husbands effectively empowers the wives' voices.

The women's situation comes in only at the petition's end, where they explicitly ally with their husbands against the rich merchant employers as they ask for "some comforte in this their distressed case for their better releiffe during their poore husbandes Captivitye whoe have susteyned greater losse then the marchantes did, noue [now] are like to perish for mere want as their said husbandes." Even here they join with their husbands equally, if only in shared destitution. However, the closing pledges—and privileges—the services of the wives, with the feminine phrase "Oratrices and all theirs" praying for the council members. These women's shared experience has led them to a shared petition in which their presence gradually seeps into the document and, as a group, they claim the responsibility of providing the prayer that serves as their part of the bargain of the body politic.

Some women employ the opposite tactic; although they speak for their husbands, they emphasize the suffering they themselves feel because their husbands are absent, using pathos to evoke pity. For example, in 1578, Ursula Morton justifies asking Lord Burghley for the release of her husband Robert from the Gatehouse prison by citing the loss of her money and house, her lack of friends, and her brother's impending death (SP 12/125/31). Without Burghley's intervention, "your said oratrice and hir husband are like to be utterlie undone . . . And your said orator & oratrice accordinge to there bounden dewtie shall praie to god for the preservation of your honor." Morton perhaps focuses more attention on herself because her husband is in an English jail for suspicious actions.[25]

At the same time, Morton's closing prayer assumes a strong degree of agency by binding her husband to pray with her for Burghley. Women who make such promises in their petitionary letters not only voice their husbands' desires but also commit them to a kind of economic action, to engage in the economy of prayer that was part of the system of Elizabethan gift exchange. In 1580, Anne Alen wrote to Elizabeth petitioning that her husband Martin's sentence of exile be lifted (SP 12/146/122). Alen praises the Queen for her "abundante clemencye" in commuting Martin's original death sentence to exile; she then shifts attention to herself, explaining that she "is broughte to extreme povertie and necessitie, like to pearishe for lacke of relief. In tender consideracion whereof, youre saide oratrice most humbelie besecheth your highenes, for the tender mercie of god, to be so good and generous to hir saide husbande as to graunte to him your gracious pardon." Alen does not suggest that Martin himself merits clemency in his own right; rather her suffering is the catalyst for her request, and it is she who beseeches Elizabeth. By emphasizing her humility and loyalty, Alen hopes her character can serve as a legitimate warrant of Martin's good conduct and promises that, if pardoned, Martin will "contynue the rest of his lief to Labor and traveill in his vocacion for the relief of him of your saide oratrice & theire ffamilie in the waie of honestie and trouthe." Alen has not merely committed her husband to prayer; in effect she obliges him to reform his behavior for the rest of his life. In doing so, Alen goes beyond merely speaking for her husband; she claims authority over his actions.

In addition to their standing as wives, women petitioners also draw authority to proceed from their duty to protect their children and their children's inheritances. Like Shakespeare's Constance in *King John*, who lobbies the French king to protect her son Arthur's claim to the English throne, historical women had the responsibility to make claims on behalf of their children. For example, in 1587, Margaret Delamarch petitioned the Privy Council's intervention because her husband's brothers had wrongfully taken charge of her husband's property. Delamarch's husband distrusted his brothers and had "willed manie times before his death shold have nothinge to doe therewith [his goods], nor anie waies medle with his children nor their porcions" (PC 2/14/330).[26] The Council determined to call all parties before them to ensure that Delamarch and her children received their rights. In this manner, husbands could transfer their authority to their wives, who were effectively given permission to petition. Similarly, Anne Lanesdall in 1576 petitioned the Queen's help in recovering the stolen titles to her copyhold lands from George Bowes, "to the utter disenherison and undooinge of your said Oratrix and children for ever" (SP 15/24/80). Her husband Christopher, who had been one of Elizabeth's guard, left the land for her use and that of their children. If Bowes is not stopped, Lanesdall implies, she will have failed in her duty to her husband and children.

Asking that Bowes should be punished "for example set," Lanesdall employs another common persuasive device: the concern for potential negative effects on the community. After a dispute with her landlord, Elizabeth, Lady Russell indignantly petitioned the Council to punish Lovelace by stripping him of his commission as a justice of the peace "to the example of other hereafter . . . or els it is better to be a meane Justice of Peace then a Noblewoman, that dependeth only upon god and her Ma[jes]ty her most gracious soveraigne" (SP 12/245/135).[27] Even the formidable Bess of Hardwick, in the course of her stormy public battles with her husband, petitioned for the Privy Council's assistance in ending the estrangement between herself and the earl, "the separacion of whome maie geve daungerous example to the worlde" (SP 12/207/17). Voicing such concerns validates these women's proceedings. In preserving their familial rights, they also protect society's values. Such rhetorical moves signal that women perceive their actions as having an effect on the community at large. By demonstrating their concern for the welfare of their community, they declare their membership in the public weal. More than that, they effectively invite the people in power whom they are addressing to join them in an alliance that protects the common good. If the petition is granted, then the women petitioners *de facto* win a measure of social capital and political influence.

Although petitioning as wife was the more popular choice, some women preferred to petition alone to emphasize their rights as daughters. In 1583, Jone Dennys, although married to a feltmaker named Nicholas, emphasizes her status as "daughter unto one Robert Scott late of Mottrome in the Countye of Chester late deceased" when she claims that she and her mother have been cheated out of their rightful inheritance by John and Edward Brodell (SP 12/163/34). Dennys's standing in the case is founded on her rights as her father's child; therefore, she emphasizes the father-daughter connection. In relating the story, she uses the phrase "yor said Oratrixes father" or some variant thereof several times. Repeating the phrase as often as possible reminds the Council that she is entitled to make this claim.

Jone Dennys acts alone in petitioning for her rights; neither her mother, her siblings, nor her husband are mentioned as plaintiffs in the case. Dennys states that her whole family has suffered; but after that she uses singular nouns and pronouns throughout: "yor Oratrixe ys verye poore, and not able to sue for *her* right by thordynarye course of the Lawe." This is her individual petition, her poverty, and her right, not a petition from the whole Scott family. Moreover, Dennys closes with a singular prayer, "she shall daylie praye unto god for your honorable preservacions Long to contynewe." Note the singular pronoun in "She shall pray," not even the commonly used phrase "she and hers" will pray. Dennys stands alone. There may have been practical reasons for this choice; her siblings may have been too young to join her, or she was the most persuasive. Regardless, Dennys's petition leaves an impression of a lone woman confronting two men who have cheated her terribly. Another hand on the petition notes: "the Plaintyf to be called with all," so Dennys's rhetoric was at least effective enough to win a personal audience with the Council.

A woman might also petition alone if she were the one who possessed court connections. In 1599, Margaret Powell petitioned Robert Cecil for financial relief because she and her first husband "a longe tyme" served his parents, the Lord and Lady Burghley, as well as his uncle Justice Cooke (SP 12/273/65). Powell only mentions her second husband to call him "an other honest man, whome it hath pleased god to visite with longe and greevous sicknes." Powell needs only to establish that he is worthy of help and that his illness has consumed their resources; her primary claim derives from the service of her first husband and herself.

Wives who positioned in support of their families clearly had a stronger position. Yet there were times when a woman needed to petition against her husband. Perhaps at such times, women took inspiration from Shakespeare's *Richard II*, which stages the far more problematic circumstance of a wife petitioning *against* her husband when the Duke and Duchess of York each appeal to their nephew, King Henry, the Duke to condemn his son Aumerle for treason, the Duchess to plead for her son's life. Mother and son sink to their knees to humble themselves before Henry, only to be joined by York, who is not to be outdone by their gesture. The Duchess promptly distances the Duke's action from theirs, setting herself squarely at odds with her husband as she dismisses his insincerity:

> Pleads he in earnest? Look upon his face.
> His eyes do drop no tears, his prayers are in jest.
> His words come from his mouth; ours from our breast.
> He prays but faintly, and would be denied;
> We pray with heart and soul, and all beside. (5.3.98–108)

Rarely in drama do we see a wife petitioning thus, not merely disagreeing with her husband, but contradicting him, criticizing his actions, and undermining his words. The Duchess asserts that the Duke's actions are false; hers stem from true zeal and integrity. Caught between his uncle's indignation and his aunt's refusal to move before she hears the word "pardon," Henry grants her plea, telling Aumerle: "Your mother well hath prayed" (5.3.143). Her tearful supplication has won her son his life. Although productions often stage the scene comically, an early modern audience must have perceived the difficulty of the Duchess, who challenges her husband through her role as a mother. Archival petitions reflect that same reality; when wives petitioned against their husbands' wishes, they needed to ground their authority in a way that society would perceive as legitimate.

By studying these documents, we can see how women rhetors shift tactics by choosing to foreground other aspects of their identities, making these petitions an excellent place to consider the manifold ways women writers establish new connections with their audiences by emphasizing additional shared values, and how by occupying multiple roles, they create more spheres where women's public speech is seen as acceptable, thus opening new avenues for women's participation in the body politic. For Isabel Frobisher, the explorer Martin Frobisher's wife, the petition is a means of regaining her wifely status, and so she crafts a complex self-representation that emphasizes her role as a good mother, a loyal wife, an even more loyal subject, and even a martyr of sorts. In an extraordinary 1574 petition to Elizabeth, Frobisher describes how she has dissuaded her husband from taking part in several treasonous plots, including an assassination attempt and plans to free the duke of Norfolk and the earl of Desmond from the Tower (SP 12/95/92).[28] As a result, Martin's co-conspirators have persuaded him to go before the Privy Council to deny that Isabel is his wife. His denunciation has cost Isabel her good name; lacking community support, she and her children are in danger of starvation. Maintaining that she has preserved Elizabeth's safety, she begs the Queen to force Martin to acknowledge her as his lawful wife.

Because these political intrigues have undermined her wifely status, Frobisher emphasizes her standing as Elizabeth's subject, basing her claim to Elizabeth's help on her loyalty to the Queen. In each of the four conspiracies she outlines, Frobisher explains that she contradicted her husband's wishes because "I had a care of the dutie I owe to your majestie." Calling herself a "true subjecte," Frobisher notes that she had feared "some trouble mighte growe theron (as I thoughte) towardes your majestie." The duty she owes Elizabeth enables her to condemn her husband's plans, so that wifely submission is abandoned in favor of her obligation to serve the monarch. Her care for the Queen is her sole motivation and the justification for her request. This framing carries implications for considering the creation of female networks of power, given that from the outset of her reign, even in her first speech to Parliament, Elizabeth cast herself as the mother to her people.[29] In 1563, she famously answered a petition from the House of Commons urging her to marry by promising them, "I assure you all that though after my death you may have many stepdames, yet shall you never have any more mother than I mean to be unto you all" (72). When Frobisher responds to that rhetoric by fervently proclaiming that all of her actions stem from her loyalty to

Elizabeth and her desire to ensure that England is protected, she effectively invites the queen to enter into a mother-daughter alliance that recasts the entire body politic as feminine.

In return for her care and loyalty, Frobisher claims that she has suffered miserably at the hands of men—both her husband and the male co-conspirators who have turned Martin against her. Her pain validates the justice of her claim: "A truer cause never came before your majestie neither greater tormente offereth to a poore womman then hath bene to me Sithence I have revealed the laste conspiratie." She has lost her husband, impoverished her children, and endured "the losse of all . . . frendes" as a result of the damage to her reputation. Using the language of torment, Frobisher claims the authority of virtual martyrdom, since all that she has done was "for the dutie that I owe unto yor Majestie." As she writes, she nonetheless tries to shield Martin from the Queen's wrath, showing that despite his callous treatment, she is still a faithful wife. As a result, Frobisher's petition weaves together devotion to Elizabeth, her own suffering, and her attempts to protect her family, proving that she is genuinely a loyal wife, mother, and subject who deserves the queen's intercession.[30]

Where Frobisher tries to reclaim her wifely status, Margaret Harper is glad for separation, petitioning the Privy Council to enforce a decree granting her an annual stipend of nine pounds from her husband (SP 12/230/36). Her argument relies heavily on contrasting her ethos as a respectable, well-connected, and God- and law-fearing woman with a picture of her husband Edward Maxey's lawlessness and profligacy. Maxey, she alleges, "is a fugitive person, leadinge his lyfe in obscure places, frequentinge lewde & vicious companye, & most willfully wastinge & spendinge his goodes & substance, not only to the great impoverishinge of hime selfe, but also to the utter undoinge of yor saide Suppliant." Harper also adds pathos to her petition, noting that she has suffered from his abuse. She asks that Maxey be ordered to "put in Suerties for the saftie of yor said Suppliantes person, for that she goeth daily in daunger & hazard of her lyfe, by hime." In painting such a vicious picture of her husband, Harper makes her request for financial support seem like a reasonable claim.

However logical her request for sureties and revenue, Harper's tactics are relatively unusual, and she is careful to provide corroboration of her accusations. Claiming the backing of the church, she enumerates the members of the High Commission who made the original order for their separation and allowance, "the right Reverent ffather in god, the Lord Archbishope of Caunterburie his grace, the right worshippll the Deane of Westminster, Mr Doctor Awbery, Mr Doctor Lewyn, & Mr Doctor Cosyn." Support from ranking English religious leaders is powerful testimony to the justice of her appeal. By contrast, Maxey's willingness to defy such men by refusing to pay out of an "obstinate minde, without the feare of god, or regard of Laue or authoritie," speaks ill of his character, confirming the truth of her assessment of him.

Harper further adds to her ethos by ensuring the Council knows her first husband was Sir William Harper, a former Lord Mayor of London. She identifies herself explicitly as "yor pore distressed Suppliant Margaret Harper late wyfe of Sir William Harper of the Cyty of London knight, decessed, & nowe wife of Edward Maxey gent." Harper emphasizes the prestigious first marriage rather than the unfortunate second union to the point of keeping the first husband's name.

Harper's demeanor in the petition itself further underscores her trustworthiness; her humility and submissive rhetorical posture enhances her ethos. She reasonably explains the circumstances of her request for a yearly revenue: that Maxey is profligately spending all of their money, to her "utter undoing." Equally, she refrains from making exorbitant demands; she is not claiming the right to oversee all their income, nor is she asking for a huge allowance. Harper also flatters the Council, citing their "accustomed goodnes" to others, and submits wholly to their authority, asking that Maxey pay sureties, only "yf it stand with yor honors good lykinge." Her offers to pray continually for the Council members' health, prosperity, and felicity, although conventional, still serve to mark the contrast between her behavior and that of Maxey. Through such devices, Harper criticizes her husband Maxey while still maintaining a good reputation.

Ultimately, these letters show that regardless of their class or education, women were able to craft multi-faceted rhetorical arguments. Knowing that they might never appear in person before their audiences, these writers worked carefully to infuse the missives with as strong a sense of "self" as they possibly could, whichever self they chose to emphasize. Their petitions appeal to their audiences, employ a variety of literary tropes, and manipulate epistolary conventions, particularly the *remuneration*, or prayer. Through their petitions, these women fashioned unique self-representations that illustrate some of the many ways that sixteenth-century women negotiated the limitations placed on their right to speak.

Not only do these petitions therefore act as exemplars of their writers' creative rhetorical skills, but they also serve to provide a record of early modern women's political engagement in the sixteenth century. Juxtaposing fictional petitions alongside historical petitionary letters reveals that sixteenth-century society regarded petitioning as a dramatic, important event with consequences for both the governor and the governed. On the stage and on the page, they considered what it means to petition the government as well as how a petitioner, particularly a female petitioner, could do so effectively. Such cultural records of petitioning further illuminate the study of the genre, adding nuance to the discussion of petition texts and helping to reveal how the petition came to be such a potent tool for women's use. This kind of documentary record—both of text and context—enables us to appreciate more fully the role of the petition throughout women's political history. For these positions, petitions represent a discursive moment when women make claims on the crown and act as subjects in their own right. By exercising their claims to this political right, women set the foundations for future women to engage in other kinds of petitioning, and ultimately, as Lucretia Mott asserted, started a process that other women could use, gradually enabling woman to become visible in her nation.

NOTES

1. *Discourse on Woman*, p. 13. The speech was printed in 1850. For more on early modern women's legal rights, see Laurence (227–49).

2. The text reads, "In entering upon the great work before us, we anticipate no small amount of misconception, misrepresentation, and ridicule; but we shall use every instrumentality within our power to effect our object. We shall employ agents, circulate tracts, petition the State and national Legislatures, and endeavor to enlist the pulpit and the press in our behalf" (qtd. in McMillen 209).

3. Gwilym Dodd traces the policy shifts that led to large numbers of private petitions in the reign of Edward I (19–25). The First Amendment reads, "Congress shall make no law respecting an establishment of religion, or prohibiting the free exercise thereof; or abridging the freedom of speech, or of the press; or the right of the people peaceably to assemble, and to *petition the Government for a redress of grievances*" (emphasis mine).

4. Some 153 petitions by New Hampshire women written from 1695–1700 are extant; eighty-seven percent of them were written by individual women relating to matters such as domestic violence and property rights (Blaine 64).

5. This essay thus responds to Cheryl Glenn's call to expand the boundaries of the map of rhetoric by including voices hitherto ignored by history (1–6).

6. Elizabeth Foyster demonstrates how various cases of petitions about domestic violence led to the 1839 Custody of Infants Act in the United Kingdom, which allowed women to sue for custody of children under seven years of age (129–31, 156–7). Foyster also notes that seventy collective petitions for changes to property law were presented to Parliament in 1856, one of them garnering 26,000 signatures (248). Blaine observes that a large number of women petitioners were those whose property was affected by the colonial wars, leading the New Hampshire legislature to provide monetary assistance to widows of soldiers who lost their lives while on duty (68–70). Marie Malloy traces the gradual effect of petitions on divorce laws across the American South, noting that often the changes stemmed from a paternalistic and protective attitude that sought to maintain existing class and racial boundaries (ch. 5).

7. Elizabeth, Lady Russell, and the other residents of the Blackfriars wanted the Privy Council to stop Richard Burbage's attempt to build a theater in their district, so they wrote a petition using a beautiful italic hand for the opening and the signatures, the body of the text in secretary hand, and then laid out the names of the residents in two neat italic columns, with Lady Russell and Lord Hunsdon's signatures at the start, privileging the higher class members of the neighborhood (SP 12/260/116, November, 1596). Another example would be in February 1586, when the inhabitants of the town of Norton Lynsey petitioned for help against a malefactor vandalizing their church; sixteen of the inhabitants signed the petition or made their mark next to their names. Two of the signatories were women, Isbell Bolies and Agnes Blicke, both of whom signed in an italic hand unlike the secretary script used for the rest of the petition, suggesting the women may have signed it themselves or a separate scribe added their names (SP 12/186/86). "SP" is the United Kingdom National Archives designation for the State Papers collection. All letters with manuscript number SP 12 in this essay belong to this collection; the second two numbers represent the volume and document number, respectively.

8. The phrase "utter undoing" is frequently used and seems to carry a specific meaning that cannot be dismissed as mere hyperbole. In February 1590, Joan Johnson joined her late husband's business partners in petitioning for letters of reprisal against the French towns Conquett, Brest, and Nantes because pirates from those towns killed her husband and stole his ship and its cargo (SP 12/230/115). In their petition, the group alleges that the seizure of their property is "contrarie to all equity and to the utter undoing of ye said poore widdow for ever, & to ye great damage & hinderaunce of your honors poor Orators." The distinction between the "utter undoing" of the widow and the "great damage & hindrance" of the men suggests that the phrase holds significance. On the one hand, the group may be making a practical distinction; as a widow, Johnson would likely face greater financial difficulties than the other owners. But the phrase also figures the woman as particularly wretched and helpless.

9. Please note that I have regularized the long s, u/v and i/j but otherwise have preserved the original spelling of manuscripts and early printed texts.

10. See, for example, the papal nuncio Francesco Chieregato's letter to Vigo da Campo San Pietro on May 19, 1517. Brown, *Calendar of State Papers, Venice*, item 887.

11. This is not to suggest that appealing to Requests was unpopular. By 1562, Elizabeth had to increase the number of judges from two to four to keep up with the volume of petitions from her subjects (Elton, 187–88).

12. "SP" is the United Kingdom National Archives designation for the State Papers collection. All letters with manuscript number SP 12 in this essay belong to this collection; the second two numbers represent the volume and document number, respectively.

13. Lawrence Green details carefully several of the manuscript exemplars still extant (103–4).

14. Day adds four letters by women to his 1595 printing of *The English Secretorie*. Of Fulwood's 111 exemplars, only five are by women (Barnes 122).

15. SP 12/184/46. The four documents are catalogued together: 46I is Blackwell's petition to the Council; 46II is the Parson's certificate sent to the Council; 46III is Blackwell's petition to Walsingham; and 46IV is the certificate for Walsingham.

16. The *Heroides* were available two centuries before Petrarch re-discovered Cicero's letters in 1345. John Richmond traces the textual trans-

mission of Ovid's work, noting the popularity of the *Heroides* from the twelfth century onwards (462).

17. Plural petitioners use the masculine form when there are both men and women involved in the petition. Individual women occasionally use the masculine "orator" rather than oratrix." See for example, Mary Hart's July 3, 1578 petition to Lord Burghley (SP 12/125/5). Margaret Shaw switches from "oratris" to "orator" over the course of her petition (SP 12/126/38, October, 1578).

18. It is difficult to say if there is any significance to the choice of "oratrix" versus "suppliant." In one petition from March, 1581, Jane Shelley, who uses "suppliant" throughout her petition, refers to herself as "oratrix" once but crosses it out immediately in favor of "suppliante," suggesting the choice may have been meaningful to her (SP 12/148/39). It is also possible she simply preferred consistency.

19. The letters are dated July, 1579. The bargeman was not seriously wounded, and when Appletree's lack of intent became apparent, both young men were issued pardons.

20. Written in the same hand, both petitions echo certain other phrases; whether the scribe introduced the phrase to both petitioners or whether he incorporated good ideas from the first into the second is impossible to say. It is likely that Actton's petition was written first since she does not mention the Queen's pardon in her plea while Appletree does so and such a pardon would have supported her request for Barnabe's release.

21. Margaret Aston similarly "exhibited" her proofs against John and Richard Daniel when she petitioned the Earl of Leicester about a land dispute in 1575 (SP 15/24/31).

22. For Mary Harte, see SP 12/125/5, on July 3, 1578 and SP 12/125/9, on July 6, 1578. Mary Scott's letter to Anthony Radcliff was forwarded to Walsingham together with other recusants' responses (SP 12/183/24, October 18, 1585). Scott also requested that Radcliff include a letter from herself to Walsingham on the same date (SP 12/183/25). One week later, she wrote directly to Walsingham again (SP 12/183/54, October 25, 1585).

23. The mariners of the *Emmanuel* had been detained in 1584 because one of the crew neglected to remove his hat before a procession of the Blessed Sacrament and the *Julian,* or *Gillian,* had been detained in Spain during the 1585 embargo (Fury 115). Unable to effect the mariners' release, the Council attempted to alleviate the wives' suffering by

ordering Dixie to summon the ships' owners to ask for their assistance. The owners, John Byrd and John Watts, protesting their losses and citing the lack of precedent for such intervention, declined to help, and Dixie forced them to write their own letters to the Council explaining why (SP 12/187/57). The mariners received no help; the men of the *Emmanuel* were condemned to death and five of the *Julian's* crew perished of starvation in prison (Fury 168). Byrd and Watts, who received letters of reprisal against Spanish ships, presumably were able to re-coup their fortunes, since both men backed ships again.

24. Cheryl Fury notes that such a state of affairs would be typical, since barring a small advance, merchant seamen were not paid until the successful conclusion of a voyage, for in the event of shipwreck or other loss of goods, the mariners themselves were held responsible and could have their wages docked or withheld altogether (93–101).

25. Morton's plea was successful in at least earning investigation. On July 30, twelve days after her petition, the Council ordered that her husband be examined further to be certain that he had no ill intentions in trying to leave the country (PC 2/12/234).

26. "PC" is the United Kingdom National Archives designation for the Acts of the Privy Council collection. All letters with manuscript number PC in this essay belong to this collection; the second two numbers represent the volume and document number, respectively.

27. All that survives of this petition is an abstract of its contents sent to Burghley, Russell's kinsman.

28. This petition is described in the *Calendar of State Papers* as that of a petition from "a poor woman to the Queen" (Vol. 1, p. 478, item 92). However, it is manifestly clear that Frobisher is the woman in question. Wheater writes that Martin Frobisher had joined Thomas Stukeley's conspiracy with Philip II of Spain to invade England and that he was supposed to convey Sir Warrham St. Leger and Jerome Brett, Stukeley's English cohorts, to Spain (856–57). Drawing on an unknown source, Wheater notes that Frobisher's wife helped to reveal the plot: "Her hostility was brought about by her personal dislike for St. Leger; and 'some jarre happened between Furbisher and her.' What was the direct result of her interference we do not know" (857). For a full account of Frobisher's relations with St. Leger, who was betraying his co-conspirators and reporting to the Privy Council, see McDermott (89–92). To the best of my knowledge, no one has hitherto associated this petition with Isabel Frobisher, but the author's references to Warrham St. Leger, Jerome Brett,

and Thomas Stukeley as her husband's confederates and her husband's subsequent repudiation of her make Isabel's authorship of this petition certain.

29. In Elizabeth's speech to Parliament in 1559, she declared "every one of you, and as many as are English, are my children and kinsfolks" (59). For more on Elizabeth's crafting of this image, see Carole Levin, *The Heart and Stomach of a King,* especially chapter four, "Wanton and Whore," pp. 65–90.

30. It is unclear whether Elizabeth responded to Frobisher's plea; the next time Frobisher enters the historical record, she is petitioning Francis Walsingham for help collecting one of Martin's debts to support herself and her grandchildren by her first husband, so it seems she was able to retain her standing as his wife (SP 12/151/17). At the time of her death in 1588, she was living in Snaith, her first husband's hometown, so it is to be hoped she received better treatment there (*Parish Registers,* 72).

WORKS CITED

Acts of the Privy Council. 1558-1603. National Archives, United Kingdom, PC.

Anonymous. *A newe enterlude drawen oute of the holy scripture of godly queene Hester.* London: William Pickering and Thomas Hacket. 1561. STC 13251.

Applegarth, Risa. "Rhetorical Scarcity: Spatial and Economic Inflections on Genre Change." *College Composition and Communication,* vol. 63, no. 3, Feb. 2012, pp. 453–83.

Barnes, Diana. "Editing Early Modern Women's Letters for Print Publication." *Editing Early Modern Women.* Edited by Sarah C. E. Ross and Paul Salzman, Cambridge UP, 2016, pp. 121–38.

Beemer, Cristy. "God Save the Queen: Kairos and the Mercy Letters of Elizabeth I and Mary, Queen of Scots." *Rhetoric Review,* vol. 35, no. 2, 2016, pp. 75–90.

Blaine, Marcia Schmidt. "The Power of Petitions: Women and the New Hampshire Provincial Government, 1695–1770." *International Review of Social History,* vol. 46, supplement, 2001, pp. 57–77.

Brown, Rawdon, editor. *Calendar of State Papers and Manuscripts Relating to English Affairs Existing in the Archives and Collections of Venice and other Libraries in Northern Italy.* Vol. 2, HMSO, 1867.

Brigg, William, editor. *The Parish Registers of Snaith, Co. York, Part II, Burials, 1537–1656*. York Parish Register Society, 1919.

"The Constitution of the United States, Amendment 1." National Archives, https://www.archives.gov/founding-docs/bill-of-rights-transcript. Accessed July 29, 2018.

Dasent, John Roche, editor. *Acts of the Privy Council of England*. Vol. 18, Her Majesty's Stationery Office, 1899. *British History Online*, www.british-history.ac.uk/acts-privy-council/vol18. Accessed 5 Feb. 2018.

Day, Angel. *The English Secretorie, Wherin is contayned, a perfect method, for the inditing of all manner of epistles and familiar letters.* London, Robert Walde-grave and Richard Iones, 1586. STC 6401.

Daybell, James. *The Material Letter in Early Modern England: Manuscript Letters and the Culture and Practices of Letter-Writing, 1512–1635*. Palgrave Macmillan, 2012.

—. *Women Letter-Writers in Tudor England*. Oxford UP, 2006.

Dodd, Gwilym. *Justice and Grace: Private Petitioning and the English Parliament in the Late Middle Ages*. Oxford UP, 2007.

Donawerth, Jane. "Women's Poetry and the Tudor-Stuart System of Gift Exchange." *Women, Writing, and the Reproduction of Culture in Tudor and Stuart Britain*, edited by Mary E. Burke, Jane Donawerth, Linda L. Dove, and Karen Nelson, Syracuse UP, 2000, pp. 3–18.

Dyson, Humfrey, compiler. *A Booke Containing All Such Proclamations As Were Published During the Raigne of the late Queene Elizabeth, Collected Together by the industry of Humfrey Dyson.* London, Bonham Norton, and John Bill, 1618. STC 7758.3.

Elton, G.R. *The Tudor Constitution. Documents and Commentary.* 2nd ed. Cambridge UP, 1982.

Foyster, Elizabeth. *Marital Violence: An English Family History, 1650–1857.* Cambridge UP, 2005.

Fury, Cheryl. *Tides in the Affairs of Men: The Social History of Elizabethan Seamen, 1580–1603.* Greenwood Press, 2002.

Glenn, Cheryl. *Rhetoric Re-Told: Regendering the Tradition from Antiquity through the Renaissance,* Southern Illinois UP, 1997.

Green, Lawrence. "Dictamen in England, 1500–1700." *Letter-Writing Manuals and Instruction from Antiquity to the Present,* edited by Carol Poster and Linda C. Mitchell, U of South Carolina P, 2007, pp. 102–26.

Harris, Barbara. *English Aristocratic Women, 1450–1550, Marriage and Family, Property and Careers,* Oxford UP, 2002.

Higginson, Stephen A. "A Short History of the Right to Petition Government for the Redress of Grievances." *The Yale Law Journal*, vol. 96, no. 1, Nov. 1986, pp. 142–66.

Laurence, Anne. *Women in England: 1500–1760, A Social History*. St. Martin's Press, 1994.

Lemon, Robert, and Mary Anne Everett Green, editors. *Calendar of State Papers, Domestic, of the Reigns of Edward VI, Mary, Elizabeth, and James, 1547–1625*. London, Longman, Brown, Green, Longmans, and Roberts, 1856–72.

Levin, Carole. *The Heart and Stomach of a King: Elizabeth I and the Politics of Sex and Power*. 2nd ed. U of Pennsylvania P, 2013.

Magnusson, Lynne. "A Rhetoric of Requests: Genre and Linguistic Scripts in Elizabethan Women's Suitors' Letters." *Women and Politics in Early Modern England, 1450–1700*, edited by James Daybell, Ashgate, 2004, pp. 51–66.

Marcus, Leah, Janel Mueller, and Mary Beth Rose, editors. *Elizabeth I: Collected Works*. Vol. 1, U of Chicago P, 2000.

McDermott, James. *Martin Frobisher: Elizabethan Privateer*. Yale UP, 2001.

McMillen, Sally. *Seneca Falls and the Origin of the Women's Rights Movement*. Oxford UP, 2009.

Miller, Carolyn. "Genre as Social Action." *Quarterly Journal of Speech*, vol. 70, 1984, pp. 151–67.

Molloy, Marie S. *Single, White, Slaveholding Women in the Nineteenth-Century American South*. U South Carolina P, 2018.

Mott, Lucretia. *Discourse on Woman*. Philadelphia, T.B. Peterson, 1850. Library of Congress, www.loc.gov/item/09002748/. Accessed 7 Feb. 7, 2018.

Mulcaster, Richard. "Richard Mulcaster's Account of Queen Elizabeth's Speech and Prayer During Her Passage through London to Westminster." *Elizabeth I: Collected Works*, edited by Leah S. Marcus, Janel Mueller, and Mary Beth Rose, University of Chicago Press, 2000, pp. 53-55.

A newe boke of presidentes in maner of a register. Preface by Thomas Phaer. London, Edward Whytchurche, 1543. STC 3327.

"Orator." *The Oxford English Dictionary*. OED Online, Oxford UP, Jan. 2018. www.oed.com/view/Entry/132201. Accessed 5 Feb. 2018.

Richmond, John. "Manuscript Traditions and the Transmission of Ovid's Works." *Brill's Companion to Ovid,* edited by Barbara Weiden Boyd, Brill, 2002, pp. 443–83.

Sadlack, Erin A. *The French Queen's Letters: Mary Tudor Brandon and the Politics of Marriage in Sixteenth-Century Europe.* Palgrave Macmillan, 2011.

Shakespeare, William. *The Complete Works,* edited by Stanley Wells and Gary Taylor, Clarendon Press, 1988.

—. *As You Like It. The Complete Works,* edited by Stanley Wells and Gary Taylor, Clarendon Press, 1988, pp. 705–34,

—. *Henry VI, Part Three. The Complete Works,* edited by Stanley Wells and Gary Taylor, Clarendon Press, 1988, pp. 91-124.

—. *King John. The Complete Works,* edited by Stanley Wells and Gary Taylor, Clarendon Press, 1988, pp. 397-424.

—. *Measure for Measure. The Complete Works,* edited by Stanley Wells and Gary Taylor, Clarendon Press, 1988, pp. 789-818.

—. *The Merchant of Venice. The Complete Works,* edited by Stanley Wells and Gary Taylor, Clarendon Press, 1988, pp. 425-52.

—. *Richard II. The Complete Works,* edited by Stanley Wells and Gary Taylor, Clarendon Press, 1988, pp. 367-96.

—. *Titus Andronicus. The Complete Works,* edited by Stanley Wells and Gary Taylor, Clarendon Press, 1988, 125-52.

—. *Twelfth Night. The Complete Works,* edited by Stanley Wells and Gary Taylor, Clarendon Press, 1988, pp. 691-714.

—. *Two Gentlemen of Verona. The Complete Works,* edited by Stanley Wells and Gary Taylor, Clarendon Press, 1988, pp. 1-24.

State Papers Domestic, Elizabeth I. 1558-1603. National Archives, United Kingdom, SP 12.

State Papers Domestic, Elizabeth I, Addenda. 1558-1603. National Archives, United Kingdom, SP 15.

Stow, John. *Annales of England.* London, 1605. STC 23337.

Stretton, Tim. "Women, Custom, and Equity in the Court of Requests." *Women, Crime and the Courts in Early Modern England,* edited by Jennifer Kermode and Garthine Walker, U North Carolina P, 1994, pp. 170–90.

Wheater, W. "The Ancestry of Sir Martin Frobisher." *Gentlemen's Magazine,* Nov., 1868, pp. 852–58.

Whetstone, George. *The right excellent and famous Historye of Promos and Cassandra.* London, Richard Ihones, 1578. STC 25347.

6 WHEN THEY WERE BOYS AND WHEN THEY WERE GIRLS: CONSTRUCTIONS OF GENDER IN PROGRESSIVE-ERA AMERICAN CONDUCT BIOGRAPHY

Lisa Zimmerelli

Conduct literature—a genre that explicitly instructs people in certain behaviors, attitudes, and modes of interaction—is a tradition most often associated with the early modern period, peaking in popularity during the Renaissance throughout Europe. It is also a tradition particularly preoccupied <u>with normative gender and class roles</u>, as the titles attest: in addition to Castiglione's well-known *The Book of the Courtier* (1528), we have, for example, Juan Luis Vives' *The Instruction of a Christen Woman* (1523), Thomas Tusser's *A Hundred Good pointes of husbandry lately maried vnto a hunderth good poynts of huswifery* (1570), and John Heyden's *Advice to a daughter in opposition to the Advice to a sonne* (1658).

Although conduct literature circulated most prevalently in the early modern period, scholars have traced the emergence of the genre in Europe as early as the medieval period[1] and have explored various iterations of conduct books in the centuries following the Renaissance.[2] As Jane Donawerth explains in her chapter on nineteenth-century transatlantic conduct books in *Conversational Rhetoric: The Rise and Fall of a Woman's Tradition 1600–1900*, as the early modern period progressed, conduct literature gradually broadened to an audience beyond the Aristocratic court:

> From the late sixteenth century to the present, conduct books
> have advised the middle classes on how to behave: how to be
> good wives or husbands, how to educate oneself, how to con-
> verse and compose convincing letters, how to impress people
> with one's knowledge, how to behave socially, how to succeed
> and appear to be a member of a superior class. (42)

With this extended audience of a middle-class base, conduct books were
an immensely popular genre over the next few hundred years, widely
read, discussed, and even satirized, as Robert Uphaus suggests in Jane
Austen's portrayal of Mr. Collin's endorsement of *Sermons to Young
Women* in *Pride and Prejudice*.[3]

This chapter further extends the generic lineage of the conduct book
into American Progressive-Era biography published for children. Like
other chapters in this collection (Hijazi, Enoch, Sadlack, Nelson, Griffin, Miller, and Donawerth), this chapter sees genre as a fruitful lens
for reading and decoding texts to glean greater understanding of the
times in which that genre circulated. Furthermore, because this chapter
traces echoes of early modern conduct book themes into Progressive-Era
biography, this chapter also explores how cultural mythos can animate
sociopolitical agendas of the time. In short, this chapter is not just about
circulation, but recirculation.

Indeed, remarkably, throughout the centuries conduct books have
retained a few key characteristics: (1) a wide array of topics covered, including domestic duties, politics, religion, personal appearance, commu-
nications, education, and decorum; (2) deeply gendered targeting and
circulation, specifically to either boys or to girls, to men or to women;
and (3) a didactic, pedagogic, often moralistic tone which conveys a primary motivation of upward—albeit often limited—mobility through
adherence to a prescribed way of being in and interacting with the world.

Specifically, my analysis focuses on American turn-of-the-century
biographical compilations written expressly for boys and girls: four sets
of biographical compilations that include a book for girls and a book
for boys, one compilation whose contents are divided with the first half
covering the biographies of men and the second half the biographies of
women, and one compilation whose contents are combined. See Table 1.

Table 1

Title	Author	Date
Lives of Poor Boys Who Became Famous	Sarah K. Bolton	1885
Lives of Girls Who Became Famous	Sarah K. Bolton	1886
Historic Boys: Their Endeavors, Their Achievements, and Their Times	Elbridge Streeter Brooks	1889
Historic Girls: Stories of Girls Who Have Influenced the History of Their Times	Elbridge Streeter Brooks	1892
Historic Boyhoods	Rupert Holland	1909
Historic Girlhoods	Rupert Holland	1910
When They Were Boys	Carroll Everett	1922
When They Were Girls	Rebecca Deming Moore	1923
True Stories of Famous Men and Women of America Containing Full Accounts of the Lives and Heroic Deeds of About Half a Hundred Illustrious Men and Women who have made our Country Great and our Flag Respected Throughout the World	"a corps of distinguished writers"	1898
When They Were Children: Stories of the Childhood of Famous Men and Women	Amy Steedman	1914

In the remainder of this chapter I call these biographical compilations "conduct biography." After providing a brief history of the tradition of biography in America, I turn to what literary theorist Gérard Genette calls "paratexts"—the table of contents, prefaces, and introductions—in order to explore the three characteristics of conduct biography as I have outlined them above, albeit with a Progressive-Era American spin:

1.   They highlight and celebrate a range of professions, people, and activities. However, that range is clearly limited to acceptable parameters marked by race, class, politics, and gender.
2.   They are marketed primarily toward either boys or girls, clearly indicated by their titles and separate publication cycles. However, the authors of the distinct conduct biographies strongly suggest that they are meant to be read as a set, by both boys and girls, and a small subset of compilations for both boys and girls published (represented by the two I include for this study) indicate a shift toward a shared readership.
3.   A didactic tone carries the explicit message of the possibility of progress—individual and national—by following a set of virtues

cast as particularly American. Reminiscent of the early modern conduct literature focused on court behavior, the biographies expressly state their intent to instruct boys and girls on proper "American" behavior.

As an unexpected sub-genre within the conduct book tradition, Progressive-Era American conduct biography offers important insights to the prescriptive, gendered constructions of what was cast as uniquely American girlhoods and boyhoods. Moreover, putting conduct biography in conversation with some of the earliest iterations of conduct literature highlights the residues of the mythos of the Renaissance on the American cultural imagination.

THE BIOGRAPHICAL TRADITION IN AMERICA

Biography was one of the most popular genres of the long nineteenth century, and during the Progressive Era in America in particular, biography heralded individual attainment and served as a powerful reminder of a national brand of morality and ethic. As historian Scott Casper explains, "Biographical Mania," as it was referred to in its own time, manifested itself in a myriad of ways: commercial publishers put out hundreds of biographies annually, including biographical dictionaries and compilations, sometimes themed around a certain industry or profession; moral biographies circulated by religious tract societies; and weekly columns in periodicals that were devoted to biography. In addition to the dozens of biographies of Jesus, even Satan had a volume devoted to his life.[4] Volumes of biography were found in homes, libraries, schools, political clubs, prisons, ladies sewing circles and the like across America (Casper 1–3).

The importance of the genre to an emerging collective American psyche—a psyche rebounding and coalescing after the Civil War—cannot be overestimated. Explains Casper: "biographers and critics and readers alike believed that biography had power: the power to shape individuals' lives and character and to help define America's national character" (3). Biography served as commemoration, documenting and recording a particular kind of life story to public memory; it also served as recommendation, suggesting a kind of life to lead.

In other words, "Biographical Mania" was not simply a consumptive trend (a description I would argue could be applied to the psychobiographies of the 1970s and 1980s); it was rather a constructive trend, educating its readership on the possibility and potential of the "everyday" individual in America. Moreover, it coincided with and affirmed America's emergence as an independent nation. In short, the life presented was not presented as unique; it was the American landscape that was presented as unique. So, American biography of this period is a rich site for investigating what biography scholar Rob Wilson calls "a master narrative affirming the very hold of self-Americanization. The self is still the site and ground of affirmative socialization, and biography conspires in this task" (169).

From the mid-nineteenth century until before the second World War, I would assert that the form of biography most conspiring in the task of American socialization was hagiography, also sometimes referred to as "pious," "hero," or "destiny" biography. It followed a rather prescriptive celebratory narrative and was so popular that Herman Melville parodied the genre in his class polemic novelistic biography *Israel Potter*. The first line of Melville's 1855 parody reads:

> Biography, in its purer form, confined to the ended lives of the true and brave, may be held the fairest meed of human virtue— one given and received in entire disinterestedness—since neither can the biographer hope for acknowledgment from the subject, nor the subject at all avail himself of the biographical distinction conferred. (3)

Despite its enormous popularity in the nineteenth and twentieth centuries, the hagiographic biography of this period has received relatively light scholarly attention, especially within rhetorical studies. Indeed, the word "biography" does not show up in the index of Patricia Bizzell and Bruce Herzberg's *Rhetorical Tradition* nor in either of the two volumes devoted to this period in the series "A Rhetorical History of the United States," edited by Martin Medhurst. Biography gets just the briefest of mentions in Jane Donawerth's *Rhetorical Theory by Women before 1900* and Nan Johnson's *Nineteenth-Century Rhetoric in North America*.

It is worth mentioning that the next generation of biographies— those that emerged in the post-World War II period—the literary, social, and psychobiographies of a single person, often a statesmen or literary figure—received much more attention and inspired a surge of interest in the tensions inherent in life writing. Within literary studies, history, feminist studies, and sociology—and largely influenced by James Clifford, Clifford Geertz, and Jacques Derrida—the biography of this later period came to be seen as symbolic, with inherent structures of interpretation reflecting the complex relationship between the biographer and his or her subject.[5]

So why the lack of attention to this earlier and more robust collection of biography? For one answer, we can look to the biographers themselves, who often engaged in a bit of meta-analysis in their prefaces and introductions. Many prefaces include discussion of biography as a genre; the authors or editors often critique the genre of biography and explained how their biography was distinct from or better than or contributed to all of the other hundreds of biographies circulating around. Take, for example, Roy Floyd Dibble's preface to his compilation *Strenuous Americans*, published in 1923. Dibble writes:

> Although many books have been written about America's most eminent sons and daughters, we have relatively few genuine biographies . . . Like the persons whose careers they record, they too have generally been representative specimens who illustrated the particular whim and foibles of a particular race, living in a particular nation, during a particular age. With distressing frequency, their literary efforts are characterized by lopsided emphasis, by sprawling incoherence, by parochial banalities, and by maddening prolixity; above all, most of these authors have constantly employed a tone of tombstone panegyric. They have buried their subjects under heavy slabs of adulation hardly less ponderous, and rarely more artistic, than the granite slabs that now mark the graves of those subjects. But these weighty tomes, whether single, twin or triple, have led to at least one happy result: almost nobody reads them. (1)

rambling on and on

"Maddening prolixity." The irony. Despite whatever literary sensibilities these biographies might violate—for their contemporary or for modern audiences—I make the case in this chapter that we need to return to the underexplored archive of turn-of-the-century conduct biography, partly because of its sheer volume and influence in the period—assuredly, it was doing cultural work—but also partly because any genre that seems at first blush to have such uniformity and coherence invites further study.

My larger archive of nineteenth and Progressive-Era biography demonstrates that these biographies were not as uniform as both their contemporary critics or modern critics often claim; it contains: biography of individual famous men and women in American history (on Abraham Lincoln, Andrew Jackson, Frances Willard, etc.); biographical compilations of famous men and women in American history and similar compilations which include all of Western history (e.g., *Great Men and Famous Women*); biography of the everyday, contemporary person (e.g., *Portraits and Biographical Records of [name of county or city]*; biography of certain professions (e.g., *Pioneer American Educators*); gender-specific biographical compilations (e.g., *Famous American Belles of the Nineteenth Century* and *Buckeye Boys who Have Become Presidents*); and the compilations for children that I am studying for this chapter.

WHO SHOULD BE EMULATED? RACE, CLASS, GENDER, AND POLITICS IN CONDUCT BIOGRAPHIES

Prefatory matter—the things that accompany a text, such as the title page, preface or introduction, and illustrations—is what Gérard Genette calls a paratext, a liminal space within and outside a book (1). According to Genette, such material is transactional—the author's attempt to exercise some control over the reception of the text and the response of the reader (2). As Genette says,

> More than a boundary or a sealed border, the paratext is, rather, a threshold . . . a zone between text and off-text, a zone not only of transition but also of transaction: a privileged place of pragmatics and a strategy, of an influence on the public, an influence that . . . is at the service of a better reception for the text and a more pertinent reading of it. (2)

In addition to being transitional and transactional, I also read paratexts as rhetorical, with signals contained therein that help communicate and mediate the rhetorical project of the text and give us insights into the generic features of a collection of texts.

If my archive were complete with the physical copies of these books as they were published and circulated, I would first investigate the covers of these books as well as the included illustrations. However, many of my copies are reprints and facsimiles, which often lack a picture of the hard cover or make mention of an illustration that is missing in the reprint. I therefore start my analysis instead with the tables of contents in these conduct biographies.

The set *When They Were Girls* and *When They Were Boys* contain only Americans from the nineteenth century. The set *Lives of Girls Who Became Famous* and *Lives of Poor Boys Who Became Famous* contain Americans and Europeans and British from the nineteenth century. The set *Historic Girlhoods* and *Historic Boyhoods* contain only a few Americans and mostly British and Europeans from the Renaissance through the early nineteenth century. The set *Historic Girls* and *Historic Boys* contain American, European, and British men and women from classical times until about 1800. Finally, the combined volume *True Stories of Famous Men and Women* contains only American men and women from the beginning of the nation until 1900, and the combined volume *When They Were Children* contains American, European, and British men and women from classical times through the late nineteenth century. In not restricting their content to Americans or to the temporal restraint of American nation formation in the seventeenth through nineteenth centuries, the majority of writers suggest that they view America as squarely within and contributing to the Western intellectual and socio-political tradition.

Ostensibly, the editors and authors claim that criteria for their selection of the men and women include: that they come from many walks of life, are representative of other men and women, occupy an important place in their profession or field, or greatly influence society in some way. Closer examination of the apparent selection criteria reveals a more homogenous group and perhaps a more sinister motivation. The following analysis takes a stance of curiosity regarding the motivations of the editors and writers in including some men and women over others. Read rhetorically, I assert that these tables of contents reveal much about the purpose of the conduct biographies and present an implicit argument. My conclusions are also informed by my reading of the biographies, how the men and women are depicted, what's highlighted, etc. within the narratives themselves.

First, a note about who is not included in these tables of contents. With the exception of Pocahontas and a few Native American leaders, men and women of color are not included. Even the typically tokenized Frederick Douglass and Sojourner Truth are not included. Among the Americans, Catholic and Jewish women are not included, and activists of a certain vein—Emma Goldman, Mother Jones, Elizabeth Gurley Flynn, and Carrie Nation—are not included.

Consequently, when I refer to "boy" or "girl" or "man" or "woman" in this chapter, let me make perfectly clear that I am referring to a construction of white, Protestant, "respectable" boyhood and girlhood and manhood and womanhood. Let me also make perfectly clear that I am not suggesting that nineteenth-century biographies of marginalized men and women do not exist. Hallie Quinn Brown, for example, published *Homespun Heroines and Other Women of Distinction* in 1926. However, the mainstream publishing venues—e.g., George W. Jacobs & Co., F. A. Owen Publishing Co., Thomas Y. Crowell Co., F. A. Stokes Co.—were not publishing these biographies. Brown's collection was published by a small Ohio press called Aldine. Moreover, this exclusion also prompts us to consider if the proliferation of slave narratives and autobiographies by Black men and women during this era is perhaps partly in response to such an obvious absence in the volumes of circulating life stories at the time.

I assert that this absence was not innocent, but was part of a larger, white supremacist project in America at this time. As has been well established by rhetorical scholars, nineteenth-century progressive social reform movements were often substantiated through racist scientific discourse. Widely disseminated medical tracts explained and categorized the "races" of man according to various physiological, behavioral, phenotypical, and cognitive differences. Nineteenth-century neurologist George Beard, for example, authored two very popular books in the 1880s on a disease he termed "neurasthenia." Defined by "nervelessness" or "a lack of nerve force," Beard argued that neurasthenia was the result of modern civilization and led to emasculated American manhood. Social reformers picked up this thread in earnest, and reformers such as Howard Pyle, Walter Rauschenbush, and others called for a more virulent, robust manhood, one which emphasized the importance of physical strength and health, of vim and vigor.

Beard explicitly connected neurasthenia to "brain workers," as opposed to what he called savages, barbarians, semi-barbarians or partially civilized people (146). According to Beard, the "Caucasian" race, because it was doing all of the thinking in America, was suffering physically. White boys needed more exercise, needed to be outside more, needed to confront danger more, etc. This implicit and explicit message gets picked up in the literature of this time, including in the conduct biographies.

In particular, Arthurian legends were enormously popular (and these legends specify that the men in Arthurian legends were "sturdy lads, descended from Anglo Saxon stock"). As historian Jeanne Fox-Friedman explains, Arthurian legends and/or the rhetoric of Arthurian heroism seeped into the discourse of children's books in various tales of chivalry partly in response to concerns over diseases like neurasthenia. Fox-Friedman explains how *Historic Girls* and *Historic Boys* editor Elbridge Streeter Brooks and others invoked the medieval period and its hero tales as models for youth. In fact, the Middle Ages were often referred to as "the childhood of the race" (142)—and they weren't referring to the human race. According to Fox-Friedman,

> Such training would enable these virile young men to rule over the more primitive peoples of the world at a moment in which nineteenth-century America was creating its own imperialist empire . . . The robust nature of medieval life was to be the instrument by which modern America would re-energize its quest for progress. (145, 148)

In other words, this argument was so prevalent, so woven into the fabric of the nineteenth-century cultural imagination, that audiences would have understood the implicit messages of these conduct biographies. These were not only qualities that boys should aspire to and girls should support; they were qualities that would ensure the continued superiority of the "Caucasian" race.[6] Consequently, and as I detail in the rest of the section, although the table of contents span eras and nations, they almost uniformly indicate a doctrine of white supremacy.

The selection criteria pre-1800 for women seem to be fairly limited to nobility (e.g., Queen Elizabeth, Mary Queen of Scots, Queen Victoria, Catherine the Great) to motherhood (the mothers of all the great presidents or kings), or to marriage (e.g., Josephine Bonaparte and Martha Washington). A few women gain admittance into these volumes by their accomplishments, such as Joan of Arc, but this is the exception. As conduct literature, the message is clear for women: one's role is clearly more important than one's activity, and the measure of a successful life is proper fulfillment of that role. This is consistent with the rhetoric of Republican Motherhood, the idea that one contributed in critical ways to the formation of America as a nation by their conduct as mothers and wives, raising good boys and maintaining a proper, well-managed home. In the case of the queens for example, depictions of their leadership in the narratives are often couched in domestic rhetoric, as opposed to particular skill in diplomacy or warfare. Holland, for example, writes of Queen Victoria, "Throughout her long reign she showed those same qualities of self-reliance, of calmness, and of devotion to duty" (252).

The selection criteria for men pre-1800, however, is solely based on accomplishment—e.g., Christopher Columbus, Mozart, Daniel Webster. Heroic deeds in war seem also to be a particularly important factor. Some importance is given to statesmanship (e.g., Benjamin Franklin is usually included); however, this is much more prevalent post-1800. As opposed to the female nobility, who are presented as being born into the role, often unwillingly assuming the responsibilities of her reign when it is time to do so, great focus is given to how male kings and lords earned the title through deeds and heroic acts, not through just birthright. In its function as conduct literature, these biographies place a high value on a boy's individual heroism and personal attainment and accomplishment.

The selection criteria post-1800 for men and women are slightly less gendered in the conduct biographies. Almost all of the men and women are American; all are either reformers or representative of a certain profession—art, music, literature, medicine, higher education. However, although the women are not chosen based on their domestic roles—on their roles as mother or wife—many of the narratives nonetheless contain an account of her home-life, not only from when she was a girl, but also from when she had her own home—how she maintained it, beautified it, etc.—even as she pursued her reform work or profession. Notably, not all reform work is represented equally. Women's rights, war humanitarian efforts, and education are represented. Abolitionism, remarkably, barely gets mention. In fact, when describing Susan B. Anthony, for example, Moore stresses, "Sometimes she pleaded for the freedom of the slaves, sometimes for temperance, but always for her favorite cause—rights of women" (36).

In its function as conduct literature, the selection implies a kind of repudiation of class structures that bound European and British women. Only certain women pre-1800 and non-American could accomplish great things—mainly those born into or married into nobility. In contrast, American women, and particularly American women in the age of progress, could contribute in significant ways to the pressing socio-political issues of the day. Simultaneously, however, these conduct biographies imply that some reform work was more acceptable than other reform work—that which did not threaten the racial status quo and that which fit within a woman's "natural" inclination toward care-giving and education.

AN EVOLUTION OF DISTINCT BOOKS AND SEPARATE
SPHERES INTO A COHERENT, SHARED AMERICA

Despite deeply gendered outward marketing and appearances (published a year apart, aesthetically gendered covers), the rhetoric of the prefatory matter in the conduct biographies suggests interesting parallels and congruencies. Genette explains that the function of the preface, at its most simplistic, is *"to get the book read* and *to get the book read properly"* (197). The paratexts of these biographical compilations speak directly to their intended formative role for a young American readership, and—notably—there is little variation. For example, the "Publisher's Note" for the 1925 edition of Sarah Bolton's *Lives of Girls Who Became Famous* recalls the importance of it as a companion text to *Poor Boys Who Became Famous* and boasts of their collective success: "Who can measure the good that these two books have accomplished? How many other ambitious boys and girls have been spurred on to high endeavor by these stories of what other boys and girls have done?" (Bolton *Girls* iii).

Indeed, all of the books in my archive state their readership as co-gendered and their motivation as encouraging a generation of boys and girls to emulate distinctly American behaviors, dispositions, and actions. For example, editor Helen Owen writes in her preface to Everett's *When They Were Boys*: "It is our desire to place these stories before the boys and girls of to-day in order that they may realize that it is possible to surmount any obstacle in the path of success" (2), and Elbridge Streeter Brooks similarly writes in his preface to *Historic Girls*: "This volume seeks to tell for the girls and boys of to-day the stories of some of their sisters of the long-ago,—girls who by eminent position or valiant deeds became historic even before they had passed the charming season of girlhood" (1).

At first glance, it might be tempting to argue that these separate compilations were merely a reflection of separate spheres ideology, the prevailing discourse that men should lead in political/public space and women should occupy the domestic/private space. Separate spheres ideology manifested itself everywhere in America during this time: young men and women sat on opposite sides of lecture halls at university; women led prayer circles for women and men led them for men. But, taking a cue from Jessica Enoch, who argues that women-only educational spaces were not only constraints, but also opportunities (11), I look to these conduct biographies as both material representation of separate spheres ideology and rhetorical opportunities to challenge such gendered materiality.

When considered together, as a set, as they are instructed to be read, the separate conduct biographies hint at a reformulation of gendered separate spheres into one coherent, shared America.[7] Textually, that coherence is realized in the two compilations containing the stories of both men and women published for boys and girls. Interestingly, *True Stories of Famous Men and Women of America*, published in 1898, still conforms to separate spheres within its covers, with the first two-thirds including lives of men and the last third including the lives of women. However, Amy Steedman's 1914 *When They Were Children* is organized simply by date. Her preface further indicates the fully integrated and combined nature of her conduct biography: "We shall learn to know these great men and women all the better for hearing something of what they thought and did when they were children" (viii).

PATRIOTIC DIDACTICISM: THE ROLES OF BOYS AND GIRLS IN THE MAKING OF AMERICA

The conduct biographies were often published by companies that also marketed to schools and teachers, such as DC Heath and Company, which published textbooks, and The Union Press, which sold Sunday School literature. I am not *presuming* that these texts may have been read in a formative way; rather, I am asserting for certain that these sets of biographies for boys and girls were *explicitly* engaged in the educative formation of children during the Progressive Era. All conduct biographies also make reference in their prefaces to certain desirable qualities that they cast as uniquely American and necessary for nation building. Their didactic rhetoric is tinged with American patriotism, with the insistence that the attainment of certain "American" ideals and one's adherence to "American" scrappiness is necessary to America's destiny as a great nation.

Each compilation constructs in its prefatory matter a kind of conglomerate model woman and model man, a summation and amalgamation of all of the traits evidenced collectively by the biographies contained within the covers of each book. Notably, the named characteristics of this model woman and model man are consistent in both the conduct books for boys and for girls—industriousness, resilience, and patriotism. This suggests the primacy of one's American identity over one's gender,

[handwritten marginal notes: "Handbook/instructor manuals", "How to be a good woman", "Qualities of a woman"]

and given the heavy reliance of the various nineteenth-century social movements in the United States on women for organization, leadership, and financial support, is also hardly surprising. Nonetheless, closer analysis reveals subtle gendered distinctions.

First, all conduct biographies stress the quality of industriousness. Writes publisher Helen Mildred Owen in *When They Were Girls*: "We may then learn that success does not come overnight, but that years of careful, painstaking work are often spent before the contribution that one has for the world is completed" (10); and in *When They Were Boys* that all of the boys "[rose] from humble beginnings" (1). Similarly, Bolton writes in *Lives of Girls Who Became Famous*, "All of us have aspirations. We build aircastles, and are probably the happier for the building. However, the sooner we learn that life is not a play-day, but a thing of earnest activity, the better for us and for those associated with us" (iv). She writes in *Lives of Poor Boys Who Became Famous*, "These lives show that without WORK and WILL no great things are achieved" (1). In the girl conduct biographies, industriousness is usually coupled with the suggestion of humility and patience; whereas in the boy conduct biographies, industriousness is facilitated by hard work and courage. Note that boys rise from humble beginnings in *When They Were Boys*. Nowhere is it implied that they must retain some of this humility. Boys can become great. Girls are inherently good, and when they work hard, they can contribute to the greatness of America. The introduction to *True Stories of Famous Men and Women* demonstrates this starkly:

> What schoolboy [asks]—what their trials and opportunities when they were young like myself?—were they like other boys or were they always superior beings, born great, and continually in the midst of prominent scenes or doing wonderful acts? He wants to know what opportunity, what hope, there is for him to be like [great men] . . . In like manner do the noble sisters of humanity, heralds of liberty and angels of mercy . . . pass before the young girls and women who read this volume, with the magnetism of their lovely and loving characters and the exalted inspiration of their noble lives and beneficent deeds. (5–6)

Also, consistently highlighted as a uniquely American trait is resilience in the face of obstacles. Owen includes an almost identical line in her prefaces to *When They Were Boys* and *When They Were Girls*: "Many of these men, in their boyhood, overcame great obstacles: some of them

were very poor, some were unable to go to school, and some lacked physical endurance. But they were all able to rise above these conditions and
forge ahead toward their goal" (1–2); similarly she writes in *When They
Were Girls*: "As girls, some of them were wealthy, some of them were very
poor; but they all had obstacles to overcome. Each one had her own way
to make" (3). Poverty is an obstacle repeated in other collections. Sarah
Bolton writes in her prefaces to the boy and girl collections, respectively:
"These characters have been chosen . . . that the youth who read this
book may see that poverty is no barrier to success" (Bolton, *Boys*, i) and
in the girls conduct book, "If poor, with Mary Lyon's persistency and
noble purpose, we can accomplish almost anything" (iv).

The boy conduct books, additionally, add specific qualities pertain-
ing to that gender: Brooks writes in *Historic Boys* that his selections
"show that, from the earliest ages, manliness and self-reliance have ever
been the chief groundwork of character" and that the men "bravely front
danger, difficulty, or death" (2). The girls aren't expected to risk certain
death. Instead, the girl conduct books make mention of those qualities we often hear in nineteenth-century separate spheres rhetoric about
women: she is charming, tender, true. In employing a generic singular
"he" or "she" throughout the prefaces and introductions, the conduct biographers establish that the men and women are not presented as unique;
rather, the American landscape is unique, lending itself to the formation
of this kind of American man or women, the kind of American man or
women who can "do" great work in the world. We see the description of
that American brand of work ethic that still echoes in national political
challenges of social reform today: One need only work hard enough—
day by day, hour by hour—and success and greatness will surely follow.

Collectively, the conduct biographies indicate a shared goal, a shared
reason why boys and girls should work hard with resilience and forti-
tude: the progress of America. All of the prefaces comment on the role
of men and women in responding to change, facilitating progress, and
inspiring patriotism in America. This capacity for progress is presented
as uniquely American, evidenced in the introduction to *True Stories of
Famous Men and Women of America*:

> [Americans] have the grandest heroes and heroines that any na-
> tion can boast, and to read their lives is to kindle every latent
> ember of patriotism into a glowing blaze, and to awaken every
> noble sentiment of the human soul. Their influence has gone
> out like beacon-lights to all the world, and their names stand

as synonyms of patriotism, exalted courage, freedom, wisdom, humanity, charity, love, and mercy. It is through them that the glory of America shines above that of all other lands foremost and uppermost in the vanguard of progress. (8)

Women's contribution to progress and instilling patriotism is particularly highlighted. This is not surprising given the prevailing rhetoric of Republican Motherhood at the time of many of these women's lives—and I would argue that echoes of the rhetoric of Republican Motherhood reverberate well into the Progressive Era. Writes Brooks, for example:

> In these progressive days, when so much energy and discussion are devoted to what is termed equality and the rights of woman, it is well to remember that there have been in the distant past women, and girls even, who by their actions and endeavors proved themselves the equals of the men of their time in valor, shrewdness, and ability. (i)

Owens similarly writes in *When They Were Girls*: "No matter how small our part in the world may seem, it is possible for us each to do our work in such a way that it will prove to be a forerunner of greater things to come" (3). As these lines attest, the progress of America is articulated as both providing opportunities for women to step into other spheres of life *and* demanding of women their continued efforts to ensure its forward momentum.

In sum, the conduct book prefaces indicate the motivational component of the books. They are clearly intended to be read as conduct literature; the girls and boys reading the texts are explicitly instructed in these prefaces to learn from and model the characters, behaviors, and actions of the men and women portrayed as models for their own lives. It would be easy to dismiss Progressive-era biographical compilations as two-dimensional hagiography; however, as influential mid-twentieth century sociologist C. Wright Mills reminds us, biography is the form that most captures and reflects the sociological imagination. Progressive-Era American conduct biographies both typify and challenge; they hold up a mirror, but they also project an image of future possibility through adherence to certain ways of conducting oneself in America. For their co-gendered youth readership, girl and boy conduct biographies contained competing narratives that were simultaneously traditional and subversive; these narratives both codified and disrupted race, gender, and class conventions and made distinct arguments for a vision of America and a path of American progress to which children should aspire to contribute.

NOTES

1. See, for example, the collection *Medieval Conduct*, an anthology of conduct literature written in the vernacular across Europe from the 13th–15th centuries.

2. See, for example, Jacques Carré.

3. Austen was quite familiar with conduct literature. For example, she admitted to reading—enjoying even—Thomas Gisborne's 1797 *An Enquiry into the Duties of the Female Sex* in a letter (Uphause 334).

4. Kersey Graves.

5. Although dated, Leon Edel's *Literary Biography* (1957) is the seminal work in this area.

6. An anomaly in my archive seems directly to address this racist agenda. Titled *Americans All: There Was No Race in Democratic America That Did Not Produce Its Hero*, published in 1925, author Chellis V. Smith opens with a polemic on the founding fathers and the proposition that all men are created equal. He follows with biographies of men representing a wide range of ethnicities. Smith writes: "There was born here in the New World a new race of men, a new ideal of brotherhood, a new bond of fellowship. The golden thread binding all is a word of holy union. It is the word *American*" (12).

7. Indeed, I believe my analysis is consistent with the argument I make in previous essays that many more rhetors offered variations of separate spheres ideology with a nuanced understanding of and strategic use of difference. For example, Frances Willard introduces a feminist theological resolution in *Woman in the Pulpit* in her Social Gospel philosophy grounded in the belief of the potential and power of female and male combined religious and political engagement (Zimmerelli, *Willard*)

8. Mary Lyon was a staunch advocate of women's education in Massachusetts, establishing the Wheaton Female Seminary in 1834 and Mount Holyoke Female Seminary in 1837, where she served as president for twelve years.

WORKS CITED

Ashley, Kathleen, and Robert L. A. Clark, editors. *Medieval Conduct.* Minnesota UP, 2001.

Bizzell, Patricia, and Bruce Herzberg, editors. *The Rhetorical Tradition: Readings from Classical Times to the Present.* 2nd ed., Bedford/St. Martin's Press, 2001.

Bolton, Sarah K. *Lives of Girls Who Became Famous*. Thomas Y. Crowell Company, 1886.

—. *Lives of Poor Boys Who Became Famous*. Thomas Y. Crowell Company, 1885.

Brooks, Elbridge S. *Historic Americans: Sketches of the Lives and Characters of Certain Famous Americans Held Most in Reverence of the Boys and Girls of America, for Whom Their Stories Are Here Told*. Thomas Y. Crowell & Co., 1899.

—. *Historic Boys: Their Endeavors, Their Achievements, and Their Times*. G. P. Putnam's Sons, 1889.

—. *Historic Girls*. G. P. Putnam's Sons, 1890.

Carré, Jacques. *The Crisis of Courtesy: Studies in the Conduct-Book in Britain, 1600–1900*. Brill, 1994.

Castiglione, Baldassare. *The Book of the Courtier*, 1528.

Casper, Scott. *Constructing American Lives: Biography & Culture in Nineteenth-Century America*. UNC Press Books, 1999.

Denzin, Norman K. *Interpretive Biography*. Sage Publications, Inc., 1989.

Dibble, Roy Floyd. *Strenuous Americans*. Boni and Liveright, 1923.

Donawerth, Jane. *Conversational Rhetoric*. Southern Illinois UP, 2012.

—, editor. *Rhetorical Theory by Women Before 1900*. Rowman & Littlefield, 2002.

Edel, Leon. *Literary Biography*. Toronto: U Toronto P, 1957

Everett, Carroll, and Charles Francis Reed. *When They Were Boys*. F. A. Owen Publishing Company, 1922.

Fenner, Mildred Sandison, and Eleanor C. Fishburn. *Pioneer American Educators*. Publisher Unknown, 1947.

Fox-Friedman, Jenny. "The Chivalric Order for Children: Arthur's Return in Late Nineteenth- and Early Twentieth-Century America." *King Arthur's Modern Return*, edited by Debra Mancoff, Garland Press, 1998, pp. 137–58.

Genette, Gérard. *Paratexts: Thresholds of Interpretation*. Cambridge UP, 1997.

Graves, Kersey. *The Biography of Satan, Or, A Historical Exposition of the Devil and His Fiery Dominions. Disclosing the oriental origin of the belief in a devil and future endless punishment; also, an explanation of the pagan origin of the scriptural terms, bottomless pit, lake of fire and brimstone, chains of darkness, casting out devils, worm that never dieth, etc.* Peter Eckler Publishing Company, 1924.

Heyden, John. *Advice to a daughter in opposition to the Advice to a sonne*, 1658.

Holland, Rupert Sargent. *Historic Boyhoods*. George W. Jacobs & Company, 1909.

—. *Historic Girlhoods*. Part One and Part Two. George W. Jacobs & Company. 1910.

Johnson, Nan. *Nineteenth-Century Rhetoric in North America*. Southern Illinois UP, 1991.

Melville, Herman. *Israel Potter*. Jonathon Cape, 1925.

Mills, C. Wright. *The Sociological Imagination*. Oxford UP, 1959.

Moore, Rebecca Deming. *When They Were Girls*. F. A. Owens Publishing Company, 1923.

Our Famous Women. An Authorized Record of the Lives and Deeds of Distinguished American Women of Our Times. 1884.

Peacock, Virginia Tatnall. *Famous American Belles of the Nineteenth Century*. J. B. Lippincott Company, 1901.

Rennick, Susan. *Buckeye Boys Who Have Become Presidents: Six Sons of Ohio and Their Part in the Nation's History*. The L. W. Walter Company, 1911.

Smith, Chellis V. *Americans All: There Was No Race in Democratic America That Did Not Produce Its Hero*. Lothrop, Lee & Shepard Co., 1925.

Steedman, Amy. *When They Were Children; Stories of the Childhood of Famous Men and Women*. F. A. Stokes & Co., 1913.

True Stories of Famous Men and Women of America For Young People. W. E. Scull, 1898.

Tusser, Thomas. *A Hundred Good pointes of husbandry lately maried vnto a hunderth good poynts of huswifery*. London, 1570.

Uphaus, Robert. "Jane Austen and Female Reading." *Studies in the Novel*, vol. 19, no. 3, Fall, 1987, pp. 334–45.

Vives, Juan Luis. *The Instruction of a Christen Woman (1523)*. Edited by Virginia Beauchamp, Elizabeth Hageman, Margraet Mikesell. U Illinois P, 2002.

Watson, Martha and Thomas Burkholder, editors. *The Rhetoric of Nineteenth-Century Reform*. Michigan State UP, 2008.

Wilson, Rob. "Producing American Selves: The Form of American Biography." *Contesting the Subject: Essays in the Postmodern Theory and Practice of Biography and Biographical Criticism*, vol. 1, edited by William H. Epstein. Indiana UP, 1991, pp. 167–92.

Zimmerelli, Lisa. "'The Stereoscopic View of Truth': Frances Willard's Woman in the Pulpit as a Feminist Rhetoric of Theology." *Rhetoric Society Quarterly*, vol. 42, no. 4, September 2012, pp. 353–74.

7 Listening to Remember: Bernice Johnson Reagon and Embodied Memories of Civil Rights

Elizabeth Ellis Miller

In winter 2010, then-President Barack Obama invited a group of musicians to the White House to perform the "soundtrack of the civil rights movement" ("White House"). To introduce the event, Obama encouraged the audience to listen and to remember the movement that changed society and made his Presidency conceivable ("White House"). He called out John Lewis in particular, referring to him as the "man whose sacrifices made it possible for me to be here tonight" ("White House"). In the mode of remembering the activist significance of this music, the audience heard from the Freedom Singers, a group comprised of civil rights veterans Bernice Johnson Reagon; Rutha Mae Harris; Charles Neblett; and Toshi Reagon, Bernice Reagon's daughter. The Freedom Singers performed "Ain't Gonna Let Nobody Turn Me 'Round," and Bernice Reagon urged the audience to sing along. She explained, "I know this is a show, but you have to sing this song. You can never tell when you might need it" ("White House"). The crowd enthusiastically joined in ("White House").

As civil rights song leader turned professional historian and public memory creator, Reagon understood the importance of freedom songs as sites for engaged, embodied memory. Rather than encourage passive listening, she sought instead to help the audience experience the songs' memorial ends as most powerful when felt through their bodies. Indeed, this night's work was no anomaly: Reagon spent nearly five decades working to cultivate embodied remembering practices through freedom songs. This work has won a Peabody award, a MacArthur Fellowship, and the attention of the nation. Reagon is today considered a foremost expert on the civil rights movement and particularly its freedom songs. All of this despite the fact that her memorial career began in the 1970s, a moment when Black women were beginning to expose and analyze the pervasive sexism that plagued the civil right movement (Beal). What is more, she engaged in this work alongside the burgeoning Black Power movement, which in many ways reified and extended this sexism and silencing of African-America women, again offering little opportunity for women's public leadership (Joseph). Given the well-known obstacles Black women faced in garnering a public space for themselves in the mid-to-late twentieth century, what enabled Reagon to craft a position for herself as movement and freedom song expert?

This chapter takes up the theme of the section, "Circulating Genres," through attention to Reagon's strategic use of genre in the space and time of her career. Here, I show how Reagon navigated the rhetorical constraints outlined above through remaking the genre that enabled her civil rights activism in the first place: the freedom song. Within the civil rights movement, Reagon crafted a position of leadership for herself as song leader. Then, once the movement ended, she shifted to memorializing freedom songs, again locating her activism in the genre she helped create and through which she had extensive experience leading before national audiences. At the center of this memorial work is her 1980 album, *Voices of the Civil Rights Movement*, a hybrid text that includes a sonic archive of freedom songs along with a songbook that narrates their role in the movement and connects them to women who led through song such as Reagon, Fannie Lou Hamer, and Rutha Mae Harris. Reagon began work on *Voices* in the 1970s, and thus examining this text reveals key strategies Reagon developed early in her career to authorize her role as public intellectual and expert on the movement for Black freedom. In *Voices*, Reagon developed this ethos by leveraging a strategy important to women across many locales and eras: genre blending and appropriation.

Like the Elizabethan women Erin Sadlack studies in the chapter initiating this section, Reagon refigured genre conventions to shape her ethos and garner new audiences. Scholar Lisa Zimmerelli theorizes this strategy as an important one for religious women in the nineteenth century U.S. as well. In her examination of debates over women's preaching, Zimmerelli reveals how the genre of defense of women's preaching began as the merging of other genres, including the spiritual memoir and letters (5). Women such as Frances Willard, Julia Foote, and Louisa Woosley engaged in "conscious blending of various genres and multiple rhetorics" to craft a "truly modified, transformed genre" (9; see Zimmerelli's chapter in this volume for an examination of genre-making and conduct biography). To make their arguments and enable their activism, these rhetors blended genres and leveraged hybrid texts to achieve their goals. In the twentieth century, Reagon engages in a similar practice, merging the concept album with the songbook to create a hybrid memorial text well-suited to the needs of ethos development and embodied memory.[1]

Through the focus on *Voices* as a civil rights memorialization, this chapter also extends studies by Jessica Enoch, Rosalyn Collings Eves, and Laura Brown to participate in conversations about how women have intervened in public memory and resisted erasure through a range of rhetorical practices. For feminist scholars, studying public memory entails not just examining the rhetoricity of memorial texts but also exploring *processes* of commemoration, and important for the focus of this collection, this emphasis on memorial processes opens up new avenues for examining women's rhetorics across and in relationship to time and space. Memory studies thus provides another method for investigating feminist circulations, one that centers the rhetoricity of movement through attention to relationships among past, present, and future. As Enoch explains, feminist memory studies "examine the ways that women's pasts have been leveraged and the rhetorical ends these remembrances served; analyze the dominant and alternative modes of production groups have used to remember women and . . . investigate the constraints groups have faced and the negotiations they have made in their attempts to commemorate women" (65). Taking on questions of constraints, Eves and Brown analyze the memorial practices of twentieth-century African-American women: Eves studies the ways that Black women turned to cookbooks as alternative sites for memory and identity (294), while Brown examines Bennett College women's rhetorical choices surrounding commemoration of the 1960s sit-ins in Greensboro, North Carolina (59). Drawing from these previous studies, this chapter shows another kind of negotiation: strategic archiving and preservation of key memorial supports, and then circulation of these artifacts in a sonic text. By collecting freedom songs in a key moment, Reagon creates a position for herself as civil rights movement music expert and secures her role in narrating past civil rights campaigns. Enoch's chapter in this volume employs "historiographic fantasies" to theorize rhetorical practices of re-membering and forgetting.

To reveal Reagon's memorial-activist practices and the strategies she cultivates through the *Voices* project, I first provide background on Rea-gon as civil rights activist and song leader and then her turn to archiving and memorial work. In sections 3 and 4, the chapter analyzes *Voices* through the lenses of *ethos* and *embodied remembering* to reveal the strat-egies Reagon developed to resist erasure and secure public memories of freedom songs and women's roles in writing, leading, and disseminating the songs.

REAGON'S ACTIVIST TRAJECTORY

Bernice Johnson Reagon was born in southwest Georgia in 1942. The daughter of a minister, Reagon first learned of the power of song in church and through religion (Hopkinson 32). Then, in the civil rights movement, Reagon began to understand and leverage religious song to-ward social change. Recruited to the civil rights movement in 1961 as a college student at Albany State, Reagon quickly rose to a position of lead-ership through her experiences with music (Hogan 67, 259). She recalls after her first time protesting segregation at the City Hall in downtown Albany, the group retreated to Union Baptist Church. Once in the space of the church, Reagon was called on to lead everyone in a song. Drawing from her background singing in church, Reagon lined out the hymn, "Over My Head I See Trouble in the Air" (Hogan 39). Throughout her work in Albany, Reagon led groups in freedom songs and helped select and adapt songs from African American religious history to expand the repertoire. This work in Albany reverberated throughout the rest of the civil rights movement, showcasing how music might function as protest. As key song leader in Albany, then, Reagon played a significant role locally and nationally through her work with music of the movement.

Leading through song was a strategic choice for Reagon, given the sexism that pervaded the movement and constrained women's rhetorical possibilities. Some women, including Fannie Lou Hamer and Dorothy Height, negotiated these constraints and developed speaking roles for themselves (Brooks, Houck and Dixon). Another avenue for leadership, however, was to craft rhetorical positions through alternative genres. For Reagon and many others, one such genre was the freedom song. Key to this rhetorical possibility for women was the organizational structure of the Black church. Within many Black churches, song leading was one of few positions open to women at the time, and given the movement's reliance on the leadership structures of African-American church traditions, song leading was a rhetorical role available to women in the movement as well. As Reagon defines the role, the song leader "is the galvanizer, the person who starts the song and thus begins to pull together a temporary community formed in the process of that specific song rendition" ("The Civil Rights" 600). The song leader selected and performed songs to encourage collective participation. Within the movement, song leaders were also genre creators; together, they helped to craft freedom songs as the unique musical genre of the movement.

In the mid-and-late 1960s, the civil rights movement splintered, and for many activists, Black Power ideologies and strategies began to resonate. These changes provided the context for Reagon, and many other women, to refigure their activism. Women's rhetorical possibilities in the Black Power movement were limited in different ways than in the civil rights era. During the Black Power movement, occurring from 1966–1975, activists largely turned away from religious genres like freedom songs in which many women had centered their rhetorical work. Black Power was instead animated by militancy and secularism, and for these reasons, the movement was largely dominated by men and afforded few opportunities for women's formal leadership. Yet at the same time, historians argue, women were still active toward Black Power's central goal: the creation of a new Black identity. As in the civil rights movement, despite pervasive sexism women found innovative ways to engage in activism. From this vantage point, women's contributions to Black Power are wide-ranging and endure beyond the movement's beginning and end. In historian Ashley Farmer's conception, this activism is most visible by focusing on how women reconceived of Black womanhood. As she writes, "If we now know that Black women disagreed with the real and imagined roles that Black men assigned them, what new models of womanhood did they develop in response?" (12). By recovering these "gendered reimaginings," scholars can "foregroun[d] the importance of considering Black women as Black Power theorists in their own right and interrogating the reciprocal relationship between their intellectual and activist work" (15). Considered in this way, even as Reagon stepped away from leading organized protests as she did in the civil rights movement, she was nonetheless still engaged in activism by participating in the Black Power project of creating and imagining Black identity.

For Reagon, this activism centered on civil rights memory and history. Here, she built on her civil rights expertise with music to craft a role for herself as public intellectual and historian, thus an authority on African American music and its role in the civil rights movement. Toward these ends, Reagon explored how formal education might support and embolden her activism, studying history at Spelman College and then in a doctoral program at Howard University. In the spirit of Black Power's focus on Black identity, Reagon sought to expand what she had learned about African American musical culture through her upbringing and the civil rights movement and then to share it with the public. Reagon explains how her formal training as historian extended learning that began as an activist,

> The civil rights movement . . . taught me that singing was not entertainment, it was something else. I had all these older people in my life who had stories about traditional songs we'd used in the movement, but the stories were about the role those songs played during slavery. And they were resistant struggle stories. So I was learning about a part of my history that I already had. I already knew the songs, but I didn't know the stories. . . . ("Interview" 5)

Through degrees in History, Reagon pursued the stories of the freedom songs that had captivated her as an activist as she also worked to document and recast the repertoire she had helped create. In 1975, she finished her doctorate and dissertation, "Songs of the Civil Rights Movement 1955–1965: A Study in Culture History." Her dissertation is the first text she created to preserve movement music in which she presents thirty-two civil rights songs and argues they are important resources for remembering the movement. To reveal this connection, she writes in her opening, "In the case of the civil rights movement, its songs provide data of high historical value and are necessary for an understanding of the movement and the relationships between the major actors, reactors, observers, and affected institutions" (6). This dissertation serves as the first full-length historical treatment of freedom songs after the conclusion of the movement. Through this text, Reagon began forming her role as public intellectual and civil rights movement and music expert. The project was both scholarship *and* a revision of her earlier activism for the new context.

Recognizing the limitations of the scholarly genre of the monograph, Reagon explored alternative genres and sought a broader audience for the arguments she developed in her dissertation. Here, she continued developing her role as public intellectual and movement expert by pursuing opportunities to work on public memory projects; indeed, as historian Brittney Cooper observes, "the kinds of Black feminist intellectual projects that emerge during the 1970s are, by and large, products of Black women's public work rather than, for instance, traditional academic theorizing" (117). Working in this vein, in 1972 Reagon began a full-time position at the Smithsonian, where she designed the Program in Black American culture. Through her post at the Smithsonian, she worked on numerous programs, including the Newport Folk Festival. At the same time, she also initiated a musical group, Sweet Honey and the Rock, to extend singing as activism in the present (Perez 7–9). By the late 1970s, Reagon was ready to circulate her dissertation work, but in a different form for public audiences. Understanding the importance of sound, Reagon merged print and sonic genres, the songbook and the concept album, to create *Voices of the Civil Rights Movement: Black American Freedom Songs, 1960–1966*, a hybrid, multimodal memorial text that includes audio recordings of songs in addition to a booklet of text and photographs.

By crafting a hybrid text for a public audience, Reagon resisted dominant narratives of the civil rights movement being written in the field of professional history at the time as she also created a path for herself as a Black woman and academic. Historian Charles Eagles observes that during the 1970s, the field of history took up study of the civil rights movement in earnest. He writes, "After the first burst of books around 1970, the civil rights movement increasingly became a subject for historical study. Even though journalists, participants, and others continued to write about it too, historians along with other academics began to dominate the field" (822). This decade of scholarship centered on a male-dominated view of the movement. Studies, predictably perhaps, focused on figures like Martin Luther King, Jr. and "employed traditional, political, institutional, and biographical approaches" (822). In Eagles' characterization, it was the 1980s before professional historians began studying women's roles and shifting their attention away from the most visible leaders and locales (826). Reagon leveraged *Voices* as a counterpoint to these early narratives with their traditional focus and male-dominated narratives. Her text invites audiences to remember the civil rights movement as deeply musical, and subsequently collective and inspired by women's voices and leadership, in addition to men's.

Given the gendered bias inherent in the field of history and the books being written, her work in the text was also to authorize her role as public intellectual and expert on remembering the movement. Here, *Voices* does important ethos work for Reagon, creating a pathway for her career and revealing her varied expertise on the civil rights movement—experiential, embodied, and scholarly. Black women public intellectuals in any period have encountered challenges and resistance, and the late 1960s through 1980 were no exception. In Cooper's estimation, this moment was in fact one of cultural upheaval. The publication of the 1965 Moynihan Report, which coupled Black poverty with single-motherhood, brought with it "a resurgence of the cultural distrust of Black women's political ideas and leadership abilities" (115). Analyzing these challenges and writing in 1966 for *Ebony*, Ponchitta Pierce asserts "The Negro woman intellectual is easily one of the most misunderstood, unappreciated, and problem-ridden of all God's creatures. In fact, if it were left to many Negro males alone to decide, she would not even exist" (144). As Cooper and Pierce observe, the late 1960s ushered in new waves of public suspicion for Black women speaking and writing about intellectual and political issues. These were among the challenges Reagon faced in authorizing her role as public intellectual and expert on civil rights history.

Since *Voices* is an unusual, hybrid text, some description of its features is necessary before moving to analysis. This text includes two major components, one sonic and one print: (1) a recorded album, the sonic component and (2) a booklet of liner notes, the print component. As a sonic album of songs and sounds combined with the booklet comprised of images and text, *Voices* merges two distinct genres, the concept album and the memorial songbook. The concept album emerged in the mid-twentieth century, a product of technologies that enabled artists to craft sonic texts with longer running time than ever before. Rather than produce one song at a time, artists could now create albums comprised of groups of linked songs. A general principle for linking the songs was choosing a theme or unifying concept; for example, in 1958 Rosemary Clooney and Bing Crosby released *Fancy Meeting You Here*, an album that "takes mostly old tunes about falling in love in exotic places and divides them into effective duets" (Decker 98, 105). Memorial songbooks emerged in the United States as early as the nineteenth century and continued to play a key role in music culture throughout the twentieth.

The memorial songbook of the mid-twentieth century typically included photos, lyrics and music for songs, and some text, whether excerpted from other publications or written for the book. In addition, they often included essays to open and close the book that offered detailed analysis of the songs' cultural significance (Miller 11–12).

Through her concept album, the sonic component of *Voices*, Reagon includes two dominant themes of freedom songs, freedom songs sung at mass meetings, and freedom songs composed by ensembles who traveled around the United States performing for various audiences. In addition to this sonic component, an important part of *Voices* is the accompanying booklet that functions more like the memorial songbook than standard liner notes. In this 25-page booklet, Reagon offers commentary on the songs, tells their stories, and narrates their role in the movement. The descriptions are interwoven with photographs of activists singing. Taken together, the sonic and print components of *Voices* work to remember a particular narrative of the civil rights movement, one that centers on songs and singers, African-American history, as well as women and collectivity.[2] The remainder of the chapter turns to analysis of *Voices*.

GENRE MERGING AND ETHOS: *VOICES* AS SONGBOOK-CONCEPT ALBUM

Through *Voices*, Reagon intervenes in conversations about who speaks for the civil rights movement and how best to remember it. As the last section indicated, at the time Reagon was working on *Voices*, many academic histories of the civil rights movement had appeared, and by and large, they worked to erase women's contributions, hers included. Taken together, the history books of the 1970s then would suggest that civil rights memories belonged to men, both those who were writing it and those who lived it. Besides these gendered biases against women in the field of history, Reagon faced additional challenges as a woman taking up the role of Black public intellectual. Many expected this role to be filled by Black men in the tradition of W. E. B. Du Bois and Martin Luther King, Jr. (Cooper 116). To negotiate these challenges, Reagon develops her ethos position by genre merging, employing academic essay-based prose in addition to images and sounds to showcase her scholarly expertise *and* her experiential, embodied knowledge of the movement. This strategy supports her ultimate argument for remembering civil rights activism as collective-based, women-led, and song-centered.

Ethos, traditionally understood as credibility or character, has been significantly refigured by feminist scholars (Ryan et al.; see also Osherow and Sadlack in this volume). Such work redefines ethos by calling for attention to the broader rhetorical situation a rhetor moves through and engages such concepts as genre, location, materiality, embodiment, and culture (Ryan et al vii, Applegarth "Working With" 219). Particularly important for understanding Reagon's rhetorical savvy is the idea of ethos as intricately connected to genre. Risa Applegarth argues that for marginalized rhetors, genre can provide important access to ethos ("Genre, Location"). She writes, "Because genres organize rhetorical resources as well as structure rhetorical constraints, genres significantly shape one's possibilities for *ethos*. Locating one's text—and oneself—in a genre begins the work of locating oneself relative to a particular audience" (50). By turning away from the scholarly genre of the monograph and toward a hybrid merging of sonic and print genres, Reagon creates an ethos that highlights her academic and activist experiences. She has professional training as a historian in addition to lived experience as a civil rights activist, and by drawing on the features of two genres merged into one, she can reveal both of these kinds of expertise at once.

To cultivate this ethos, Reagon opens the booklet by calling her audience's attention to the need for histories of the civil rights movement that center on activist experience and move beyond academic categories. In this print text that operates similarly, in features and in purpose, to the memorial songbook, the first entry is a short scholarly essay, "The Song Culture of the Civil Rights Movement." Here, Reagon takes advantage of a long-form written text to craft a careful argument about the kind of texts needed to capture freedom song's significance. Situating her own story as an activist in an academic essay, she raises questions about history books' capacity to capture civil rights memories; the subtle argument is that scholarly texts cannot reveal the complexity of African-American culture and its connection to the movement for Black freedom. In the first pages of the text Reagon asserts:

> The development of this anthology of civil rights movement song was, for me, a way to pay homage to experiences which clarified my personal and professional direction. I grew up in Doughterty County, just outside of Albany, Georgia, in a community steeped in Black Southern cultural traditions. . . . All the established academic categories in which I had been educated fell apart during this period, revealing culture not to be

luxury, not leisure, not entertainment, but the lifeblood of a community. (2)

To open *Voices*, Reagon begins by observing that African-American culture surpasses academic categories; it must be understood through the communal, lived experience of the people. She goes on to make this point overtly, "As I read the numerous studies on the civil rights movement, I look for the people who made up the numbers; I look to see if they are a faceless mass or an eloquent and strongly focused community. The few successful studies acknowledge the songs as the language that focused the energy of the people who filled the streets and roads of the South during that period" (2). Reagon speaks back to the histories of civil rights that leave out ordinary activists. She makes clear that academic history may miss the heart of the movement if it does not center on the experiences of these activists; she connects this point to singing experiences in particular. Through this argument, Reagon engages in what Karlyn Kohrs Campbell refers to as "subversion, using the master's tools to undermine, even sabotage, the master's house" (112). In the analytical essay-based prose that opens the songbook, Reagon leverages academic argument to claim the categories and modes of meaning-making that comprise traditional history are inadequate; in themselves, they cannot capture the movement, memories, or its music. Instead, academic ways of knowing must be coupled with activist experience and songs, essential knowledge-bases for civil rights histories: we have to listen to the stories and songs of activists themselves to understand the "lifeblood" of the movement for Black freedom.

Through this coupling, Reagon cultivates her ethos by skillfully manipulating academic argument to create a need for civil rights movement experts with on-the-ground experience as activists, and then reveals herself to be such a figure. Indeed, in this opening essay, Reagon showcases her experiential knowledge of civil rights by explaining that she was present for important protests and events. After asserting the claim that academic categories fail to capture the "lifeblood" of African-American community, Reagon then recalls some of her own key activist experiences:

> As a singer and activist in the Albany Movement, I sang and heard the freedom songs, and saw them pull together sections of the Black community at times when other means of communication were ineffective. . . . In Dawson, Georgia, county seat of 'Terrible Terrell' where Blacks were seventy-five percent of the

population, I sat in church and felt the chill that ran through a small gathering of Blacks when the sheriff and his deputies walked in. They stood at the door, making sure everyone knew they were there. Then a song began. And the song made sure that the sheriff and his deputies knew we were there. (2)

Again employing the resources of the songbook genre—narrative prose—Reagon weaves her own story into the freedom song narrative she develops. The story of the songs, she maintains, is her story and experience as well: *she* was there. This portion of the essay draws on activist testimony that Reagon herself provides: she has observed the rhetorical power of the songs firsthand, and this firsthand knowledge shows Reagon is well-suited as a civil rights expert.

Besides these moves to make clear civil rights history belongs to those who lived it, Reagon cultivates her ethos by revealing her professional and academic training. Here, she employs another feature of the songbook, the possibility for sub-arguments interwoven together. The following list reveals the section headers for the sub-arguments that comprise the remainder of the booklet:

- "Freedom Songs: Language of Black Struggle"
- "Roots: Notes on Black American Choral Song Style"
- "From the Tradition: A Contemporary Statement"
- "Mass Meetings"
- "Ensembles" (Voices)

As this list conveys, like the essay that opens the book, the remainder of the text weaves together scholarly conversations about movement music interlaced with activist experiences, Reagon's and activists she knew and with whom she worked. Through the sections, "Freedom Songs: Language of the Black Struggle," "Roots: Notes on Black American Choral Song Style," and "From the Tradition: A Contemporary Statement," Reagon's sub-arguments draw on scholarly works and reveal her engagement with other historians and music scholars. She thus leverages these sources to bolster her ethos, continuing to show her scholarly and professional expertise. Yet, through the latter two sections, "Mass Meetings" and "Ensembles," Reagan returns to centering activists' experiences, her own included. Through the text that comprises the songbook, Reagon subverts the notion that civil rights movement histories can be told by figures with no activist experience and reveals herself as both academic and experiential expert on the songs.

In addition to these prose features of the songbook, Reagon also crafts her ethos through the multimodality of the songbook and its accompanying concept album. Besides telling audiences she was there during the movement, she shows them as well. Images are interwoven with the essays that comprise the songbook, and readers see Reagon singing in the context of the movement. On page 27, for example, in the Ensembles section of the book, a photograph depicts Reagon performing with the Original Freedom Singers in 1963. The image provides visual evidence for Reagon's experiential authority. Seen standing and singing with Charles Neblett, Cordell Reagon, and Rutha Mae Harris, audiences gain a sense of Reagon's leadership through song within the movement and her relationships with other key activists. This image is interwoven with her explanation of the rhetorical prowess of the Freedom Singers:

> The three SNCC ensembles [including the Freedom Singers] developed to the highest degree the use of music to carry the Movement's message to audiences far removed from the struggle. Through nationwide tours, these groups catalyzed support for SNCC Movement activities at a time when public attention was focused primarily on media-recognized leaders and large direct-action events rather than on the more dangerous and lonely grassroots organizing activities. (26)

Together, the description and image continue to show Reagon as movement music expert; even within the movement, readers learn, she played a key role in circulating freedom songs to wide audiences. Her public persona as freedom singer becomes a kind of analogue to the authority she garners for herself in *Voices*.

Finally, Reagon draws on the affordances of the concept album—sound—to extend her ethos. In the "Ensembles" portion of the album, two songs feature Reagon as lead singer and soloist. Here, the sounds of her voice offer sonic evidence of Reagon's experience. Listeners get to see her singing, read about the importance of the Freedom Singers she helped create, and then hear her voice as well, thus gaining a layered sense of the activist experience Reagon has persuasively asserted must serve as the basis for narratives and studies of the movement. Yet, taken as a whole, the images and sounds of *Voices* feature *other* activists; Reagon seems most interested in highlighting a wide variety of African-American voices. In this way, the handful of images and songs that center on her presence and singing should be viewed as strategic selections, carefully chosen evidence to make clear Reagon's integral role in the community of civil rights activists. These features of the songbook and album thus afford Reagon opportunities to reveal herself as trained historian with extensive experience as an activist and freedom singer.

CIRCULATING MULTIMODAL MEMORIES OF COLLECTIVES, WOMEN, AND RELIGION IN THE MOVEMENT

Besides revealing *who* is best suited to speak for the civil rights movement, *Voices* also seeks to make clear *how* it should be remembered. Juxtaposed against the scores of books about civil rights many other professional historians were producing at the time, *Voices* challenges the notion that the movement for Black freedom can be captured by a monograph as it also refutes narratives that focus on individuals and male leaders. By weaving together images, sounds, argument, and narrative, *Voices* instead encourages *embodied remembering*, full-bodied engagement with presentations of the past through a range of sensory experiences. Reagon invites audiences to see and hear this movement by engaging in multisensory listening practicing, what Steph Ceraso theorizes as multimodal listening, "a full-bodied awareness that heightens listeners' experience of the sensory, material, and environmental aspects of sonic interactions" (106). Through these multimodal memories, Reagon's text blends genres to call for a different view of the civil rights movement, one where collectives, women, and African American religious music are of key importance.

To invite audiences to remember with their bodies, Reagon creates reciprocity between the songbook and the concept album. These two components of *Voices* work together in lock-step: Reagon blends these genres to craft a hybrid memorialization that centers on sound, image, and story. Listening to the album is heightened by looking through the book: seeing the events, places, and figures heard about on the album enriches the sounds' meaning and contextualizes songs and voices. Likewise, the narrative of the book gains new layers accompanied by the sounds; one's understanding of the power of the songs' stories is expanded by listening to them as well.

For example, the "Mass Meetings" section of the album and booklet work reciprocally to reveal the sights and sounds of these key civil rights events. In the booklet, audiences garner a sense of the meeting through image and narrative. They learn that these events were held in churches, and then see an example of one that occurred in Montgomery. Listening to the first portion of the album, "Mass Meetings," they gain sonic details for the events that cannot be represented in the booklet. These details include sounds of freedom songs recorded at the meetings, like "This Little Light of Mine," and also other sonic evidence of the events such as the "Freedom Now" chant and a portion of a sermon by Reverend Lawrence Campbell. Through reading about the meetings, audiences garner visual and narrative evidence of the events, and then listening they gain an affective sense of the meetings—the excitement, the spiritual fervor—through the sounds.

Drawing on the work of historian Brittney Cooper, we can see how through the embodied remembering *Voices* calls for, Reagon not only makes a case for particular memorial practices, but she also extends and refigures her activism by acting as a Black feminist intellectual. In Cooper's view, this centrality of the body constitutes "a form of Black female textual activism wherein race women assertively demand the inclusion of their bodies and, in particular working class bodies and Black female bodies by placing them in the texts they write and speak" (43). In this way, Reagon's memorialization participates in a Black feminist intellectual tradition that Cooper traces back to the nineteenth century and to Anna Julia Cooper in particular (3). By inviting audiences to listen with their bodies, Reagon's project in *Voices* is not only a memorialization but an intellectual and theoretical project as well.

Through the sounds, images, and text of *Voices*, audiences experience a movement that did not rise and fall with individuals. Speaking back to the male-dominated approach to civil rights history and its narrow focus on leaders like Martin Luther King, Jr., *Voices* seeks to show that such simplified stories excise the rhetorical work of women and collectives, and the extensive African-American historical tradition that they called on for their work. Here *Voices* works against narratives that would preclude the on-the-ground rhetorical work of communities and the longer history from which this work emerged. Through embodied remembering, audiences garner a view of the movement as carried out by collectives of ordinary African Americans. The sounds, stories, and visual evidence make clear that there is no one individual responsible for the gains of the movement. Images highlight diverse Black people of different ages, classes, and genders. Reagon's writing emphasizes this dimension of the movement as well; she writes for instance, "*Voices of the Civil Rights Movement: Black American Freedom Songs, 1960–1966* documents a central aspect of the cultural environment of the civil rights movement.

It is a series of musical images, seen both distantly and at close range, of a people in conversation about their determination to be free" (3). Finally, the accompanying sounds corroborate this story of the movement carried out by women and men, young and old, rural and urban. Songs offer listeners a chance to hear this collective voice; the majority of the "Mass Meetings" portion of the album is devoted to showcasing the sounds of many singing at once. Danielle Griffin's chapter in this collection on early modern women's petitions offers further insight into collectivism as rhetorical strategy.

The multimodal memories created through *Voices* further argue for a movement where African-American women played central roles. Reagon works against the narratives that would erase women's rhetorical contributions and suggest men were the most important figures. Through *Voices*, Reagon memorializes influential musical women including Fannie Lou Hamer, Janie Lee Culbreth, Betty Mae Fikes, Rutha Mae Harris, Brenda Darden, Mabel Hillary, Joycelyn McKissick, Dottie Miller, Bertha Gober, Mamie Brown, Diane Smith, and Cleo Kennedy. At times these women are mentioned next to songs that they adapted, and in other places, Reagon describes the significance of their leadership and its import for the songs and includes images of them singing. This leadership does not simply include singing; Reagon makes clear the women were key to the creation of the freedom song genre. Describing the development of the song, "Oh Pritchett, Oh Kelly," Reagon writes, "While the form and voicings remained consistent, new lyrics by Bertha Gober and Janie Lee Culbreth addressed the local Albany, Georgia, struggle of November and December 1961" (10). Movement women were central to adapting older songs and revising their lyrics, important invention work for the cultivation of the freedom song genre. Then, through visual and sonic evidence, audiences interact with memories of women's leadership through image and sound. For instance, in the image depicting song-leaders at the Newport Folk Festival in 1964, Reagon highlights Brenda Darden, Rutha Mae Harris, Cleo Kennedy, and Betty Mae Fikes, and the visible performance and leadership they provided at this large, public event. The sounds of the songs on the album extend this representation of women's significance as leaders; through songs like "Go Tell It on the Mountain," led by Fannie Lou Hamer, listeners gain a sense of women's vocal leadership. Overall, then, *Voices* provides audiences with multimodal memories of women's freedom song activism as both behind-the-scenes invention work and visible, vocal, and public leadership that must be remembered.

Finally, Reagon calls audiences to embrace the civil rights movement as an extension of a much longer tradition rooted in African-American religion. In the opening, she writes, "Music has always been integral to the struggle for freedom. The music culture of the civil rights movement was shaped by its central participants: Black, Southern and steeped in oral tradition" (3). The section "Roots: Notes on Black American Choral Style," offers extensive commentary on the musical patterns of this tradition, marking out how to understand the sounds of the songs in relationship to African-American religious history. The songs bear out more evidence of this including old hymns sung at movement events such as "Leaning on the Everlasting Arms" and "Walk with Me Lord." Listeners learn too about how freedom songs emerged from singing traditions in African-American churches. Overall, through *Voices* audiences listen and peer in on the civil rights movement, learning about the collective of women and men who made it sing, and connecting this singing to a longer African-American tradition.

CONCLUSION

In an interview in the 1990s, Reagon explained that while her academic colleagues do appreciate her public memory work, she is often asked, "But when are you going to do your monograph?" (Perez 20). Her response is telling: "One of the things I encourage them to understand is that the world is changing. Students who are studying history, even though they are going to have to contend with a world in which information still continues to be transmitted through the printed word, are also going to have to become fluent in some of the mediums I've been working in" (Perez 20). Indeed, Reagon became fluent in multimodality at the beginning of her career, decades ago. Remarkably, in the late 1970s and early 1980s, as Reagon considered how to circulate the arguments of her dissertation, she understood the affordances of sound and image as necessary to achieve her rhetorical ends. Through this engagement with multimodality in *Voices*, Reagon authorized her career as movement memory expert as she also circulated an embodied experience of civil rights. She recognized that text alone was inadequate for remembering freedom songs and their rhetorical work, and so she crossed boundaries and merged genres to remediate her text, cultivating her ethos and garnering a wide audience for multimodal memories of the movement. In these ways, Reagon's work in *Voices* participates in and extends a tradition important to rhetorical women across space and time.

NOTES

1. Through the focus on *Voices* as sonic memory text, the chapter also responds to feminist work on women's rhetorical use of emerging technologies. Sarah Hallenbeck reveals the importance of this line of inquiry, examining women's rhetorics around bicycling in the nineteenth century. Hallenbeck uncovers the ways women intervened in debates about gender and the bicycle, leveraging expertise in technological innovation (xiv). In outlining her study, Hallenbeck notes the need for studies of women's scientific and technological rhetorical practices, a gap her book helps fill (xiv). Turning to the twentieth century, this chapter extends this conversation and explores how Reagon merged the concept album, a sonic genre enabled through technologies of sound, with the songbook to gain a broad audience for her memorialization of freedom songs.

2. While *Voices* may be unique in its merging of genres, it is not the first sonic concept album or songbook produced to cultivate memories of civil rights. During and after the movement, allies to the movement such as Guy Carawan, Alan Lomax, and Pete Seeger produced songbooks and albums including *Freedom is a Constant Struggle, Story of Greenwood, Mississippi*, and *We Shall Overcome: Songs of the Freedom Riders and the Sit-Ins*. These white men took up documenting the music of civil rights through academic connections to folklore and professional experiences with music. Within the context of the ongoing movement, they defended this role by arguing that African-Americans were "too busy living the Movement to worry about the needs of history" (Turner 44). After the movement ended, however, Reagon began to see the needs of history as very much the activism in which she wanted to engage, and to do so, she chose to merge the songbook and concept album, taking advantage of the affordances and resources of each.

WORKS CITED

Applegarth, Risa. "Genre, Location, and Mary Austin's Ethos." *Rhetoric Society Quarterly*, vol. 41, no, 1, 2011, pp. 41–63.
—. "Working With and Working For: Ethos and Power in Women's Writing." *Rethinking Ethos: A Feminist Ecological Approach to Rhetoric*, edited by Ryan et al., Southern Illinois UP, 2016, pp. 216–36.

"A White House Concert with Bob Dylan, Jennifer Hudson and More." NPR, February 10, 2010.

Beal, Frances. "Double Jeopardy: To Be Black and Female." *The Black Woman*, edited by Toni Bambara, Washington Square P, 2005, pp. 109–22.

Brown, Laura Michael. "Remembering Silence: Bennett College Women and the 1960 Greensboro Student Sit-Ins." *Rhetoric Society Quarterly*, vol. 48, no. 1, 2018, pp. 49–70.

Brooks, Maegan Parker. *A Voice that Could Stir an Army: Fannie Lou Hamer and the Rhetoric of the Black Freedom Movement*. Oxford: U of Mississippi P, 2014.

Campbell, Karlyn Khors. "Inventing Women: From Amaterasu to Virginia Woolf." *Women's Studies in Communication*, vol. 21, no. 2, 1998, pp. 111–26.

Carawan, Guy and Candie. *Freedom is A Constant Struggle. Songs of the Freedom Movement*. Oak P, 1968.

—. *We Shall Overcome*. Oak P, 1963.

Ceraso, Steph. "(Re)Educating the Senses: Multimodal Listening, Bodily Learning, and the Composition of Sonic Experiences." *College English*, vol. 77, no. 2, 2014, pp. 102–23.

Cooper, Brittney. *Beyond Respectability: The Intellectual Thought of Race Women*. U of Illinois P, 2017.

Decker, Todd. "Fancy Meeting You Here: Pioneers of the Concept Album." *Daedalus*, vol. 4, 2013, pp. 98–108.

Eagles, Charles. "Toward New Histories of the Civil Rights Era." *The Journal of Southern History*, vol. 66, no. 4, Nov. 2000, pp. 815–48.

Enoch, Jessica. "Releasing Hold: Feminist Historiography Without the Tradition." *Theorizing Histories of Rhetoric*, edited by Michelle Baliff, Southern Illinois UP, 2013, pp. 58–73.

—, and Jordynn Jack. "Remembering Sappho: New Perspectives on Teaching (and Writing) Women's Rhetorical History." *College English*, vol. 73, no. 5, May 2011, pp. 518–37.

Eves, Rosalyn Collings. "A Recipe for Remembrance: Memory and Identity in African-American Women's Cookbooks. *Rhetoric Review*, vol. 24, no. 3, 2009, pp. 280–97.

Farmer, Ashley. *Remaking Black Power: How Black Women Transformed an Era*. U of North Carolina P, 2017.

Hallenbeck, Sarah. *Claiming the Bicycle: Women, Rhetoric, and Technology in Nineteenth-Century America*. Southern Illinois UP, 2015.

Hogan, Wesley. *Many Minds, One Heart: SNCC's Dream for a New America*. U of North Carolina P, 2007.

Houck, Davis, and David Dixon. "Introduction: Recovering Women's Voices from the Civil Rights Movement." *Women and the Civil Rights Movement, 1954–1965*. U of Mississippi P, 2011. pp. ix–xxi.

Hopkinson, Natalie. "Rock and Soul." *The Crisis*. 2003, pp. 31–33

Joseph, Peniel. *Waiting 'Til the Midnight Hour: A Narrative History of Black Power in America*. Henry Holt and Company, 2006.

Miller, Elizabeth. "Remembering Freedom Songs: Repurposing an Activist Genre." *College English*, vol. 81, no. 1, Sept. 2018, pp. 50-72.

Musgrove, George Derek. *Rumor, Repression, and Racial Politics: How the Harassment of Black Elected Officials Shaped Post-Civil Rights America*. U of Georgia P, 2012.

Perez, Marvette. "Interview with Bernice Johnson Reagon." *Radical History Review*, vol. 68, 1997, pp. 4–24.

Pierce, Ponchitta. "Problems of the Negro Woman Intellectual." *Ebony*, June 1966, pp. 144–49.

Reagon, Bernice Johnson. "Since I Laid My Burden Down." *In Hands on the Freedom Plow: Personal Accounts by Women in SNCC*, edited by Faith S. Holsaert et al., Rutgers UP, 1998, pp. 146–50.

—. *Voices of the Civil Rights Movement: Black American Freedom Songs, 1960–1966*. Smithsonian Institution, 1980.

—. *Songs of the Civil Rights Movement 1955–1965: A Study in Culture History*. Dissertation, Howard U, 1975.

—. "The Civil Rights Movement." *African American Music: An Introduction*. Routledge, 2006, pp. 598–623.

Ryan, Kathleen, Nancy Myers, and Rebecca Jones. *Rethinking Ethos; A Feminist Ecological Approach to Rhetoric*. "Introduction: Identifying Feminist Ecological Ethe." Southern Illinois UP, 2016. pp. 1–23.

Turner, Kristen. "Guy and Candie Carawan: Meditating the Music of the Civil Rights Movement." MA Thesis, University of North Carolina, Chapel Hill, 2011. UMI, 2011.

"White House Concert Honors Music of Civil Rights Era." CNN, February 10, 2010.

Zimmerelli, Lisa. "A Genre of Defense: Hybridity in Nineteenth-Century Women's Defenses of Women's Preaching." Dissertation, U Maryland, 2010.

8 STAGING GENDER POLITICS ON A WORLD STAGE

Adele Seeff

In 2005, in a democratic South Africa, the South African Broad-
casting Company (SABC) issued a competitive call for proposals for
made-for-television updatings of Shakespeare's plays.[1] The SABC
stipulated Black actors only, the use of Black South African vernacular languages, and contemporary settings.[2] Four adaptations aired in
2008: one of *King Lear*, one of *Romeo and Juliet*, and two versions of
Macbeth by two different directors. In this chapter, I focus primarily on
one of the versions of *Macbeth*—*Death of a Queen*—with reference to
the other—*Entabeni*—because in different ways both appropriate *Macbeth* to represent the destruction of powerful women. *Death of a Queen*,
however, is also committed to portraying an ideal of female leadership.
Here, then, I work alongside my fellow contributors within this volume
to trace the literary sojourn of Shakespeare's women and Shakespeare's
concerns about gender from early seventeenth-century England to South
African television at the beginning of the twenty-first century, exploring
how these figures and anxieties evolve in this contemporary South African context.

What does the use of a malleable Shakespearean text authorize in
the socio-political South African context? Shakespeare's cultural stature,
enhanced by its thorough cinematicization, provides authority to local
film projects seeking an international audience. Accordingly, *Death of
a Queen* and *Entabeni* graft Shakespearean narratives onto South African themes and preoccupations through the medium of internationally recognizable film genres and styles, thus simultaneously localizing
and globalizing Shakespeare. Or, as the editors put it in their Introduction to this volume, citing Laurie Gries, the circulation of early modern

texts, however appropriated, to a South African context, permits "people, ideas, images, and discourse [to] become persuasive as they move through the world and enter various associations" (Gries 12). Furthermore, the dramatic potential of *Macbeth* in a global film/television market of art forms and ideas liberates storytellers who might otherwise be silenced. In a post-apartheid South Africa, Shakespeare's cultural capital facilitates social, political, and ideological comment.

According to scholar Mark Thornton Burnett, "Macbeth anatomizes anxieties about women and worries about the security of male identity."[3] It is this strand that I focus on in this chapter. I am interested in exploring the way that Marina Bekker, the scriptwriter for *Death of a Queen*, appropriated a Shakespeare drama as a window into African folklore, legend, and myth to reimagine relations between men and women, the nature of female and male power, and the nature of both masculinity and femininity. In this way, her adaptation is utopian in the context of post-apartheid South Africa but always tethered to the Shakespeare play, to the legend of the Rain Queen, and, as firmly, to the social and political condition of women in twenty-first century South Africa. In this way, I would suggest that Bekker herself may be described as kaleidoscopically mapping the "relationship between rhetoric and mobility" (Royster 277). Bekker travels across time and geography, and, by modifying the genres of tragedy, epic, legend, and film, she reimagines the nature of female leadership. Needless to say, the 1606 play written in patriarchal England decides nothing for its viewers and audiences, leaving them instead with a deep appreciation of the play's ambiguity and complexity. The South African adaptations take advantage of these compelling Shakespearean qualities to craft an old tale in new ways.

Death of a Queen is grounded in actual political events of the recent South African past and in legend, myth, and ritual. I refer here to the legend of the Rain Queen, the sacred matriarchal figure of the Balobedu peoples in remote rural northwestern South Africa. The program's setting and the history of the Balobedu peoples provide a cover for a revisioned representation of the current state of women in South Africa. The setting and the rituals and legend associated with the Rain Queen[4] also allow international audiences, Shakespeare scholars and teachers, and the worldwide Shakespeare industry to engage, through the lens of Shakespeare, with a historical struggle on many levels, not the least of which is the condition of women in South Africa. I leave it to others to decide whether or not this isolated, pastoral setting meshes with their expectations of a South "African" story. I do not endorse the implied exoticism. I do endorse the deep pleasure to be derived from encountering the beauty of this region of Africa. The program was shot in the austere bushveld of Hammanskraal in northwestern South Africa. I use *Entabeni* as a reference because it emphasizes similar social issues but in a contemporary urban corporate setting. Since it depicts the psychic fragmentation of its central female character through the use of a *doppelganger*, a rhetorical device borrowed from *film noir*, thus doubling the number of powerful women arrayed against Macbeth, its story is more difficult to capture in the allotted space.

What makes *Macbeth* of all Shakespeare's plays the most commonly adapted to film, television, opera, and the novel in the twentieth and twenty-first centuries? For many scholars, it is the ontology of the supernatural. James I, a Scottish king, only recently arrived on the English throne, had authored a book on witchcraft.[5] Originally thought to have been written to flatter James I, *Macbeth*, featuring three riddling witches, exhibits a high degree of ambiguity toward the witches and their influence on human events. Another obvious answer is the ease with which the play is transposed to contemporary contexts. The fact that one of the contexts most frequently chosen by adapters is the representation of the equivocal nature of gender relations and the nature of male and female power that the play makes available is another explanation for the play's popularity.

In a play derived from various chronicle histories, the early modern dramatist depicts as protagonist a brave, noble warrior, Macbeth, who is seduced both by the prophecies of the three soothsaying witches (ambiguously gendered but unambiguously supernatural) and the re-enforcing manipulations of his wife, Lady Macbeth, to seek the throne by committing regicide. Shakespeare is careful to show us how conflicted Macbeth is in contemplating this enterprise while the king, Duncan, also his cousin, is under his roof as a guest. The playwright is equally careful in representing Lady Macbeth as Macbeth's unwavering, manipulative instigator as he vacillates, weighing the moral consequences of killing his king. Her actions in the first act, both in relation to Macbeth and to the murder (she is the one who returns the bloody sword to Duncan's groomsmen to implicate them in the killing), have led to centuries of caricaturing of her character. At the same time, the relationship of Macbeth and Lady Macbeth has been a critical focus: its intimacies, its knowing and not knowing, its failures, and ultimately its fall from grace. Over the course of the play's five-act structure, Lady Macbeth is portrayed in many guises: as manipulative, ambitious (for her husband) wife who makes killing the king a test of Macbeth's manhood; as supportive wife who seeks to protect her husband in a public setting;[6] and as wife who withdraws in ignorance. "Be innocent of the knowledge, dearest chuck / Til you applaud the deed," (3.3.51–52)[7] her husband tells her as he plans the murder of his friend Banquo. The revelation in the fifth and final act of Lady Macbeth's vulnerability and likely suicide, however, and her attempt to reassert herself subvert all previously held views of her. Critics have tended to see Lady Macbeth's suffering as merely humanizing her. In fact, even though we only see her once in the final act, we hear of her in profoundly affecting ways, and her presence dominates the last act.

Shakespeare's subversion in Act Five of his representation of the "fiend-like queen" and the issue of where to place moral accountability as Macbeth, completely unbeknownst to his wife, embarks on a tyrannical rampage of killings to secure his position as king, has opened the way for feminist criticism of the play, crucially of Lady Macbeth and the other woman in the play's cast of characters, Lady Macduff, whose husband is a target of Macbeth's murderous suspicion. Macduff flees to England to join Malcolm, the murdered king's son, and it is in Macduff's absence that Macbeth arranges to have Lady Macduff and her children murdered.

Such a brief summary of the play omits such major themes as the nature of sovereign power, the many paths to sovereignty, and the origin and responsibility of the witches. But it distills for the reader one of the mysteries that lies at the heart of this play: how does Lady Macbeth realize her journey from Macbeth's letter to her in Act 1, Scene 5, in which he describes his encounter with the three witches: "This have I thought good to deliver thee, my dearest partner of greatness, that thou might'st not lose the dues of rejoicing by being ignorant of what greatness is promised thee" (1.5.10–13) to his comment to her cited earlier, "Be innocent of the knowledge, dearest chuck / Til you applaud the deed," (3.3.51–52) which provides the fulcrum on which their relationship turns from a partnership to a fall from grace. And, to complete the triptych I am gesturing toward here, how are we as audience members or readers to make meaning of her final appearance in Act 5, Scene 1 (not the last we hear of Lady Macbeth but it is her final appearance), sleep-walking, re-enacting in her sleep the murder? Her sighing evokes the following from the Gentlewoman in attendance, "I would not have such a heart in my bosom for the dignity of the whole body" (5.1.7–8).

Scriptwriter Bekker responds to the challenge of representing the Africanized Lady Macbeth. She moves swiftly over the struts of the *Macbeth* plot, seamlessly plotting *Macbeth* onto her drama of Prince Malôrô, the Macbeth surrogate, within this context the Rain Queen's trusted cousin and councilor—regicidal as is his prototype, Macbeth, and Prince Malôrô's formidable wife Grace/Lady Macbeth. Grace, the Lady Macbeth surrogate, the demonized woman, is the metonymy for sexual politics, the gendered nature of power, and the role of the supernatural.[8] As Erin Sadlack, Lisa Zimmerelli, and Elizabeth Ellis Miller demonstrate in their contributions to this volume, gender-bending facilitates discourses of feminist power. She is constructed here as an embodiment of manipulation, irresistibly compelling and beautiful, head cocked and coiled in reptilian pose, slithering serpent-like around her husband as she catches him in her verbal snares.

As an Africanized construction of Lady Macbeth, Grace, like her prototype in Shakespeare's play, is a woman "barred from battle by prevailing gender ideology,"[9] consigned instead to a constraining domestic sphere. Shakespeare, as we know, subverts and complicates that ideology as Lady Macbeth commits her courage and vitality to a warrior-like, anti-maternal evil, "Come you spirits / That tend on mortal thoughts, unsex me here / And fill me from the crown toe top full / Of direst cruelty" in 1.5.47–60. Lacking her own counter-language, she uses the language of patriarchy. She spurs and taunts Macbeth to perform regicide. Grace, too, is passionately power-hungry on her husband's behalf and committed to his taking back patriarchal power, "It is time for men to rule again" (*Death of a Queen*, television script), convinced, and trying to persuade Malôrô, that they are doing the ancestors' will. Grace never sees the witches; instead, she confuses the witches with the ancestors throughout production.

Like Ava, the Lady Macbeth figure in *Entabeni*, and unlike Shakespeare's Lady Macbeth, who acts as a forceful accessory to her husband's murderous actions, Grace acts both independently and with her husband to promote his regicide. Ava in *Entabeni* is aided by her *doppelganger*, who appears to her with instructions. Grace acts alone. It is she who goes into the dark, forbidding forest in search of the poison that Malôrô/Macbeth will use to murder the Rain Queen, the Duncan figure.

Mirroring the source play's preoccupation with succession and children, the scriptwriter allows Grace a pregnancy. Grace, of course, attributes the pregnancy to the work of the ancestors: "Our ancestors have blessed us" (*Death of a Queen*, television script). Grace's pregnancy, however, produces no offspring. Wandering the palace corridors at night, sleepless like Lady Macbeth, her prototype, Grace returns to the Rain Queen's grave in the forest to ask for forgiveness. There, she miscarries, and the Macbeth couple remain sterile. Grace's bloody miscarriage signals her surrender to madness and to death. In a "mock" *patlah* (a riff on Lady Macbeth's invocation of the spirit world, "Come you spirits") cited earlier,[10] Grace chillingly summons the ancestors: "I call on the ancestors to strengthen me. You took my child. You killed my baby! Dry the milk in my breast" (*Death of a Queen*, television script). These lines plaintively echo Shakespeare's, "Come to my women's breasts / And take my milk for gall, you murd'ring ministers," (1.5.54–55). This scene re-creates Shakespeare's sleepwalking scene and secures a kind of dominance for Grace, an assertion of an autonomous, female self which has the same haunting quality as the analogous scene in Shakespeare's play.

Does the retelling of Shakespeare's play within this South African context muffle or amplify the representation of female power? I would argue that it does both. Lady Macbeth denies her maternal body in Shakespeare's play. However, in the African appropriation, Grace affirms her maternal body, citing the will of the ancestors in her pregnancy, announcing it with joy to her husband. But she misappropriates her actions to the ancestors; she miscarries, and the audience is witness to Grace's deterioration as a function of loss and guilt, and as a failed partner to her husband within the warrior culture of *Macbeth*, destroyed by this warrior culture as much as by her own actions.

Grace too dies onscreen—smearing poison on her lips—in precisely the same way that Malôrô, her husband, murdered the sleeping Rain Queen—also shown onscreen. Her exercise of power over her husband has been remorseless and unyielding, her access to evil empowering. Her death, unrepentant though it may be, lays bare her own conflicts and terrible vulnerabilities and movingly dramatizes for the viewer the costs of her actions. She dies in her trebled corporeality: as woman seeking to undo her maternal body, as female warrior, and as witch. I resist the description of her as "fiend-like queen" (5.8.82).[11] Bekker does not include a translation of this Shakespearean phrase in any of the four African languages in use in her adaptation.

To understand how easily Marina Bekker manages the transposition of *Macbeth* to television, one must first understand the impact of patriarchy's subjugation of women in the South African context, most particularly since 1994, the advent of democracy. In other words, one must understand gender politics in South Africa. While the anti-apartheid struggle brought an end to the crippling oppression of apartheid—where one could live, job discrimination by ethnicity, regulation of sexual relations, separate education and legislative control of the language one could be educated in, and absence of freedom of movement within the country—the new Constitution, liberal as it was in granting freedoms to all, is described by one scholar as an "aspirational document."[12] However skewed and uneven as the dispensation of democracy was for many Black South Africans,[13] for women who, on paper, were granted rights to full humanity, the ironies must have been bitter indeed. The anti-apartheid struggle had tended to eclipse gender issues. At the same time, as with all liberation movements, women suffered abuse not only from the state but from their male comrades as well. More importantly, since 1994, there has been an astonishing rise in sexual violence that cuts across all classes and ethnicities.[14] Despite a thirty-percent representation of women in parliament, South Africa has one of the highest rates of gender-based violence and HIV-AIDS infection in the world. South Africa is described as a rape culture.[15] According to Helen Moffatt, one in three women can expect to be raped in her lifetime. Controversy surrounds the reasons for this escalation in violence in intimate spaces. Women are now articulating the urgent need for their constitutional rights and are arguing for freedoms along intersectional axes: social, economic, political, and cultural dynamics of power that are determined by racial, gender, class, and sexual identities. In spite of the prevalence of rape and other gender-based violence against women and babies, it is startling to learn that the first legislation protecting women from violence dates from 1998: the *Domestic Violence Act No 116*, 1998. Far less surprising is the fact that very few women avail themselves of these "protections."

Against this background—and we should remember that the call for proposals went out in 2005 and the programs were aired in 2008—it is easy to find the proximate causes for *Death of a Queen* in the dire and seemingly intransigent plight of South African women today. *Death of a Queen* represents a vision of South African society that allows South African men and women to navigate the complexities of belonging to both global systems and to local traditions while aspiring to leadership. But there is another context, equally compelling. In 2005, an actual, historical succession crisis occurred, a power shift in the nature of leadership in twenty-first-century South Africa. *Death of a Queen* is set in Limpopo province, South Africa, among the Balobedu nation. This is the world of the Rain Queen: homogeneous, "traditional" and agrarian. It has remained so even with the coming of Europeans and Christianity. In 2005, the Balobedu Rain Queen, Queen Makobo Constance Modjadji VI, died under mysterious circumstances, leaving her kingdom stunned with grief. Her rivalrous brother, suspected in her death, succeeded her, rupturing four hundred years of female rule. The legend is an originary story of female rulers who, four hundred years ago, had to assume leadership after the men were decimated by war. *Death of a Queen* appropriates Shakespeare by using *Macbeth* as a cultural lens onto the legend of the sacred queen and onto present-day Balobedu national politics. Scriptwriter Bekker then widens the lens to include the rest of South Africa.

Macbeth's ongoing debate about paths to kingship maps neatly onto the Balobedu struggle between matrilineal and patrilineal sovereign power. At the time of this writing, the Rain Queen is once again in the South African news.[17] In April 2018, current President of South Africa Cyril Ramaphosa spoke at the coronation of the new Rain Queen, Masalanabo Modjadji VII, "This is a celebration of a unique royal leadership with a rich history that dates back over 400 years," he said. "This is the first and only queenship in the country and on the continent," he added. How the Rain Queen makes rain, a matter of supreme importance in Africa, the actual succession process, sacred female ruler to female ruler, how a mate is chosen for her by her Council—all is shrouded in secrecy, as is the ancestors' influence in quotidian life. The power of the legend and its legacy in contemporary politics gives *Death of a Queen* its special status.

The legend's founding in matrilineal succession provided the impetus for Bekker to exploit the sexual ambiguity built into *Macbeth* from Act 1, Scene 3, when Macbeth and his warrior comrade, Banquo, first encounter the witches on the heath: "You should be women / Yet your beards forbid me to interpret / That you are so." She flips gender in this African intertext, re-shaping as female, key male figures in the *Macbeth* plot. Bekker re-writes as female two important characters gendered male in Shakespeare's play, highly significant in the context of this utopian vision of strong women. She endows each of them with unusual leadership qualities. The first of these is MaModumedi, surrogate for Macduff (loyal thane to King Duncan and then to his son, Malcolm[18]), unambiguously loyal guardian and teacher to Puno and the Rain Queen while she is alive. MaModumedi, oral historian of the Balobedu people, who explains to Puno the four-hundred-year legend of the Balobedu, teacher of spiritual values and the right relation to the ancestors, is a wonderful instance of gender-bending, both in dramatic terms and in terms of gender dynamics. The second is Puno, the Rain Queen's young daughter and legitimate heir, a composite of Duncan's son and heir, Malcolm, who becomes king after Macbeth's death in Shakespeare's play. Duncan in Shakespeare's play is transposed to the young Rain Queen, the object of Malôrô's/Macbeth's ruthless ambition.

Gender-bending achieves two things. It supports Bekker's examination of gendered power relations in the context of the Balobedu people; this, in turn, allows her to re-configure gender politics in a South African context.[19] For Bekker, this was an opportunity to imagine a transformed female leadership where the desire for reconciliation directs action, where benevolence and inclusivity are prized values of governance.

Where should we locate Bekker's representation of Grace/Lady Macbeth in terms of feminist criticism of Shakespeare's plays? For centuries, Lady Macbeth has drawn vilification and has shared moral responsibility with the witches, who according to this view, she summons in her notorious, "Come, you spirits / That tend on mortal thoughts, unsex me here," speech (1.5.47–48) to provide her with the necessary courage—gendered male—to persuade her "too full o' th' milk of human kindness" husband to commit murder. However, since the early 1980s, with the emergence of feminist criticism of Shakespeare and the emergence of such scholars as Peter Stallybrass, Jonathan Goldberg, Madeleine Gohlke, Marjorie Garber, Lisa Jardine, Catherine Belsey, Janet Adelman, Terry Eagleton, Carol Neely, Nicholas Brooke, and Mark Thornton Burnett against the backdrop of the development of the women's movement, interest in the competing ideologies that the play sustains has also radically shifted the critical perspective on Lady Macbeth and the witches. According to Eagleton, the witches are the heroines of the play. It is they who through "planting"[20] ambitious designs in Macbeth expose the hollowness of the hierarchical order of the male warrior code, a code that relentlessly dominates Scottish society and women by means of violent oppression and ceaseless warfare. This "hypermasculine world," according to Goldberg in "Speculations: *Macbeth* and Source," is consumed by a lust for power, particularly the power of succession at the expense of women.[21] In the end, "all masculine attempts at feminine deprivation—including Lady Macbeth's wish to unsex herself—are robbed of ultimate success."[22] One could argue that Eagleton leads us directly to Burnett's celebration of Lady Macbeth. She wishes to assume a masculine warrior-style of leadership (the only kind she knows), and then if her leadership in the enterprise of killing the king fails, she remains female. However, as a woman, she acts to assert herself in the sleep-walking scene. We, as readers and audience members, are left to assess the impact of Lady Macbeth on Shakespeare's play. We are told by the gentlewoman in attendance that Lady Macbeth has pen and paper by her at all times. Writing and reading were largely male privileges in the period. The serving woman is loyal to her, refusing to divulge information to the doctor and disobeying the doctor's injunction to "Remove from her the means of all annoyance / And still keep eyes upon her" (5.1.80–81). "The cry of women," portending Lady Macbeth's death, heard as Macbeth prepares for his final battle, suggests a solidarity of women, not isolation at all.

Her death haunts the play, as it haunts Macbeth, prompting the most nihilistic language in the play, "She should have died hereafter. / There would have been a time for such a word" (5.5.20–21), followed by "Life's but a walking shadow, a poor player / . . . It is a tale / Told by an idiot, full of sound and fury, / Signifying nothing" (5.5.27–31). In Bekker's appropriation, Malôrô is present at Grace's death and watches helplessly over her. He is never alienated from her as Macbeth is from Lady Macbeth in the source play. The young actress's powerful performance together with the power of the script contribute to the impression of her character as resistant, insisting on her autonomy, rejecting powerlessness. This is Bekker's counter to *Macbeth*'s dystopian take on female power.

Grace's death is the hinge upon which Bekker turns to Puno (heir to the throne, Malcolm in Shakespeare's play). Scriptwriter Bekker's decision to re-write the "déjà-vu ending" and to graft her own (re)construction onto *Macbeth* provides a redefinition of femininity and masculinity, recuperating the tragic ending of both her sources, Shakespeare's play and the matriarchal legend, restoring order in a very non-Shakespearean manner. What is the potential in Africa for benevolent, matriarchal, matrilineal power? What is the nature of female sovereignty? Puno, not yet a woman, as we shall see, an assimilation of male and female leadership characteristics, offers a vivid contrast to Grace's tragically failed leadership.

The South African production revises Shakespeare's text to give women agency. In the final scenes, MaModumedi functions as both warrior (she leads the attack on Prince Malôrô and strikes his death blow) and protector/teacher of Puno, a choric role. MaModumedi (the name means "mother of the believer") helps ensure that power is returned to the women. She also represents the supremacy of female leaders as inevitable, always stressing the role of magic, ritual, and the proper relationship to the ancestors. Female leadership is enabled by the white stones, properties of female sovereignty, which, according to legend, endow the sacred queen with the capacity to make rain. As I noted earlier, the way in which the Rain Queen brings rain has never been revealed. Black stones, on the other hand, found in the belly of the sacred crocodile, are the properties of male leadership, of kingship.

Puno's mother, the former Rain Queen murdered by Malôrô, the Macbeth figure, now an ancestor, appears before her daughter in a dream sequence to give her the white stones. In the closing scene, Puno turns to the dying Malôrô and says, "Uncle, you don't have to die!" (*Death of a Queen*, film script). Malôrô hands Puno the black stones with a curt, "You're going to need these" (*Death of a Queen*, film script): a self-conscious transformation of *Macbeth*'s conclusion. As with all Shakespeare's tragedies, *Macbeth* demands the protagonist's death as essential to the establishment of a new order. The question of *which* new order, though, always remains unclear. Healing the wounds of a tragic past and fears for the future was the filmmakers' responsibility towards the spiritual transformation of the nation. By swallowing the white stones and the black stones, Puno reconciles tradition (leadership gendered female) and the succession rupture (leadership gendered male), inventing the way forward and urging Malôrô/Macbeth to live.[23]

For the filmmakers this scene was "excruciatingly important."[24] The altered ending represents the filmmakers' sense of responsibility toward the spiritual transformation of the new South African nation and the hope for the emergence of opportunities for female leadership, female autonomy, rights, and freedoms. Rain falls in the final moments of the program, heralding the physical and spiritual transformation of a nation through reconciliation, its most urgent need. The production thus becomes a working-through that is not idle entertainment but a part of South Africa's social-moral history: a nation's search to heal its recent traumatic past in relation to an ancient past. Bekker and Grobbelaar—scriptwriter and director/cinematographer—fulfill television's stated role at the time—2005–2008—articulated in the SABC's Mission Statement. Television, as bard, has responsibility for healing a nation traumatized by the legacies of apartheid.

Bekker does not adopt the source play's preoccupation with male violence and the warrior code (to be a man, Macbeth must be violent: the murder of Duncan is the test of Macbeth's virility). Macbeth insists, "I dare all that may become a man. / Who dares [do] more is none." And Lady Macbeth responds swiftly, " "What beast was't, then, / That made you break this enterprise to me? / When you durst do it, you were a man; / And to be more than what you were, you would / Be so much more the man" (1.7.51–56). Bekker steers clear of the different and ambiguous models of masculinity that Shakespeare's play offers us: Duncan, the king at once nurturing like a woman, "I have begun to plant thee and will labor / To make thee full of growing" (1.4.32–33), yet obviously enjoying cruelty and violence (his evident pleasure at the report of Macbeth's violence on the battlefield in the second scene of the play); Macduff, loyal to the dead king, Duncan, and his ambiguous son, Malcolm, who abandons his wife and son to Macbeth's murderers; and Malcolm himself, masquerading as licentious to test Macduff's loyalty and then depending on Macduff to destroy Macbeth in the final battle as his father Duncan had depended on Macbeth to fight his battles. In their place, Bekker creates a quartet of contrasting women: the Rain Queen, Grace, MaModumedi, and Puno representing for the viewer dystopian and utopian visions of the female. Each of the four is a foil to the other three.

And Shakespeare's text? "I used it as a cover. I could never have done it without Shakespeare," was scriptwriter Marina Bekker's comment.[25] She and director Pieter Grobbelaar seized on the Balobedu sovereign (already gendered) crisis to represent a South African gendered Macbeth. In doing so, they, in company with the authors and artists that Karen Nelson, Michele Osherow, and Nabila Hijazi evaluate in this volume, crossed "a variety of local, national, and international boundaries" (Introduction). Bekker and Grobelaar radically re-imagined *Macbeth*'s cast and Shakespeare's tragic ending to offer a revisionist feminist indigeneity for the South African nation: a utopian image of the South African feminine principle with, it must be said, dystopian bass chords.

NOTES

1. This chapter is dedicated to Kethiwe Ngcobo, former Head of Drama at the SABC; to Marina Bekker, scriptwriter for *Death of a Queen*; and to the memory of Queen Makobo, Constance Modjadji VI. I would like to thank Karen Nelson for her invaluable editorial support.

2. Each program—a half-hour in length—aired over a six-week period. All had huge viewing audiences, garnered various awards, and served as linguistic reclamation projects to celebrate the 1994 addition of nine indigenous languages to the existing roster of South Africa's official languages, previously only English and Afrikaans.

3. See Mark Thornton Burnett, p. 3. See also Janet Adelman, p. 131, for the argument that *Macbeth* "represents primitive fears about male . . . autonomy itself, about those looming female presences who threaten to control one's actions and one's mind, to constitute one's very self, even at a distance."

4. See the work of anthropologists E. Jensen Krige and J.D. Krige.

5. The date of the play is assumed to be 1606. James I was crowned in 1603, and the topic of witchcraft was current in early sixteenth-century England.

6. I refer here to the banquet scene in 3.4 where the ghost of his friend Banquo, whose murder he has engineered, appears to him and Macbeth loses his composure. Lady Macbeth explains her husband's strange behavior as a "fit" and sends all the guests home.

7. William Shakespeare, *Macbeth*. Folger Digital Texts. All quotations from Macbeth are taken from this edition.

8. I would like to thank Susan O'Malley for pointing out the irony in the choice of this name.

9. Susan Snyder.

10. A *patlah* is an African ritual generally held in the early hours of the morning when the ancestors are likely to be responsive. The supplicant asks the ancestors for help.

11. I contest this ascription for Lady Macbeth and Ava in *Entabeni* as well.

12. Pumla Dineo Gqola, p. 112.

13. Much has been written on the lack of access to education, housing, and jobs for Black South Africans. This topic is outside the scope of this chapter. However, this situation affects roughly eleven million young people who continue to be mired in a "post-liberation, unequal capitalist society," as David Everatt observed, p. 133.

14. See Helen Moffet. See also Pumla Dineo Gqola.

15. See Helen Moffett; see also Lisa Vetter. Kethiwe Ngcobo, currently CEO of Infuzion Media, commented on widespread abuse toward women: "Researchers in South Africa blamed high rape statistics, both during apartheid and in the transition, on the gender and racial inequalities spawned by the social and political apartheid system and its aftermath. The particular ways in which patriarchal traditions intersected with cultural and religious customs tended to create patterns of male control that subordinated women from all class and ethnic groups in South Africa."

16. *Entabeni*, by contrast, does not erase its heterogeneous narratives: Kumkani, the Macbeth surrogate as successful businessman; the witch as ancestor, homeless but thoroughly subversive; and white Macduff, "uncle" to the Malcolm surrogate. According to both scriptwriter Marina Bekker and director/producer Pieter Grobbelaar, the Tribal Elders and the ancestors were appeased by the use of Shakespeare's *Macbeth* and the choice of another nation—the Bapedi—as covers for the Balobedu crisis.

17. Peter Ramothwala, "New Balobedu Queen Ushered in With Rainfall." Masalanabo Modjadji will be installed as Rain Queen Modjadji VII after she has graduated through the Lobedu customs.

18. The plot follows Macduff to England where Malcolm is in hiding. It is during his absence that his wife, Lady Macduff, and her son are killed by murderers dispatched by Macbeth to kill Macduff.

19. As a leader, the Rain Queen in Bekker's representation is as ambiguous as Duncan of whom Macbeth says, "This Duncan / Hath borne his faculties so meek, hath been / So clear in his great office, that his virtues / plead like angels" (1.7.16–19, Folger Digital Texts). Yet, why does Duncan hang back in battle while seeming to relish in bloodshed as he does in 1.2? Duncan is certainly part of the warrior culture in which Macbeth rises. Time and space forbid a full analysis of the female Duncan, the Rain Queen in *Death of a Queen*. Suffice it to say here that she is figured as torn between tradition—staged by the drama of the rain ceremony—and modernity—suggested by her interest in computers.

20. Terry Eagleton, 48. Whether or not Macbeth had long harbored his regicidal route to the throne or whether the witches seduce him with their "double-tongue'd" prophesies about Macbeth's future has long been a debate in critical writing about the play. Shakespeare constructs sufficient evidence on both sides of this debate, leaving the reader/viewer to decide.

21. Goldberg, 257.
22. Goldberg, 257.
23. According to African legend, the black stones found in the belly of the crocodile represent male divine kingship, in contrast to the white stones, which represent female divine sovereignty. These stories are passed on from elder to child over centuries. Every child grows up with the warning not to harm a crocodile, and every African knows the male power this animal possesses, especially in the realm of kings and chiefs. Grobbelaar was careful to include ethnographic visual detail throughout.
24. Pieter Grobbelaar, "Good Storytelling."
25. Marina Bekker. Telephone Interview. March 25, 2010.

Works Cited

Adelman, Janet. *Suffocating Mothers: Fantasies of Maternal Origin in Shakespeare's Plays, 'Hamlet to 'The Tempest.'* Routledge, 1992.
Bekker, Marina. Telephone Interview. 25 Mar. 2010.
—, and Grobbelaar, Pieter. Personal interview. 10 Mar. 2010.
Burnett, Mark Thornton. "The 'fiend-like Queen': Rewriting Lady Macbeth." *Paregon*, vol. 11, no. 1, 1993, pp. 1–19.
Eagleton, Terry. "The Witches Are the Heroines of the Piece." *Macbeth: Contemporary Critical Essays*, edited by Alan Sinfield, MacMillan, 1992, pp. 46–52.
Everatt, David. "Standing on the Shoulders of Giants." *Fees Must Fall: Student Revolt, Decolonisation [sic] and Governance in South Africa*, edited by Susan Booysen, Johannesburg, Wits UP, 2016.
Goldberg, Jonathan. "Speculations: *Macbeth* and Source." *Shakespeare Produced: The Text in History and Ideology*, edited by Jean E. Howard and Marion O'Connor, Methuen, 1987.
Gqola, Pumla Dineo. "How the 'Cult of Femininity' and Violent Masculinities Support Endemic Gender-Based Violence in South Africa." *African Identities*, vol. 5, no. 1, 2007, pp. 111–24.
Gries, Laurie E. "Circulation as an Emerging Threshold Concept." *Circulation, Writing, and Rhetoric*, edited by Laurie Gries and Collin Gifford Brooke, Utah State UP, 2018, pp. 3–26.
Grobbelaar, Pieter. "Good Storytelling," unpublished presentation at INPUT, Warsaw, 2009, courtesy of Marina Bekker, Mar. 2010.
Krige, E. Jensen and J.D. Krige, *The Realm of a Rain Queen: A Study of the Pattern of Loved Society*. Oxford UP, 1943.

Moffett, Helen. "'These Women, They Force Us to Rape Them': Rape as Narratives of Social Control in Post-Apartheid South Africa." *Journal of South African Studies*, vol. 32, no. 1, 2006, www.tandfonline.com/doi/abs/10.1080/03057070500493845. Accessed July 2018.

Ngcobo, Kethiwe. Personal interview. Johannesburg, 10 Mar. 2017.

Ramothwala, Peter. "New Balobedu Queen Ushered in with Rainfall." *Sowetan Live*, April 9, 2018, www.sowetanlive.co.za/news/south-africa/2018-04-09-new-balobedu-queen-ushered-in-with-rainfall/. Accessed 31 July 2018.

Royster, Jacqueline Jones. *Traces of a Stream: Literary and Social Change among African American Women*, U of Pittsburgh P, 2000.

Shakespeare, William. *Macbeth*. Folger Digital Texts, www.folgerdigitaltexts.org/?chapter=5&play=Mac&loc=p7. Accessed 10 July 2018.

Snyder, Susan. Introduction. *Macbeth*. Folger Shakespeare Library, Simon & Schuster, 2003.

Vetter, Lisa. "Addressing Domestic Violence in South Africa: Reflections on Strategy and Practice." *UN Women Watch*. Centre for the Study of Violence and Reconciliation, South Africa, 2005, www.un.org/womenwatch/daw/egm/vaw-gp-2005/docs/experts/vetten.vaw.pdf. Accessed 16 Feb. 2018.

III Connections through Circulation

9 To "meddle with a multitude": Gender at Work in the Petitions of Early Modern Women Servants

Danielle Griffin

In her groundbreaking call to regender the rhetorical tradition in *Rhetoric Retold*, Cheryl Glenn attempts to "[remap] rhetorical territory" (1) from antiquity to the Renaissance. Of Renaissance women, she notes, "The Renaissance Englishwoman continued to be marginalized from the body of linguistic performance. The literary participation of even the most erudite and talented was limited to patronage, religious writing, and translation" (119). In this section of her book, Glenn goes on to explore such genres as translation and a "rhetoric of silence" (153) to theorize such women as Margaret More Roper and Anne Askew as significant rhetors in a canon that greatly privileges their male counterparts.

Since Glenn's influential call in 1997, feminist historiographers have cultivated a variety of innovative methods and methodologies to research the history of women rhetors and our own ideological underpinnings as a discipline.[1] In light of these developments, I am interested in how we can further "remap" the rhetorical history of Renaissance rhetoric to expand the margins of the early modern era to theorize the rhetorical contributions of working women—women who were marginalized from the rhetorical tradition not only by gender but also by class. In light of Glenn's initial (and continuing) call, I examine in this chapter two petitions from the early modern period that address and are attributed to maidservants, *A Letter sent by the Maydens of London* (1567), which is also analyzed by Karen Nelson in another chapter in this collection, and

"The Petition of the Women-Servants within the City" (1700) ("Unto the Right Honourable . . ."). Both of these petitions are texts that argue for labor rights for women servants specifically, with the collective authorship afforded by the petition enabling working women the rhetorical agency to articulate arguments about gendered labor and equitable working conditions. More significantly, in arguing for equitable working conditions for women servants as a group, these petitions theorize a collective of working women that calls attention to the intersection of gender and class, contributing to our field's expanding knowledge about the ways rhetorical subjects were (and are) not only gendered but also classed. In other words, these petitions evidence awareness of a political subjectivity defined by labor. A focus on these early articulations of gendered class consciousness deepens the study of women, work, and rhetoric.

While the themes of sexuality and religion have been the subjects of a vast amount of scholarship concerning early modern women, the study of labor and gender in the period has received far less attention.[2] However, discourses of women's work—both by and about working women—evidence the significance of labor as a determinant of sociopolitical identity. In examining representations of women's labor, literature scholar Michelle Dowd states, "though sexuality is often heralded as a key component of modern subject-hood, my [research] suggests that the ideological category of 'work' played an equally significant role in the construction of the early modern female subject" (*Women's Work* 18). While Dowd's work analyzes narrative representations of women's work in literary texts such as Shakespeare's *Twelfth Night* and Isabella Whitney's *A Sweat Nosgay*, to name a few, her insights are relevant to a rhetorical approach, especially in thinking about how women workers constructed their own ethos. Matthew Kendrick employs a similar strategy in his book on labor in the early modern theater. Although like Dowd's much of his book examines representations of labor in drama, he also examines many petitions from craftsmen in the period. Of the numerous workers' petitions in the Elizabethan period, he notes, "These petitions are insightful because they demonstrate that workers, faced with the increasing commercialization of traditional occupations, were developing their own sense of the social, moral, and economic value of their labor in opposition [to] perceived economic injustice" (8). Kendrick's thoughts about the importance of a "laboring subjectivity" (165), as he describes it, are deeply perceptive, even if his project does not analyze gender as a factor in such a subjectivity.

Both Dowd's and Kendrick's emphasis on representations of labor rather than analysis of the discourse of laborers is not simply a result of the emphasis on drama and poetry in early modern studies; researching the writing of middling and lower-class persons in the early modern period presents numerous methodological difficulties, including illiteracy, scarcity of preserved archival material, and difficulty in discerning authorship. One method potentially fruitful to the recovery of laboring rhetors is that of searching for collectivist rhetorics. Feminist rhetorical scholars such as Barbara Biesecker, Wendy Sharer, and Lindal Buchanan have noted the significance of collectivity in women's rhetorics specifically. In particular, Buchanan notes the importance of collaboration to women's rhetorical endeavors: because of "the material, social, and ideological conditions around them" (58), women and other marginalized groups have relied particularly on cooperative efforts in order to make their rhetoric heard. While Buchanan's own research investigates the "supportive collaboration" (44) that facilitated nineteenth-century American women's public discourse, her insights are equally applicable to early modern working women, marginalized by class, gender, and perhaps illiteracy. Their ability to participate in rhetorical discourse would have been facilitated or even enabled by relationships forged with professional scribes, printers, and educated men and women who assisted them in the articulation and textual production of their arguments.

Recent methodologies in early modern studies have also provided promise to the growing potential for analyzing contributions by non-elite speakers and writers. In particular, the displacement of the single author has expanded the scope and function of texts available for analysis. Although the author function was first famously theorized by Foucault, scholars of early modern literature like Harold Love have offered expansive and historically nuanced views of authorship that also yield great potential for scholars in the history of rhetoric. In *Attributing Authorship*, Love defines authorship "[not as] the condition of being an originator of works, but a set of linked activities (*authemes*) which are sometimes performed by a single person but will often be performed collaboratively or by several persons in succession" (39). Although Love is not focusing on class or labor in his book, his insights are applicable to thinking about how middling and lower-class rhetors participated collaboratively in rhetorical activities during the early modern period; their struggles with literacy and other rhetorical constraints often necessitated collaboration in order to yield written texts like petitions.

In fact, the petition was a rhetorical genre that enabled authorship among a great body of marginalized rhetors. As Erin Sadlack observes in "Petitioning Power: The Rhetorical Fashioning of Elizabethan Women's Letters," "surviving petitions testify that women from all classes had the right to participate in government on this individual basis, indicating that the petition was one of women's first political rights" (229). Although the genre of the petition has received notable work from rhetorical scholars such as Alisse Portnoy and Susan Zaeske, its rhetorical analysis is almost solely relegated to the nineteenth (and sometimes twentieth) century. The early modern petition has been explored primarily by historians with very little attention from scholars of rhetoric. However, exploring the petition outside of the history of the United States can greatly expand our knowledge of the genre and of women's rhetorical endeavors. First, the political situation of early modern women living under a monarchy is drastically different from that of the numerous studies of the rhetorical efforts within American democracy. Portnoy's interest in rhetorical participation when "women's political intrusion as extraordinary" (603) is magnified when we consider societies without even the affordance of a democratic government. Furthermore, in focusing on nineteenth century women's petitions, rhetorical scholars often emphasize the work of middle- and upper-class women, with Portnoy observing that "petitions were appropriate vehicles for upper-middle-class women" (617) and Zaeske noting that women's antislavery petitions were often authored by "thousands of northern, middle-class, predominantly white women" (148). While Portnoy and Zaeske offer relevant observations about the role of the petition in enabling rhetorical agency and constituting political subjectivities, extending the historical focus of the petition yields greater insight into women's rhetorical constraints as well as the way their rhetorical subjectivities were not only gendered, but also classed.

Although the role of the petition in the early modern period has received little to no attention from scholars of rhetoric, it has received considerable attention among early modern scholars, with much of the scholarship focused on the petitions produced during the English Civil War, especially the sudden increase of printed petitions that came with the breakdown of censorship during the period.[3] Some Renaissance scholars, however, have researched the petition outside of its prominence during the English Civil War. Both Sadlack and James Daybell, for example, look at women's rhetoric in letters of petition, which contained the formal request elements associated with the petition genre but were presented in the form of a letter, and Sadlack continues to offer an in-depth look at this subject in her chapter in this collection. Daybell provides a thorough history of the petition and its use by women, noting that letters of petition were "influenced in different measure by the classical letter form of the medieval *ars dictaminis*, early modern rhetorical theory and revived theory of the 'familiar' letter" (5). He also observes that instructions for letter-writing in vernacular manuals speak to the availability and knowledge of the genre among literate women of lower ranks (5). With increased accessibility of knowledge of the form of the petition, women heavily utilized this genre for various effects:

> Female petitioners made a broad range of patronage suits, both for themselves and on behalf of family, dependants and other groups: [friends], neighbours and clients. For themselves, women wrote to procure grants of land, wardship, pensions and annuities, and to settle disputes over jointure and inheritance; they also wrote seeking favour and advice, to influence local officials, and to secure justice and release from imprisonment. Acting as patrons and intermediaries, women wrote concerning the preferment of suitors to offices, and the bestowing of titles and honours, thus performing many of the same patronage functions as men. (3–4)

In addition, some early modern scholars have done work to explore petitioning after the English Civil War, as with the anti-tithe petitioning of Quaker women in the late 1650s.[4]

While Daybell focuses on letters of petition and thus women's letter-writing, the genre of the petition was also available to illiterate women. This point is significant in examining the rhetorical endeavors of working women, as many were illiterate or could read but not write. Sadlack notes in "Petitioning Power" that the easy access to professional scribes meant that "[m]any petitioners employed such professional scribes, so that even if the petitioner herself could not write, she was still able to petition" (232). In some instances of petitions, the document even acknowledges the authors' illiteracy. Consider, for instance, the justification for the signers' and signees' act of petitioning in *The Apprentices Petition and Propositions, presented unto the Honourable House of Commons in Parliament Assesmbled* (1647): "Nor can we see any reason why a poore or illiterate man (being injured) should not seeke for redresse of his grievances, as well as a rich and learned" (qtd. in Suzuki 138). Here, the apprentices' petition makes explicit the use of the genre by illiterate persons. Such evidence points to the accessibility of the genre of the petition, and it also establishes a long precedent of petitionary activities that occurred throughout the early modern period, long before the American antislavery and antiremoval petitions of the nineteenth century.

Indeed, the extensive use of the word *petition* during the period points to the multiple shapes this fluid genre took. Petitions could be presented as the direct political request we associate with the word today, but they could also be embedded in personal or business letters or published as pamphlets. The word *petition* also functioned prominently as a verb; "to petition" often meant delivering a written request, but it could also refer to the act of making a request without a corresponding written document or gathering in public space to make such requests ("Petition, v." *Oxford English Dictionary*). For this chapter, I am interested in employing a broader definition of the petition than a document with a request delivered to Parliament or the monarch. Carolyn R. Miller's critical re-definition of "genre as social action," as opposed to genre as form, for example, allows us to think more copiously about the function that a petition might perform.[5] Keeping this fluid definition in mind expands the body of texts we might consider and therefore the rhetors who authored them. While "The Petition of the Women-Servants within the City" falls neatly into traditional generic qualifications of the petition, *A Letter sent by the Maydens of London* does not. Although the Maydens' *Letter* makes implicit requests concerning women's working conditions, it was printed and circulated as a pamphlet (not delivered) and addressed to servants' "mistresses" broadly. Despite some different deployments of genre, both texts use the affordances of the petition to articulate grievances concerning the labor of women servants. In the remainder of the chapter, I turn my attention specifically to these two petitions rather than discussing petitions in the period broadly. I show how these texts are arguments for the labor rights of working women and how, in turn, these texts reveal the intersection of class and gender. Considering the articulation of this subject position, then, I demonstrate how these petitions work to theorize a collective of working women and an early articulation of class consciousness.

Before an analysis of the texts themselves, a brief summary of each petition is useful. The Maydens' *Letter* (1567) serves as a response to an earlier pamphlet (which is no longer extant) by Edward Hake that employs stereotypes about and attacks the character of the maidens and mistresses of London. The text of the Maydens' *Letter* itself is written from the persona of a group of six servants, whose names are possibly pseudonyms, and if they are not pseudonyms, the text provides no last name for the women, effectively rendering them anonymous. Although it is written in response to Hake's tract, the text itself is addressed to their "moste woorthie Matrones & Mistresses" (A3ʳ), or the women who employed them. The Maydens' *Letter* is summarized cogently by Ilona Bell in her book chapter exploring the *Letter* and its authorship: "The gist of the Maydens' argument is that the servant/mistress relationship must be mutually rewarding, answering not only the needs but also the pleasures of both parties" (189). Here, the Maydens make arguments about the conditions of their labor as a kind of petition to their mistresses. "The Petition of the Women-Servants," on the other hand, is a much more formal petition and is addressed to the town-council of Edinburgh. In this petition, the women seek key "Necessities" from the government, such as welfare and housing for women workers who encounter hardships that affect or are a result of their employment as well as a pension program for women servants set up by the local government. Despite the variations in their construction of the petition genre, though, both documents call attention to gendered labor and argue for rights to equitable working conditions for women servants specifically—not for women as a whole, and not for servants of both sexes. Moreover, although these petitions were written and circulated over a century apart, the similarities of their requests offer another instance of "recurrence" theorized by Shirley Wilson Logan in *"We Are Coming,"*[6] and the echo of these maidservants' demands puts this reverberation into conversation with the other pieces in this section that consider the way that arguments from/about women circulate across time.

Neither the Maydens' *Letter* nor "The Petition of the Women-Servants" has received much scholarly attention. Aside from the emphasis on drama and poetry in early modern English studies, both documents have anonymous authorship, and there is no proof that the documents were authored by women at all. In fact, discerning the "author(s)" of petitions, especially when it concerns women, is the subject of much scholarly inquiry and debate. Some scholars have attempted to determine the sex of the author of petitions by discerning gendered stylistic differences (Thorne, "Narratives of Female Suffering" 137), with Patricia-Ann Lee even positing a "distinctively female voice" (244). However, Daybell claims that such gendered language is "a 'scripted' female voice that could be appropriated by both men and women" (4); therefore, such variations in style are performative and may shed light about the intentions of the petitioner but not necessarily her gender. While Sadlack explores other methodological solutions, such as examining "a petition's deviation from scribal conventions" (231) as a possible indicator of authorship, there is ultimately no way of determining with certainty whether the petitions were authored by (or to what degree they were authored by) women as the text may indicate.[7]

These questions of the authorship of the Maydens' *Letter* are explored in depth by Bell in her book chapter on the document. While Bell concludes that there is no "extrinsic data" (192) to determine whether the *Letter* was authored by a man, a single woman, or a group of women as the text indicates, she notes that the text "demonstrates . . . knowledge of and immersion in the actual daily life of London serving women" and that it "derives much of its rhetorical power from personal testimony, compellingly supported by precise accounts of serving women's daily chores and weekly schedules" (183). The use of personal experience and knowledge of the quotidian lives of women servants may support a hypothesis that the document was, in fact, authored by a woman or a group of women. In her comprehensive study of working women in the period, historian Marjorie Keniston McIntosh describes the long list of varied tasks that may make up the work of women servants: "The kinds of work done by female servants covered a wide spectrum, depending upon the type of household into which they had been hired. A domestic servant's duties commonly included cleaning, cooking, serving at meals, sewing, washing clothes, and looking after young children" (50). Engagements with such tasks are described (and sometimes bemoaned) in the Maydens' *Letter* as well as in "The Petition of the Women-Servants." Although surmising about who put pen to paper only amounts to a researched conjecture, the text is nonetheless significant in its contribution to understandings of authorship: as Bell states, "By inviting the reader to wonder whether the author could be a woman, the Maydens force us to reexamine our assumptions about what sixteenth-century women were capable of knowing and doing" (179). Similarly, Margaret W. Ferguson and Mihoko Suzuki note that "[t]he petition is predicated on the assumption that maidservants were capable of authoring it; moreover, since the text takes their perspective, we can conclude that it assumes and appeals to an audience of female servants" (579). In other words, even if scholars cannot discern exact authorship, the Maydens' *Letter* challenges assumptions about who had access to the writing and reading of petitions, because the text imagines collective women authorship and readership. Similarly, present-day historians have no evidence concerning the authorship of "The Petition of the Women-Servants"; yet its very existence imagines a community of serving women who had access to the petition genre and utilized it for political purposes.

Having considered uncertainties concerning authorship, I turn to the texts themselves and their rhetorical efforts concerning labor and collectivism. Despite authorial speculation, the articulation of a subjectivity determined by gendered labor exists in both texts. The requests of the petitions are rooted in working conditions, thus in order to make the requests, the texts define their petitioners by their labor, a move that distinguishes them from the addressees of the petitions. Early in *A Letter sent by the Maydens of London*, the Maydens envision a hypothetical scenario that exemplifies their demands. They postulate that if their mistresses were to condemn their servants as Hake's tract suggests,

> that in a verie shorte time and space, ye shoulde have gotten very fewe or no seruants at al, when such as are born in the countrey shoulde choose rather to tarie at home, and remaine there to take paines for a small stipend or wages with libertie: and such as are Citizens borne, shoulde repaire also to the countrey, or to other Cities where they might be free, than to abide as slaues and bondewomen in London. (A3ᵛ)

Such a scenario makes explicit the importance of the labor that women servants perform, and it provides a justification for the Maydens' complaint that certain mistresses "haue done their dueties to vs [servants] as slaues or bondewomen" and have made servants "take intollerable paines for a trifle" (A4ᵛ). These observations lead the Maydens to argue for days of recreation:[6] "How much against al reason were it, so straightly to deale with vs, and so straitely to vse vs, that after all the toile we take in the whole weeke, we might not enioye a piece of the holyday, to refresh our spirites, and to rest our wearied bones?" (A4ᵛ-A5ʳ).[8]

The authors of "The Petition of the Women-Servants within the City" do not request regular days of leave, but they do make similar requests based on the nature of their work. In response to the lack of support women servants face when they are no longer capable of laboring, the authors request welfare from the city and support such as funding, housing, and healthcare in order to prevent such women from becoming homeless. Their appeal describes information about the conditions of their employment: "That to our inexpressible Grief, we dayly see when any of us are rendered Incapable to serve either through Old Age, Sickness, Infirmity, or other Accidents, we are presently exploited in an Ignominious Manner to seek our Bread." The petition makes explicit the labor conditions that might lead a woman servant to "Infirmity" or cause her to become "Incapable," which in turn render her likely to become homeless if she does not have a support system or alternative employment. In both texts, as the women servants utilize the petition to make requests, the authors offer key information about their working conditions in order to justify their arguments. Thus, these texts are probably some of the earliest available documents that make arguments concerning the labor conditions of working women.

Importantly, the working conditions articulated in these petitions show that the authors' subject positions are informed not only by gender, but also by class: both petitions explicitly distinguish servants from the women for whom they work. As I discussed earlier, the Maydens' *Letter* is addressed to their mistresses. As Bell observes, "The Maydens' argument not only consistently emerges out of their experiences as servants, but it is also carefully constructed to persuade, not a general reading public, but the particular women who control the Maydens' lives and supply their very likelihood" (183). While the Maydens do make some supporting arguments that are applicable to women in general, particularly concerning marriage,[9] their act of addressing their mistresses distinguishes themselves and their class conditions from women of higher rank. This distinction—while often used pejoratively to lower-class women—is here described from the perspective of working women in order to relay their own experience and enable them to convey important information about the labor conditions they face.

Similarly, "The Petition of the Women-Servants" treats women servants as separate from and not belonging to the family they serve when it advocates for a "House or Hospital [that] will prevent the inhuman ejecting of [women servants] from Families where [they] serve." This argument works both as a logical appeal for providing such housing, as well as a pathetic appeal concerning abandoned women servants, but it also distinguishes such women as separate from the households in which they serve. The petition argues that women servants deserve rights specifically as women servants and that these rights are justified on the basis of the conditions that such gendered labor entails.

While it may seem obvious that documents concerning women servants would make explicit the connection between gender and class, this significant marker differentiates these petitions from many other petitions by wives and widows that were authored during the English Civil War and from letters of petition that individual women wrote. While these other petitions were likely to include information about the hardships women faced due to poverty or childcare, they usually do not discuss labor conditions or workers' rights as part of their argument. As a comparison, "The Humble Petition of Many Thovsands of Wives and Matrons of the City of London" (1643), which has been analyzed by many scholars of English Civil War petitions, employs a much different cultivation of ethos than the texts of women servants. In contrast to the women servants who are defined by their work, the authors of the English Civil War women's petitions are defined by their roles as wives and mothers. The petition begins, "It was the first act of God Almighties favour, to our first parent in Paradise, to ordaine him a helper meet for him; namely, a Wife; such as we are, to the number of many thousands, who doe hereby present this Petition for the rectifying of our dreadfull and increasing grievances" (A2^r). From the outset, then, the authors of this petition are defining themselves in relation to men both in title (as wives) and in function (as "helper meet for him"). This description was normal in the early modern period, as McIntosh notes, "While men were usually labeled by their employment, as a carpenter or merchant, women were normally labeled by their marital status" (7) and far less likely to be seen as having an "occupational identity" (123). Moreover, the women justify their use of the petition by giving themselves a civic significance based on childbirth and mothering: "Wives are those who people and replenish the Common-wealth with Inhabitants; . . . Wives are the Mothers of the faithfull, and the producers of all goode Subjects" (A2^r). Here, the women establish their ethos by employing traditional gender roles, a much different rhetorical strategy than that utilized by the women servant authors. Although many signees of the petition would have been working women like the Maydens and perhaps even lower-class like the authors of "The Petition of the Women-Servants," the content of "The Humble Petition" and its explicit involvement in matters of war and state necessitate that women express their gender in a much different way. For instance, the authors of "The Humble Petition" do mention their roles as working women when they say that the effects of the wars "afflicts [them as] Oyster-wives, Apple-wives, Tripe-wives . . . the very Ale-wives" (A4^r); however, these mentions are not the emphasis of the petition and are presented as secondary details. These discrepancies in the presentation of ethos reveal that women petitioners employed multiple rhetorical strategies suited to the persuasive goals of the particular petition and request.

In addition to different tactics of self-identification, the women servants' petitions and the English Civil War wives' petitions differ greatly in their employment of humility as rhetorical strategy. The deployment of humility rhetoric in petitions has been the subject of considerable scholarly criticism, yet the Maydens' *Letter* and "The Petition of the Women-Servants" illustrate that this "distinctively female voice" (Lee 244) was utilized to different degrees among women petitioners of the period. "The Humble Petition of Many Thovsands of Wives and Matrons" makes extensive use of this strategy of humility: "in all humility shewing the greatnesse of our dolors and sufferings" (A2^v); "we women are the weaker vessels, and so have the frailer flesh, and are more subject to our failings then [sic] men" (A3^r); "we poore distressed Wives this cold weather lying alone in our beds, without the warme touches and embraces of any man to comfort us" (A4^r); "the terrour of all Christian people, especially of us weake and tender-hearted women" (A4^v). The petitioners' cultivation of humility was widespread in the early modern period, but it was heightened in the language of most women petitioners. Alison Thorne notes that "[i]n deploying the rhetoric of helplessness, these female petitioners are clearly exploiting received assumptions about the physiological and intellectual inferiority of their sex as the readiest means of inducing sympathy for their plight" ("Women's Petitionary Letters" 29). Therefore, employing this hyperbolic gendered imagery would serve as a strong pathetic appeal for women and gain sympathy for their cause.

However, the emphasis on humility tropes and feminine weakness in the English Civil War petitions makes the Maydens' *Letter* and "The Petition of the Women-Servants" interesting in the relative *absence* of these supposedly genre-defining rhetorical markers. While there are occasional references to weakness or sorrow, these instances are infrequent and less exaggerated than those in the petitions of wives and widows from the English Civil War. After the accusations in Hake's tract, the Maydens say, "We were in a very euill case, and ryght good cause had we to dread and to dispaire of oure well doings . . . wer it not that we knew ye [the mistresses] to be such as are not moued wyth euery wynde" (A3^r). So, while the Maydens begin with the humility topos, they alleviate their hardship within the same sentence. Other instances of humility are conditional ("might haue bred vs siely girles" A3^r) or very brief ("unto us your pore hand maides" B5^v).

Likewise, there are much fewer instances of such vulnerability or despair in "The Petition of the Women-Servants." In addition, when the women-servants employ imagery of weakness, they pinpoint the cause of such frailty not to their gender as a whole but as a result of their working conditions: "That to our inexpressible Grief, we dayly see when any of us are rendered Incapable to serve either through Old Age, Sickness, Infirmity, or other Accidents, we are presently exposed in an Ignominious Manner to seek our Bread, from the Charity of others." In this way, the Maydens' *Letter* and the "The Petition of the Women-Servants" take into account the intersection of gender and class in the early modern period and do not treat all women as one collective group. The differences between the rhetorical strategies of these maidservant petitioners and other women petitioners also contribute to our knowledge about the range of discursive tactics women employed in varying early modern rhetorical situations. Importantly, the de-emphasis of feminine humility topoi and the reliance on descriptions of labor highlight the significance of class and work to women's understanding of their own identity and the different ways in which they expressed that identity rhetorically.

Importantly for the concerns of this chapter, descriptions of gendered labor do not merely function as part of the argument; they also work to theorize a collective that reflects an adept employment of class consciousness as argumentative strategy. Unlike letters of petition that make requests based on the interests of individual women, these petitions make requests on behalf of collective groups. While the Maydens' *Letter* is "signed" by six women, its argument is applicable to women servants in general, and textual moments showcase the petition's awareness of its collective position. When addressing Hake, the petition asks, "For what one wise man will willingly meddle with a multitude, or contende with a whole company?" (A7^r). Furthermore, the Maydens declare, "We must then of necessitie addresse our selues to Replie in defense of our liberty, and eke of our honesty, least our silence yeld vs gilty" (A8^v). The use of the plural pronoun and the broad purposes of their writing showcase the element of collective voice that undergirds the petition. As Bell states, "Regardless of who the Maydens actually were, their defense represents itself as the voice not of a single, isolated individual, but of a group of women working together to urge their employers to resist any attempt to curtail 'their lawful libertie'" (184). The *Letter* perhaps makes this knowledge of collectivism most explicit when they note of Hake, "when he recited six of us by name, and vnder those six names aboue sixe thousand of us" (A7^r). This rhetorical move from "six" to "sixe thousand" reflects the women petitioners' awareness of their own "laboring subjectivity" (as Kendrick would say) and their willingness to deploy it on behalf of interests of women servants as a whole.

Likewise, "The Petition of the Women-Servants" makes explicit the collective interests of the document's demands: "And we judge our Condition generally much better than many of these especially considering the greatness of our number." Embedded in this phrase is not only a justification for the right of these women to speak but also an articulation of the collective identity that informs the requests they are making. They boldly state in their conclusion, "And seing this Project is of so great a Concernment not only of us, but to the City, yea the whole Nation." The collective voice that these petitions represent both justifies their existence and serves as strong evidence for the merit of their requests. Both documents also realize the extent to which serving women in early modern England constituted a political subjectivity; the women servants in both petitions leverage personal experience in order to make arguments applicable to large groups of women. Even as far back as the early modern period, it seems women were aware that "the personal is political," even if they would not word it as such.

While greater numbers behind a collective document might increase its chances of political influence, the anonymity afforded by such authorship could also help to protect individual women from attacks on their character. Elizabethan letters of petition received little resistance due to the relatively "private" nature of such documents, but printed petitions and pamphlets authored by women met harsh criticism as women attempted to participate in political matters, organize as collectives, and deliver petitions and present their bodies/voices in public space. While Sadlack chronicles well the normalcy and frequency with which individual early modern women petitioned, collectives of women petitioners often had their petitions denied *because* they were women and were frequently attacked for attempting to do so. Mihoko Suzuki, for instance, observes that the petitions of male apprentices during the English Civil War received much more acceptance than those of women: "Although

Parliament and the London Common Council took seriously and responded to petitions from apprentices, Parliament was not as receptive
to women's petitions" (152). Women petitioners were regularly turned
away with the justification that women were already represented by their
husbands. Historian Amanda Whiting describes an event in which a
women's petition that reportedly had over ten thousand signatures ap-
pended to it was agreed to be read in the House of Commons; however,
the response to the petition was hardly receptive: "that the matter you
petition about, is of an higher concernment then [sic] you understand;
that the House gave an answer to your husbands; and therefore that you
are directed to goe home, and look after your own businesse, and meddle
with your huswifery" (qtd. in Whiting, "'Some Women'" 84).

Attacks on women petitioners went beyond Parliament's unwilling-
ness to hear their claims since they were already spoken for by their
husbands. In addition, there was a large print culture of newsbooks and
pamphlets that mocked women petitioners, and satires of women's petitions were frequently published, especially during the English Civil War.
Brian Patton explores this phenomenon in his article "The Women Are
Revolting? Women's Activism and Popular Satire in the English Revolution," observing that such mock petitions "refus[e] to take seriously the
opinions of women on any topic of political or religious significance"
and "frequently blend flippant antifeminist satire with earnest pleas for
an end to fighting and a restoration of proper order in the kingdom"
(76). In such printings, misogynists often attack women petitioners as
sexually promiscuous. Such an attack was particularly likely for women
servants, since they were regarded—as Dowd describes—as especially
"sexually vulnerable and potentially disorderly singlewomen" ("Desiring
Subjects" 133), because they were away from their home and parents'
supervision. Both the Maydens' *Letter* and "The Petition of the Women-Servants" anticipate attacks on the morality of the authors, as the
Maydens defend themselves from allegations made by Hake concerning the character of maidservants, while the "Women-Servants" argue
that meeting their requests "will help in some measure to restrain [their]
Pride and vain Apparel, which too much fosters Profaneness, Immoral-
ity, and Idleness amongst [them]." In other words, they leverage the opportunity to "increase Piety and Godlyness" among women servants as a
major justification for enacting the civic demands the petition describes.

Moreover, the existence of documents like Hake's initial attack on
maidservants and the later mock petitions speaks to a reaction against

women's involvement in political discourse broadly and petitioning specifically: "such oppositional accounts nevertheless acknowledge women's active involvement as a fact of contemporary politics" (Suzuki 133). For example, "The Maids Petition" (1647) is a mock response to an ordinance that granted male apprentices but not women servants lawful recreation days. Inadvertently, though, as Suzuki discerns, "the petition unwillingly calls attention to how the apprentices' demands for their rights as workers could be, but were not, extended to the women servants who occupied analogous positions of subordination in the household" (154). The existence of women servants' petitions as well as misogynistic documents attacking and mocking such requests evidence the cultural awareness of a gendered class consciousness that could—and did—have an impact on political discourse and the public sphere.

Early modern working women's efforts to recount their own experiences of labor and leverage that as an "available means of persuasion" should be seen as a historically significant cultivation of ethos, especially given such women's rhetorical constraints. Indeed, the agency that these women yielded prompts scholars of women's rhetorics to further examine the history and continued practice of rhetorical participation in non-democratic cultures. After all, such women used their experience of lower rank and labor *in order to* argue for their political betterment, not in spite of it. Whiting describes well the contradiction inherent in the petition: "Because petitioning was an act of submission, it reaffirmed the social and political order. Because, by definition, it expressed criticism and an alternative to the present—the preferred remedy—it challenged that order" (*Women and Petitioning* 2). The petitions of early modern women servants are thus an especially rhetorically rich site, as their authors had to negotiate gender, class/rank, and the right to political participation in ways that acknowledged and navigated the complexities of their rhetorical situation. A focus on work reminds rhetoricians that there is a myriad of ways in which to "retell" the herstory of rhetoric and that the continued work to do so is well worth our labor.

NOTES

1. For a helpful overview of feminist rhetorical practices in rhetoric and composition, see Jacqueline Jones Royster and Gesa E. Kirsch.

2. For more on women and work in the early modern period, see Susan Amussen; Michelle Dowd; Eleanor Hubbard; Dowd and Natasha

Korda, editors; Patricia Fumerton; Laura Gowing; Natasha Korda; Sara Mendelson and Patricia Crawford; and Marjorie Keniston McIntosh.

3. Most prominently within contemporary scholarship, David Zaret argues that the use of petitions during the English Civil War led to the "invention" of the public sphere. For studies of women petitioners during the English Civil War, see: Patricia Higgins; Patricia-Ann Lee; Ann Marie McEntee; Mihoko Suzuki; and Amanda Whiting, *Women and Petitioning in the Seventeenth-Century English Revolution*.

4. See Stephen A. Kent and Peter Smith.

5. See especially the "Circulating Genres" section of this collection, in which Sadlack as well as Lisa Zimmerelli, Elizabeth Ellis Miller, and Adele Seeff offer compelling analyses of varying genres and the ways in which they were negotiated and remade to make arguments about gender.

6. See the introduction to this collection.

7. However, there is interesting evidence to suggest that the authorship of petitions mattered much, at least during the English Civil War period. Patricia-Ann Lee describes at least one petition circulated as a pamphlet in which the "authenticity was challenged in an investigation by the House of Commons" (248). This observation merits more scholarly inquiry to understand the significance of authorship of petitions in the period; it may also yield methodological insight into questions of authorship.

8. Such a request may have referred to Sundays (as holy days), or it may have referred to time off in general. For instance, an ordinance was passed in June 1647 that granted "lawful recreation days" to male apprentices on the second Tuesday of each month (M'Arthur 704–5).

9. Specifically, the Maydens argue for women's choice in choosing whom to marry, as well as their ability to travel around the city as desired, with emphasis on taverns and theaters. Bell provides a more thorough analysis of the Maydens' arguments as applicable to women of all classes. See also Karen Nelson's chapter in this collection.

WORKS CITED

Amussen, Susan. *An Ordered Society: Gender and Class in Early Modern England*. B. Blackwell, 1988.

Bell, Ilona. "In Defense of Their Lawful Liberty: A Letter Sent by the Maydens of London." *Women, Writing, and the Reproduction of Cul-*

ture in Tudor and Stuart Britain, edited by Mary E. Burke, Jane Donawerth, Linda L. Dove, and Karen Nelson, Syracuse UP, 2000, pp. 177–92.

Biesecker, Barbara. "Coming to Terms with Recent Attempts to Write Women into the History of Rhetoric." *Philosophy & Rhetoric*, vol. 25, no. 2, 1992, pp. 140–61.

Buchanan, Lindal. "Forging and Firing Thunderbolts: Collaboration and Women's Rhetoric." *Rhetoric Society Quarterly*, vol. 33, no. 4, 2003, pp. 43–63.

Daybell, James. "Scripting a Female Voice: Women's Epistolary Rhetoric in Sixteenth-Century Letters of Petition." *Women's Writing*, vol. 13, no. 1, 2006, pp. 3–22.

Dowd, Michelle. "Desiring Subjects: Staging the Female Servant in Early Modern Tragedy." Dowd and Korda, pp. 133–44.

—. *Women's Work in Early Modern English Literature and Culture.* Palgrave Macmillan, 2009.

—, and Natasha Korda, editors. *Working Subjects in Early Modern English Drama.* Ashgate, 2011.

Ferguson, Margaret W., and Mihoko Suzuki. "Women's Literacies and Social Hierarchy in Early Modern England." *Literature Compass*, vol. 12, no. 11, 2015, pp. 575–90.

Fumerton, Patricia. *Unsettled: The Culture of Mobility and the Working Poor in Early Modern England.* U of Chicago P, 2006.

Glenn, Cheryl. *Rhetoric Retold: Regendering the Rhetorical Tradition from Antiquity through the Renaissance.* Southern Illinois UP, 1997.

Gowing, Laura. *Domestic Dangers: Women, Words, and Sex in Early Modern London.* Oxford UP, 1996.

Higgins, Patricia. "The Reactions of Women, with Special Reference to Women Petitioners." *Politics, Religion and the English Civil War*, St. Martin's Press, 1973, pp. 179–222.

Hubbard, Eleanor. *City Women: Money, Sex, and the Social Order in Early Modern London.* Oxford UP, 2012.

"Humble Petition of Many Thovsands of Wives and Matrons of the City of London, and other parts of this Kingdome, For the Cessation and Finall Conclusion of these Civill Wars, And for the restitution and revocation of their Husbands . . . , The." London, 1643. *Early English Books Online.* https://search.proquest.com/books/humble-petition-many-thovsands-wives-matrons-city/docview/2248546431/se-2?accountid=14696 Accessed 28 Feb. 2016.

Kendrick, Matthew. *At Work in the Early Modern English Theater: Valuing Labor.* Fairleigh UP, 2015.

Kent, Stephen A. "'Hand-Maids and Daughters of the Lord': Quaker Women, Quaker Families, and Somerset's Anti-Tithe Petition in 1659." *Quaker History,* vol. 97, no. 1, 2008, pp. 32–61.

Korda, Natasha. *Labors Lost: Women's Work and the Early Modern English Stage.* U of Pennsylvania P, 2011.

Lee, Patricia-Ann. "Mistress Stagg's Petitioners: February 1642." *The Historian,* vol. 60, no. 2, 1998, pp. 241–56.

Letter sent by the Maydens of London, to the vertuous Matrones & Mistresses of the same, in the defense of their lawfull Libertie, A. London, by Henry Binneman, for Thomas Hacket, 1567.

———. *English Literary Renaissance,* vol. 14, no. 3, 1984, pp. 293–304.

Logan, Shirley Wilson. *"We Are Coming": The Persuasive Discourse of Nineteenth-Century Black Women.* Southern Illinois UP, 1999.

Love, Harold. *Attributing Authorship: An Introduction.* Cambridge UP, 2002.

M'Arthur, Ellen A. "Women Petitioners and the Long Parliament." *The English Historical Review,* vol. 24, no. 96, 1909, pp. 698–709.

"Maids Petition . . . , The." London, 1647. *Early English Books Online.* https://search.proquest.com/books/maids-petition-honourable-members-both-houses/docview/2240951382/se-2?accountid=14696 Accessed 28 Feb. 2016.

Mendelson, Sara, and Patricia Crawford. *Women in Early Modern England 1550–1720.* Clarendon Press, 1998.

McEntee, Ann Marie. "'The Uncivill-Sisterhood of Oranges and Lemons': Female Petitioners and Demonstrators, 1642–53." *Prose Studies,* vol. 14, no. 3, 1991, pp. 92–111.

McIntosh, Marjorie Keniston. *Working Women in English Society, 1300–1620.* Cambridge UP, 2005.

Miller, Carolyn R. "Genre as Social Action." *Quarterly Journal of Speech,* vol. 70, no. 2, 1984, pp. 151–67.

Patton, Brian. "The Women are Revolting? Women's Activism and Popular Satire in the English Revolution." *The Journal of Medieval and Renaissance Studies,* vol. 23, no. 1, 1993, pp. 69–87.

"Petition, v." *OED Online,* Oxford UP, Mar. 2016. Accessed 9 May 2016.

Portnoy, Alisse. "'A Right to Speak on the Subject': The U.S. Women's Antiremoval Petition Campaign, 1829–1831." *Rhetoric and Public Affairs,* vol. 5, no. 4, 2002, pp. 601–23.

Royster, Jacqueline Jones, and Gesa E. Kirsch. *Feminist Rhetorical Practices: New Horizons for Rhetoric, Composition, and Literacy Studies.* Southern Illinois UP, 2012.

Sadlack, Erin A. "Petitioning Power: The Rhetorical Fashioning of Elizabethan Women's Letters." *New Ways of Looking at Old Texts,* Vol. IV, Papers of the Renaissance English Texts Society, edited by Michael Denbo, Arizona Center for Medieval and Renaissance Studies, 2008, pp. 229–37.

Sharer, Wendy. "Genre Work: Expertise and Advocacy in the Early Bulletins of the U.S. Women's Bureau." *Rhetoric Society Quarterly,* vol. 33, no. 1, 2003, pp. 5–32.

Smith, Peter. "Handmaids of the Lord in King's Lynn and West Norfolk." *Quaker History,* vol. 102, no. 2, 2013, pp. 12–27.

Suzuki, Mihoko. "Petitioning Apprentices, Petitioning Wives." *Subordinate Subjects: Gender, the Political Nation, and Literary Form in England, 1588–1688.* Ashgate, 2003, pp. 132–64.

Thorne, Alison. "Narratives of Female Suffering in the Petitionary Literature of the Civil War Period and Its Aftermath." *Literature Compass,* vol. 10, no. 2, 2013, pp. 134–45.

—. "Women's Petitionary Letters and Early Seventeenth-Century Treason Trials." *Women's Writing,* vol. 13, no. 1, 2006, pp. 23–43.

"Unto the Right Honourable, The Lord Provost, Baillies, and Remanent members, of the Town-Council of Edinburgh. The Petition of the Women-Servants within the City." Edinburgh, 1700. *Early English Books Online.* https://search.proquest.com/books/unto-right-honourable-lord-provost-baillies/docview/2248533135/se-2?accountid=14696 Accessed 28 Feb. 2016.

Whiting, Amanda. "'Some Women Can Shift It Well Enough': A Legal Context for Understanding the Women Petitioners of the Seventeenth-Century English Revolution." *The Australian Feminist Law Journal,* vol. 21, 2004, pp. 77–100.

—. *Women and Petitioning in the Seventeenth-Century English Revolution: Deference, Difference, and Dissent.* Brepols, 2015.

Zaeske, Susan. "Signatures of Citizenship: The Rhetoric of Women's Antislavery Petitions." *Quarterly Journal of Speech,* vol. 88, no. 2, 2002, pp. 147–68.

Zaret, David. *Origins of Democratic Culture: Printing, Petitions, and the Public Sphere in Early-Modern England.* Princeton UP, 2000.

10 "With Cunning Needle Told": Working the Susanna Narrative in Seventeenth-Century Domestic Embroidery

Michele Osherow

The apocryphal story of Susanna may seem an odd choice for a collection dedicated to feminist rhetoric and circulation because among the crew of bold, articulate, and even boisterous biblical heroines, Susanna seems astonishingly silent.[1] She does have the wisdom to pray to God "with a loud voice" (*KJV*, Susanna, v. 42),[2] but she apparently makes no attempt to defend herself when faced with the malicious lies of the elders. Instead, she lets a youth do the talking for her. Contemporary feminist scholars show frustration with the character,[3] but in the early modern period Susanna was an unquestionable favorite. Tellings and retellings of her story appeared on page and stage, in music and in art. Biblical scholar Nicole Tilfold, marveling at the variety of discourse surrounding Susanna, declares her "one of the most discussed female figures in the history of biblical interpretation" (432). It is an impressive claim for a woman whose story hovers in the margins of the canon. The significant plot points of her narrative are these: Susanna, beautiful, married, and raised "according to the Law of Moses" (*KJV*, Susanna, v. 3), wants to bathe in her garden. She has just sent her handmaids to fetch oils and soaps when two lecherous elders see an opportunity they refuse to resist. They threaten Susanna, insisting she surrender to their desires or they will accuse her of adultery, a capital offense. Susanna denies the men. She reasons, "It is better for me to fall into your hands, and not doe it: then to sinne in the sight of the Lord" (v. 23). The elders immediately fabricate a tale claiming they witnessed Susanna with an unknown lover in her garden. Susanna is publicly tried and condemned to death. In desperation, she offers a prayer to God who responds by "rais[ing] vp the holy spirit of a young youth, whose name was Daniel" (v. 45). Daniel vindicates Susanna by questioning the elders separately about what they saw. The elders' lies are exposed and the two are executed for bearing false witness. All ends happily because Israel is prevented from shedding "innocent blood" on that day (v. 62).

The Susanna narrative is part of the collection of non-canonical writings contained in the Apocrypha. There are two separate sources for the narrative: the Old Greek (OG) version found in the Septuagint and the more elaborate Theodotion version consisting of sixty-four verses. The Theodotion became the dominant version of the text by the end of the second century and is the basis for the Susanna story that appears in the Geneva, King James and other early English translations.[4]

The interpretations of Susanna examined in this chapter are evidence of female rhetors' ability to craft opportunities for discourse and argument. These readings were translated by needle and circulated on linens and on silks. Susanna's narrative was among the most popular subjects for domestic embroidery of the seventeenth century (Geuter 60). Biblical themes and episodes comprise over forty-three percent of extant needlework pieces (57). Susanna, along with the biblical figures of Judith, Esther, Jael, and Ruth were most frequently represented (Snook 14). The canvases featuring these biblical women, stitched by early modern women's hands, are among the unchartered rhetorical territories Cheryl Glenn encourages us to find (4). In their needlework, embroidering women emerge as scholars in their own right, plotting female figures on the maps of both rhetorical and biblical histories, and circulating women's biblical exegesis in visual displays.

Increasingly in the last decade scholars attending to early modern women have recognized ways women's textiles are akin to women's texts. Susan Frye impressively outlines the many intersections among women's visual and verbal textualities—the links between pens and needles—and suggests that attending to products of both "presents an alternative way to read canonical literature" (Frye xvi). Frye, along with Margaret Ezell, Jennifer Munroe, Elizabeth Mazzola, and Lisa Klein, argue that through needlework women "fashioned themselves as subjects" (Klein 462). Scholars of feminist rhetorical studies have impressively championed investigation of non-traditional texts in a similar drive to recover women's voices, history, and literary practices. The disciplinary turn toward material culture lead to theorizing ways non-literary texts communicate meaning, and, explains Beth Fowkes Tobin and Maureen Daly Goggin, "signals a willingness to take seriously women's productive labor as a form of invention" (*Women and Things*, 2). Tobin and Goggin explore across several rich collections the "dynamic interplay of women, gender, culture, . . . politics and needle arts" (Goggin, *Material Culture* 2). A consistent and pronounced objective is recognizing ways stitched texts operate as "meaningful epistemic spaces" (Goggin, *Material Culture* 35). Through this lens, embroidered samplers, needlework pictures, and similarly crafted items are goods "made to be seen"—not as shows of ornament, but as active sites of meaning-making (Newell 55). What has emerged across disciplines is recognition of the needle as a technology of rhetoric, enabling embroidered pieces to function as rhetorical spaces, their patterns and stitches a means to disseminate values, establish identity, build community, and "promote women's interests" (Klein 462).

That they are specifically early modern *women's* interests promoted in domestic embroidery is an accepted matter of scholarly inference. In the seventeenth century, men were employed as professional embroiderers working within guilds; domestic embroidery, however, was increasingly fashioned as a feminine activity (Goggin, *Material Culture* 40). These works are presumed to be crafted by women, though the majority of extant pieces are unattributed. According to Carol Humphrey, Honorary Keeper of Textiles at the Fitzwilliam Museum, "To be able to give an English sampler a secure provenance is relatively unusual" (12). The lack of personal information on embroidered pictures and samplers is itself a probable sign of female authorship, offers Humphrey, because "most of the population would have considered female needle skills more important than literacy" (13). Marking needlework with a stitcher's initials or year of a work's completion became more common toward the end of the century, but those meager bits often do little to uncover a stitcher's identity.[5] Textile scholar Ruth Geuter looks to the subjects of extant embroideries and locates female preference. In her view, the rather "limited group" of biblical narratives favored in the seventeenth century suggests they were selected by women. These scriptural scenes are "characterized predominantly by their focus on women, children, and relationships between husbands and wives," she explains, with a woman often appearing as "the central figure of the story as well as the design." On pieces depicting figures of both sexes, the female is "of an equal size and interest" (59).

Seventeenth-century needlework publications leave no doubt that stitching and embroidery were presumed feminine interests. Pattern books and other guides target female readers. The preface to John Taylor's *The Needles Excellency* (1631) boasts, "this Booke, some cunning workes doth teach/ . . . / So Maides may (from their Mistresse, or their Mother)/ Learne to leaue one worke, and to learne another" (unnumbered). Taylor makes clear that needlework is practiced by women across economic and social classes, from simple maids to "mighty Queenes . . . and high-borne Ladies" (unnumbered). Education for girls emphasized needlework, though servants and others attending Dames schools were not taught the 'fancy work' learned by girls of means (Brooks, *English* 12). Taylor grounds needlework as a legacy begun in "Paradice," after which "for generation unto generation/. . . . Daughters Daughters vp did grow (. . .)/ The Needles Art, they to their children show" (unnumbered). In Taylor's text, as in behavioral guides for girls and women, needlework is linked to moral behavior and to a demonstration of religious faith.[6]

Because both work with a needle and attention to Scripture were prescribed behaviors for early modern women, some question the validity of attributing feminine agency to these stitched pieces. Lena Cowen Orlin faults needlework for making women "invisible," their "eyes dropped . . . to . . . busy hands" (183), not least, she says, because their subjects show a redundancy of themes "often from hoary Old Testament stories" (189). Yet, women made use of such stories to tremendous advantage in written texts, advancing an impressive range of arguments from the importance of mothers breast-feeding their own children, to the rights of women to preach in the church, to publish, to study mathematics and rhetoric, or to occupy a throne. Women's biblical readings often clashed with dominant interpretations, and those clashes are as palpable in their stitched texts as they are in those they printed. As Tara Hamling and Catherine Richardson write *in Everyday Objects: Medieval and Early Modern Material Culture and its Meanings*, "Protestantism's focus on the Word led inevitably to intense engagement with . . . the material form of that Word" (5).If biblical needlework is a demonstration of feminine piety, it is also something more. Within this conventional form, women found the means to explore unconventional discourse and argument. Their engagement is akin to the manipulation of genre examined by Erin Sadlack in section two of this volume. Sadlack evidences ways petitioning early modern women recalibrate genre conventions to participate in politics. Similarly, these stitching women negotiate the conventions of women's work in order to participate in biblical interpretation. I agree with Heather Pristash, Inez Schaechterle, and Sue Carter Wood who write that "needlework is not just a vehicle through which women have been constructed by dominant discourses—it is a vehicle through which women have constructed discourses of their own, ones offering a broader range of positions from which to engage dominant culture" (27). Within the culture of seventeenth-century England, no text was more dominant than the Bible. Women documented by needle their negotiations of its complex themes and narratives. Their renderings offer up an impressive form of biblical commentary.

That the early modern period recognized women's domestic embroidery as a platform for biblical readings is indicated, conveniently enough, in a poetic representation of Susanna herself. Robert Aylett's depiction of the heroine in his 1622 *Susanna: or, the arraignment of the two vniust elders* features a Susanna who sits and stitches on biblical themes:

> Of cloath which she had spun of her owne fleece;
> Yet oft to shew her skill in curious peece, / . . . /
> Where thou might see, with cunning needle told,
> The subtile serpent simple *Eue* infold.
>
> . . .
>
> But not farre off, her cunning hand contriues
> An *Antidote* which out this poison driues:
> For here the child's depainted to the life,
> That trembleth vnder faithfull *Abrams* knife (13)

Aylett presents Susanna's embroidered biblical images as glosses; one stitched narrative serving as commentary on another. The ease with which the poetic narrator considers Susanna's attention to the binding of Isaac as a remedy to Eve's transgression invites us to make similar connections among any biblical episodes juxtaposed on linen. Aylett allows biblical subjects rendered in needlework to function for his heroine as they did for his female contemporaries.[8]

Women's embroidered representations of the Bible open up biblical texts, indicate women's engagement with them and frequently contest prevailing readings. Domestically embroidered works do for Susanna what other early modern representations do not: they place her within a female community of active and observant women, offer up antidotes to the dangers threatening the story's heroine, and confirm women's abilities to engage their enemies head-on. Similar arguments are communicated across worked narratives, demonstrating in these stitched texts a recognition of female agency and activism and the assertive use of needlework as a genre through which women circulate ideas. Needleworkers embroidered the Bible literally and metaphorically; the medium invited indulgence in excess and in detail. Stitched narratives were not bound to Scriptural accuracy, and several varied and contrasting episodes may be worked into a single piece. What emerges in these liberties is a stunning complexity of ideas. That these may be communicated through a biblical narrative like Susanna's—that is, one not overtly attentive to feminine enterprise—is evidence of what Roziska Parker asserted decades ago: "embroiderers do transform materials to produce sense—whole ranges of meanings" (6). It is worth noting that the Bible itself anticipates the "material turn" taken up in literary and rhetorical studies, directing attention to women's textiles as evidence of intelligent expression. Proverbs 31 knits rhetorical potency to the needle, connecting the work of a woman's hands to the excellence of her tongue. In the description of a woman of valor, women's skills with textiles are referenced some half-dozen times.[9] She who "layeth her handes to the spindle" and "maketh fine linnen" will "openeth her mouth with wisdom" (*KJV*, Proverbs 31:19, 24, 26).

Yet, for all her wisdom, the Apocryphal Susanna appears more acted upon than active, more seen than seeing. Her heroism is rooted in her chastity and faith; these traits are admirable, certainly, but lead her to accept death rather than bring dishonor to her husband's house. It is easy to link Susanna's chaste and largely silent behavior within her narrative to the idealized feminine virtues advanced by an early modern patriarchal order.[10] Curiously, however, visual representations of Susanna produced in the period suggest that chastity was not the story's primary appeal. When we consider the celebrated representations of Susanna in paintings by Jacapo Tintoretto (1550–55, 1555, 1555–56), Giovanni Francesco Barbieri ("il Guercino") (1617), Guido Reni (1620–25), Andrea Vaccaro (1650s) and others, we understand why art historians locate in these depictions the beginning of a pleasurable indulgence in a sexualized subject (Clanton 4). (See Figures 10.1 and 10.2.) The "go to" moments for representing Susanna feature her confrontation with the elders or represent the moment immediately prior to that confrontation. In these images Susanna becomes the object of everyone's desire.

Figure 10.1: Tintoretto, Susanna and Bathing (1555–56). Eric Lessing/Art Resource, NY. ART120422. Used by permission.

Figure 10.2: Guido Reni, Susannah and the Elders (1620–5). Scala/Art Resource, NY. ART27574. Used by permission.

Such representations, argued the late John Berger, make all of us view Susanna from the perspective of the elders; we are all complicit in the elders' lust (50).[11] This perspective is key in understanding the culturally proscribed view of the narrative because rather than represent Susanna's heroism, such depictions promote empathy for the elders attracted to Susanna's beauty. "Drawn by instinct to identify more with the villains than with the heroine," explains Mary D. Garrard, artists and patrons "ignored the fundamental moral point concerning the discovery of truth and the execution of justice to focus instead on the secondary plot of temptation, seduction and the erotic escapades of the Elders" ("Artemesia and Susanna" 152–153). The use of the narrative to tease and titillate was not limited to visual displays: in 1638 George Ballard rallies an audience for his verse adaptation suggesting, "to our pleasure, let us bend *Susanna*" (Section VI, D4r). The upshot of arousing a general desire for the heroine not only diminishes the elders' foul behavior, but also presents their desire to rape as "a natural result of viewing female beauty" (Clanton 121). In this way, Susanna, a woman who chooses death before compromising her chastity, became in painting the occasion for a celebration of sexual opportunity (Garrard, *Artemesia* 84).

A piece from the V&A collection worked in embroidered silk satin with colored silks and metal purl (circa 1660, artist unknown), is set in the deceptively Edenic garden and features the key characters of Susanna, the two elders and characters who appear with great frequency in stitched renderings: her two maids.[12] (See Figure 10.3.) These maids, simply called *girls* in the Greek source texts, disappear early on from the narrative. But their presence in embroidered versions invites feminine perspective and influence in a story driven almost entirely by what men see and do. The first thing to note in this piece is the needleworker's unusual choice to present Susanna fully dressed. It may seem a nod toward modesty, but it also demonstrates competent reading. Never does Susanna actually bathe in her narrative. There is no reference to a bath at all in the OG source; the Theodotian text makes clear that the day was hot and Susanna *desired* to bathe (Septuagint, Sousanna, v.15, emphasis added). But as soon as she sends off her maids for oils and soap, the elders are fast upon her (v.19). Other biblical narratives in which men observe bathing women, such as King David observing Bathsheba (2 Samuel 11), present the woman's bathing activity explicitly, but not so here.

Figure 10.3: Susannah and the Elders, Embroidered Picture (ca. 1660) © Victoria & Albert Museum, London, T.50–1954. Used by permission.

The scene in this stitched piece precedes the men's approach, directing the viewer to anticipate crisis without modeling the elders' violence outright. The picture relies on its audience's understanding of the danger to come and parses that threat. In approaching visual representations of biblical narratives, cultural theorist and critic Mieke Bal urges a distinction between what appears and what's known. "Narrative," she writes, "encourages a projection of pre-established textual meanings on the visual work, making the work itself more difficult to see because we only see or rather project, what we already know" (316–17). In this embroidered piece, it is what we do *not* see that is surprising. These elders are unusually benign. The needleworker does not make the slightest attempt to obscure these men, who, the narrative repeatedly tells us, are hiding and spying in the garden (Susanna vv.16, 18). It is not even clear that the men arrive in pursuit of Susanna: one elder looks in Susanna's direction, the other towards her waiting women. The lack of a discernible threat from these figures invites a viewer to seek out other dangers on the canvas and one reveals itself almost at dead center. This rendering signals crisis not in the prying eyes of men, but in the turning heel of a woman. The maid's exposed foot is the 'pivotal' image, emphasizing the threat that comes on the heels of the two maids' departure. The casual act of women turning their backs on one another yields opportunity to the elders. The importance of the maid's turn is highlighted by the tension it provokes in the stitched piece: the maid in yellow pulls at her companion by the arm; nonetheless, the second maid stands firm. The viewer who recognizes the scene knows that the narrative requires both women to leave the garden. But in freezing the action at this moment the needleworker asserts how vital is the presence of those maids. She uses an ancient text to signal to her contemporaries that a female community is key to women's safety. The choice confirms a rhetorical function of needlework as a platform upon which "women construct discourses with the potential to expand . . . the power they wield over their own lives" (Pristash et al.13). It is this moment of Susanna's story that the embroiderer chose to preserve with her needle, and to frame in materials more elaborate than those used to chronicle the scene.[13] We see in this single stitched narrative a number of rhetorical practices attributed to women throughout this collection. This needleworker engages in kairotic intervention in her depiction of the scene, a rhetorical opportunism similarly identified in the essays of this volume by Jessica Enoch, Nabila Hijazi, Ruth Osorio, and Adele Seeff. An emphasis on female community as a path to female resistance emerges as a theme in the work of Hijazi and Osorio.

The V&A's embroidered Susanna goes further to emphasize feminine potential by displacing male privilege as it appears in the narrative. The elders' sight of Susanna triggers the plot and the story builds continuously on verbs of perception: the elders *see*, they *look*, they *watch*, they *spy* (*KJV*, Susanna vv. 8, 9, 12, 15, 16, 20, 38, 39) while the women's sight is essentially blank, defined by what they do *not* see. But this embroidered picture shifts the power of the gaze and depicts women clearly watching one another, and it is under that gaze that Susanna is protected. The responsibility to maintain Susanna's safety is passed on to any who view the picture because the extended feminine gaze lands, ultimately, with us. The feminine gaze is an invitation into the scene initiated by the maid in yellow, passed to the maid in pink, and delivered out from the canvas by Susanna. As John Elkins explains, in visual art the gaze extending out from a canvas "functions as an invitation or communication" positioning the viewer in relationship to the depicted scene ("Visual"). Susanna's direct gaze out from the needlework situates the viewer with respect to those figures, aligning us with the narrative's female community and not with the story's transgressors.

The women's engagement with one another is reflected, too, in their show of hands. References to hands are significant in the Susanna text. Part of the ironic wordplay in the narrative is that the elders who desire to lay their hands on Susanna in a sexual sense make due with laying their hands on her in a legal one. The men specifically "lay their hands on her head" (*KJV*, Susanna v.34); it is a phrase borrowed from Leviticus to indicate that they bear witness against her (24:14). But in this embroidered piece they are women's hands that are impossible to ignore. These hands actively pull, hold, or reach out in care of one another (even if the two maids understand this care differently). The elders' hands are all but invisible in the folds of their robes. The women's helpful hands are a notable contrast to the hazards Susanna locates specifically in the hands of the elders: "For if I doe this thing, it is death vnto me: and if I doe it not, *I cannot escape your hands*" (*KJV*, Susanna v.22, emphasis added). The elders' hands metonymically indicate all that is dangerous about them; they carry a threat that is at once sexual and spiritual, domestic and social.

The V&A piece variously signals feminine alliance through the women's close proximity to one another, their gazing on one another, and their hands-on care of one another. That alliance is driven home in the needleworker's extraordinary choice to make these women's faces look exactly alike. We are prevented from attributing this to limited skill because the stitcher modifies the faces of the two elders well enough. The shared features on the faces of the women makes Susanna's appearance completely unremarkable, voiding any claim that the elders' immoral behavior was the upshot of Susanna's particular, exceptional beauty. The tendency to fault Susanna's beauty for the elders' transgression is clear: Aylett's poetic history itemizes Susanna's parts, concluding any "reasonable man turnes senselesse beast" with the heavenly sight of her (17). A 1663 commentary, credits Susanna's "bodily beauty" with provoking "impure solicitations, the usual temptation and attendant of rarity" (Waterhouse 272). The woman stitching this piece invalidates— more, exposes the absurdity of— such assertions. The presentation of a Susanna indistinguishable from her maids carries, too, the unsettling reminder that all women are vulnerable to the "voyeurism, blackmail, [and] slander" of sexual and other predators (Frye 140). Such a reminder is potentially among those rhetorically coded forms of meaning shared among a select audience. Needlework, according to Pristash, Schaechter-le, and Wood "needs to be read as a frequently coded practice;" it enabled women "to make the statements that they needed to make . . . to the people they wanted to talk to" (15).

There is a clear sensitivity toward vulnerability in embroidered Susannas. A resistance to that vulnerability, as well as a sense that women are best at watching one another's backs, may have inspired the design of another embroidered Susanna, silk on silk (circa 1650, artist unknown). (See Figure 10.4.) This center image shows Susanna as she is commonly depicted in visual representations. The image likely comes from Gerard de Jode's illustrated two-volume Bible *Thesaurus Sacrarum Historiarum Veteris Testamenti* (1585), a popular source for needlework representations of biblical subjects (Arthur 79).[15] Susanna is shown nude in her bath.

Figure 10.4: Susannah and the Elders (mid 17th Century, n.d.) Stephen & Carol Huber. Antique Samplers, Old Saybrook, CT. Used by permission.

The elders already have their hands on her; the garden gates are shut. In this rendering, Susanna's handmaids appear as dots retreating in the distance. But the lost attention of the two girls of the narrative is replaced by a heroic regiment of substitutes that frame Susanna's central image.

From the top left: Deborah, Jael, Judith and Esther. Their figures and histories function as glosses for Susanna's own. The extension of the floral motif out from Susanna's garden and into the populated frame provides a visual link between Susanna and this sisterhood, urging connections among the women's histories.

The needleworker, too, is a part of the rhetorical display. Among the epistemic constructions to be mapped in women's textiles are individual and community identities. The embroiderer responsible for grouping Susanna with Deborah, Jael, Judith, and Esther experiments with both. The feminine community she fashions from the pages of the Old Testament advertises guts more than it does God. Susanna's chastity will be replaced by risk, silence by judgment. The woman stitching such a piece engages in a show of femininity via her needle while using that needle to reshape ideas of what constitutes the feminine. Her own constitution is implicated in the shift. If, for example, stitching linens for a hope chest is a rhetorical act that signals readiness for marriage, what sort of readiness shows itself when needle-sized weapons are stitched into delicate hands?[16]

Susanna's helpless and exposed body is a marked contrast to the fiercely appareled bodies of the heroic women in each corner of the work. Among the framing elements that are so impressive are the women's shows of power. In their hands we see weapons, armor, a scepter, and a severed head. If we seek out a visual complement in Susanna's hands, we find the breasts she tries to cover. This arrangement constructs Susanna's naked body as a weapon. Her position in center reminds us that three of the four framing heroines use their bodies and the promise (and/ or deliverance) of sex to bring down Israel's enemies. Jael invites Sisera into her tent with a suggestive "Turne in, my lord, turne in to me, feare not" (*KJV*, Judges 4.18)—"turn in" being a euphemism for sex in the Bible.[17] Deborah's celebration of Sisera's fall between Jael's legs frames the general's defeat in sexually emasculating terms (5.27),[18] as does Jael's penetration of Sisera's body with her tent peg (4.22). Jael's act is an inversion of rape; she performs the sort of violence that often marks male victory in the Bible.[19] Judith famously beguiles Holofernes in order to behead him. She is able to approach her victim unguarded in his tent because "he desired her greatly . . . from the day that he had seene her" (*KJV*, Judith 12.16).[20] Esther, who will save her people and promote the destruction of thousands of Israel's enemies, enters her narrative in response to a cattle-call for beauties to help King Ahasuerus forget the wife he banished (*KJV*, Esther 2:1–8). Esther anoints herself with oils and other beauty products for a full year (v. 12) before earning her place in a procession of virgins, each on their way "vnto the kings house" where "[i]n the euening she went, and on the morrow . . . returned into the . . . house . . . which kept the concubines" (*KJV,* Esther 2:13–14). Viewed through these heroine's narratives, Susanna's nakedness denies any show of feminine vulnerability, rather, it works as a tool to expose male vulnerability and corruption.

The prophetess Deborah's methods are different from the rest, but she, too, is deliberately tied to Susanna in this embroidery. Deborah is presented in her narrative seated "vnder a palme tree" (*KJV,* Judges 4.5). In the center of this piece Susanna also appears under a tree, and though the figures of Susanna and elders imitate the de Jode illustration, no tree appears in the de Jode. Deborah's tree symbolizes her judicial authority; it is there that the "children of Israel came vp to her for iudgment" (*KJV,* v.5). To place Susanna beneath a tree invites us to recognize her capacity for judgment; and judge she does. When confronted with the elders' threat, Susanna determines: "It is better for me to fall into your hands . . . then to sinne in the sight of the Lord" (*KJV,* Susanna v. 23). In the moment following, the heroine continues to perform as a judge and prophetess might. As soon as Susanna elects to favor virtue, we read, "With that Susanna cried with a loud voice" (*KJV,* v. 24). Her cry is a human enough response, but it is also essential in a legal sense. According to Deuteronomy 22, a woman's scream indicates an unwanted sexual encounter; it could make a difference between a woman's life and death by stoning (vv. 22–25). Though she is called neither judge nor prophetess in her narrative, Susanna knows how to voice what's right in a given situation.

Susanna is often criticized for her lack of testimony at her trial (Bach 68), but she is not altogether silent. Susanna cries out, twice. She does speak in her narrative, though not to the judges who condemn her. She addresses a higher authority: "Then Susanna cried out with a loud voice and said: O euerlasting God. . . . Thou knowest that they haue borne false witnesse against me" (*KJV,* Susanna vv. 42–43). Though Susanna says little, her linguistic success is clear. The narrative explicitly states, "And the Lord heard her voice" (*KJV,* v.44). Young Daniel's entry into the narrative is evidence of God's hearing (v. 45). The necessity and potency of Susanna's voice was obvious enough to at least one early modern needleworker. In an embroidered piece at the Metropolitan Museum of Art (circa 1600–1625, artist unknown), a Susanna is shown flailing her arms in a clumsy effort to exit her bath and, most importantly, to avoid her attackers. (See Figure 10.5.) Her tiny circle of a mouth is open, implying a vocal correlative to the physical resistance she displays. This rendering engages Susanna in a discourse without end; we are invited to imagine a continual epideictic expression bent on blame. The embroidery suggests a causal relationship between women's rhetorical activities that scholars will articulate four centuries later: that engagement in one form of rhetoric prompts women toward other rhetorical turns (Pristash et al. 21).

Figure 10.5: Cushion with Susanna and the Elders (1600–1625). The Metropolitan Museum of Art. Used by permission.

Linking Susanna with such active and outspoken heroines as Deborah, Jael, Judith and Esther contradicts readings like Edward Waterhouse's, who commends Susanna for a faith that translates to inaction:

> But honest soul and wife as she was, she trusted in *God* for the right of her wrong, and the asserter of her innocence; no *Amazonian* raving, or masculine indignation, shews she to them; . . . nor did she with a *Iael*-like fortitude dissemble her anger, till she had them under the perpendicular of her fatal revenge; she did not endeavour her defence by arguments impotent to it. (274)

Exposure of the elders, the climax of Susanna's story, is, as Waterhouse notes, God's business. And God makes it Daniel's by assigning him that privilege. But embroidered Susannas suggest that this, too, could be otherwise. In piece after stitched piece, the women who serve and surround Susanna appear to know more than the maids within the textual narrative are permitted to say. In an open cut and drawn work from the Ashmolean Museum (mid-to-late seventeenth century, artist unknown), Susanna's handmaid clearly witnesses the elders accosting her mistress. (See Figure 10.6.)

Figure 10.6: Susanna and the Elders, WA2014.71.9 (17th century, n.d.) © Ashmolean Museum, University of Oxford. Used by permission.

But this needleworker confirms both the maid's and Susanna's linguistic silence by denying mouths to the female figures, a choice that serves as a strong visual reminder of women's rhetorical constraints and lack of access to "esteemed rhetorical spaces" as described in the introduction to this collection. The embroidered picture is itself a new rhetorical terri- tory that would cultivate women's rhetorical production, demonstrating how circulation of discourse is affected by the rhetor's gender identifi- cation. Put simply, the embroidered pieces make clear that there is more than one way for a woman to tell her story. What the needleworker curbs in speech, she confers through industry: her stitched maid has notice- ably and unusually large hands. Susanna's hands are proportionate to her body; the elders' hands are enormous, club-like, echoing their threat to Susanna in the narrative. What distinguishes the hands of the watchful maid are her apparently nimble fingers.

The maid's fingers prompt us to consider not only the textiles craft- ed by women's hands, but the *act* of marking in which the hands are engaged. Rhetorical scholars attend to process and product as a means to uncover intentionality of material texts. Though critical focus is predominantly toward the marks that are "readable" as text, Pristash, Schaechterle, and Wood characterize textile arts as rhetorically mean- ingful "both through their products and their practice" (16). In the Ash- molean piece, the maid's surprising hands and fingers combined with the women's conspicuously missing mouths compound Susanna's nar- rative so that the "practice," of working a needle becomes part of the "product," or story being told. In this rendering, Susanna encounters two distinct threats: one presents itself in the form of lustful elders, the other in the absence of the heroine's mouth. In the narrative, the elders exploit the ancient world's requirement for female chastity, threatening to slander Susanna with adultery if she denies them sexually. From an early modern perspective, Susanna's chastity is affirmed by her silence. Nevertheless, her inability to speak increases the danger within this scene. She is denied the means to protest. Her scream, the necessary indicator of sexual menace, is stifled. Legally, this Susanna's virtue has already been compromised. Her inability to tell her own story—to pro- test or even to pray—stresses the necessity of alternative discourses for women's narratives, and insists, particularly, on the value of texts worked by needle. The remarkable hands of the silent maid heighten an aware- ness of the practice described by Pristash, Schaechterle, and Wood. The maid's fingers are primed to tell what the women may not speak. The elders' manipulations of Susanna will be remedied through a woman's manipulation of a needle. Needlework is described by Jennifer Weardon as the "power to perform magic" through the movement of the hand (Weardon 129). Goggin defines that magic as knowledge (bodily cognitive, kinetic, and more) (*Material Culture* 5). The hands that crafted the Ashmolean Susanna reveal a knowledge not only of how to tell stories but also how to move them forward, so that we see both circulation and education in action on a single canvas. The needleworker extends the significance of Susanna's tale to another story worked on the linen. The co-mingled narratives restore potency to women represented in and beyond the embroidered work; Jessica Enoch tracks similar emphases on the juxtaposition of female image and allusion in her examination in the closing chapter of this section.

Continued feminine agency is demonstrated in the embroidered panel directly beneath Susanna's; featured there are two mermaids, two ships, and two props of vanity: a mirror and hair comb. At a glance, the association of Susanna with mermaids may look like a show of sympathy for the elders, as though they are as vulnerable in the top panel as the ships' imagined sailors are beneath. Mermaids and sirens were interchangeable in the Renaissance (Pedersen 12); linking Susanna's narrative to a siren scene may imply that her appeal is similarly irresistible and deadly.[21] But the marriage of these scenes does more than warn against the hazards of feminine beauty. It asserts the magnitude of female power and indicates the consequences awaiting those who deny or otherwise wrong it. The piece demonstrates connections made through circulation of women's stories. Juxtaposing Susanna's narrative to a siren legend connotes a brand of universal justice. Susanna's encounter with the elders, and the encounters of sirens with innumerable sailors, all occur in or before a backdrop of water. The paired scenes suggest that the wrong done to one woman in her private bath may be avenged exponentially on men in waters that are uncontained, and by an army both feminine and devastating.[22] The capacity to devastate is extended to women beyond the embroidered panel and its stitched shores. The sea-maids recruit to their ranks through the use of a hand mirror turned directly out from the worked linen. The mirror shows a reflected face not unlike that of the mermaids, but its position makes a reflection of either mermaid impossible. Instead, it offers a mock-reflection of any feminine face that inspects the embroidered piece. In this way, all who witness the abuse of feminine virtue are in implicated in the active redress of it. We might describe such a rhetorical measure as the circulation of obligation.

The use of the mirror—a stock symbol of female vanity—is refigured radically in this piece. Mirrors appear in numerous Susanna paintings including several by Tintoretto (*Susanna and the Elders* ca. 1550–55, *Susanna and the Elders*, ca.1555–56), Abraham Janssens ([by or after], *Susanna and the Elders*, early seventeenth century), Cornelisz van Haarlem (*Susanna and the Elders*, 1599) and others. In these, Susanna either holds a mirror, gazes at her reflection in a mirror, or is positioned beside a mirror that has been, or will be, used. It showcases conceit—a vanity that diminishes the elders' wrongs and highlights Susanna's instead.[23] Dan W. Clanton, for example, believes Tintoretto's 1555–56 painting of a self-admiring Susanna prompts viewers to consider, "If Susanna is so involved with her beauty, one might wonder how this Susanna would respond to the elders' advances" (125). (See Figure 10.1.) The pleasure Susanna takes in her own bare image hints at inclinations toward female sexuality and indulgence more generally. That Susanna's recognition of her beauty is enough to justify the elders' perverse intentions is made explicit in a sixteenth-century canvas by a follower of Lambert Sustris. The image presents one elder thrusting a mirror before Susanna's eyes; her sight of her own reflection is intended to legitimize the elders' aim (*Susanna and the Elders*). Susanna appears caught in that mirror, Medusa-like, by her own image. Framing her as a kind of Medusa shifts the locus of danger away from the elders bent on abuse and onto the woman "who is able to kill . . . just by looking, and being looked at" (Bal 289). The impulse to trap Susanna with her own reflection binds her to the Medusa myth and to the terror of confronting what Bal describes as "an ideology that turns women into monsters" (291).[24]

The call to bear witness to this injustice announces itself in Susanna embroideries. Again and again one or more of the maids appear in the landscape behind the elders' encounter with Susanna. Though there is no narrative equivalence of this presentation, the maids, curiously, announce their presence with raised hands. (See Figures 10.7 and 10.8.) The self-consciousness of the women's displayed hands is significant. It underscores the value of raised hands to this (or any) story being worked by needle, and at the same time, thwarts the elders' intentions. In an embroidered Susanna from the Metropolitan Museum of Art, the classic declarative gesture assigned to the elder on the left suggests that he's pursuing those intentions even now (Figure 10.7): "Behold, the garden doores are shut, that no man can see vs, and we are in loue with thee: therefore consent vnto vs, and lie with vs" (*KJV*, Susanna v. 20).

Figure 10.7: Susanna and the Elders (mid-17th century, n.d.) The Metropolitan Museum of Art, New York. Used by permission.

Figure 10.8: Detail. From Susanna and the Elders (mid-17th century, n.d.) The Metropolitan Museum of Art, New York. Used by Permission.

The text toys with the male privilege of sight: *"Behold,"* he begins, "no man can see us" (*KJV* v. 20, emphasis added). And in the written text, that's so. But when the narrative becomes a visual subject, elements of the story are refigured. Rather than deny the dramatic function of our own visual engagement, these renderings recruit us as foils to the elders, making exquisite use of the medium into which Susanna's story is translated. Each glance at this work bucks the elders' claim. *We can see them.* That embroidered maid raises a hand as if to say, "*I* can see them; and I can see you seeing them too." Susanna's deliverance, ultimately, is sourced from a woman's extended hand. Moreover, the frequency with which Susanna's maids are depicted in this way underscores the idea that launches this volume. The collection's editors reference Laurie Gries, who argues that circulation of "people, ideas, images, and discourse" increases the strength of an argument as it "move[s] through the world and enter[s] various associations" (12). The popularity of the "waving maid" figure suggests that early modern needleworkers recognized a similar rhetorical phenomenon.

Because the figure of the waving maid has no parallel moment in the written text, her signaling pervades the narrative sequence on display. In the first of the pieces from the Metropolitan Museum of Art (Figure 10.7) the maid's raised hand complements the hand raised on the opposite side of the canvas. That second raised hand (which I take to be Daniel's) clutches a stone to be hurled at the exposed elders. The maid's hand both anticipates and echoes that performance. It advertises female might and action, revising the biblical narrative in a way that reshapes women's contributions to it; textual revisions bolstering female agency and the potential of female leadership are similarly addressed in Adele Seeff's essay in section two. The attention to maids' hands in Susanna renderings drives home a practical truth: whose hand but a woman's tied the elders to that tree, or closed each finger around the stone in each fist? The woman's raised hand demonstrates women's readiness to participate and to punish. The narrative suggests this is as it should be: a death by stoning requires the hands of the all the community because it is the community that has been wronged.

The elders' affront to their community was their malicious treatment of Susanna, a woman Daniel celebrates as a Daughter of Judah (v. 57). It is a title that wholly affirms her righteousness: Judah, the first man in the Bible to admit that he was wrong, made that admission to his daughter-in-law by publicly stating צָדְקָה מִמֶּנִּי, "she is more in the right than I" (*Jewish Publication Society*, Genesis 38:26). Susanna is double-bound to her Daughter of Judah title, not only through her righteousness but also through the heritage indicated in the narrative's opening verses: "There dwelt a man in Babylon, called Ioacim / And hee tooke a wife, whose name was Susanna" (*KJV*, Susanna vv. 1–2). The presence of Jews in Babylon was due to the defeat of the Kingdom of Judah by the Babylonians in the sixth century BCE. Susanna's story takes place in Babylon. Though she bathes in the waters there rather than weeps by them, the history and sentiment found in Psalm 137 is never far removed from early modern consideration of her character. Ballard has his Susanna reciting this psalm even as the elders gaze upon her because she "wont (while bathing in the silver, spring) / This sequent Psalme most frequently to sing" (Sect. VII, Ev); the poet includes a verse paraphrase of Psalm 137's full text (Er). Other retellings quote parts of the psalm, and commentary cites the psalm's references to water and to tears (Bentley, *Fifth Lamp*, 92).

Renaissance theologians regularly used Susanna's story to illustrate God's remembrance of the faithful (Anderson cii). Embroidered pieces provoke remembrance of a kind as well, though I am not sure that it is faith we are directed to recall. Time and again, what is depicted in stitched Susannas is the story of a woman being threatened or molested just beyond her door. Susanna's enemies are domestic; the elders have repeatedly visited her home (vv. 5–6); they are men her community deems virtuous and who have been honored with titles (v. 5). Remembrance is also at the core of Psalm 137, and the repeated association of Susanna's story with that psalm infuses her narrative with an appeal to memory. The psalm's text specifically links remembrance to anticipation of vengeance and destruction:

> Remember, O Lord, the children of Edom, in the day of Ierusalem; who sayd, rase it, rase it: euen to the foundation thereof.
>
> O daughter of Babylon, who art to be destroyed: happy shall he be that rewardeth thee, as thou hast serued vs. Happy shall he be that taketh and dasheth thy little ones against the stones. (*KJV*, vv. 7–9)

If the time-intensive act of embroidery affords a woman an opportunity for contemplation of the texts she plots by needle, then she who worked Susanna's brief narrative would attend to themes of Psalm 137 as well. Parker maintained that an embroiderer's silence and concentration provided "a kind of autonomy" (10). That idea is born out in Aylett's description of his Susanna who engages in holy contemplation while at her needle: "Oft reads she . . . some holy Hymne of praise, / Yet neuer from their worke her fingers stayes" (14). It's hard to resist thinking about the ease with which the woman embroidering Susanna's story might slip into the role of bartering psalmist, particularly at v.5: "If I forget thee O Ierusalem: let my right hand forget her cunning" (*KJV*, Ps. 137). How might that verse have turned in the mind of the woman stitching her bit of Babylon? The cunning of her hands is so much in evidence, confirming her remembrance of all the right things. With each stitch, the embroiderer works a deal for vengeance: not just on Susanna's enemies, but on all those who compromise the safety of our gardens.

NOTES

1. Special thanks to Dr. David Rosenbloom (University of Maryland, Baltimore County) for his generous assistance with translation of the Septuagint, to Elisabeth Murray of the V&A Clothworkers' Centre, and Dana Macmillan of the Ashmolean Museum for their kind assistance with special collections.

2. Unless otherwise noted, all biblical citations reference *The Holy Bible, King James Version* (1611) 400th Anniversary Edition (Henderson Publishers, Inc., 2010), abbreviated as *KJV*.

3. Alice Bach, for example, describes Susanna as "naked and powerless in front of her enemies, she needs to be rescued, re-covered, by the young Daniel," p. 131. For a discussion of the male gaze and Susanna's objectification within the narrative, see Glancy.

4. The Theodotion text is believed to be an adaptation of the OG, though scholars no longer date the Theodotion from the mid-second century CE, the accepted date for the activity of Theodotion. Instead, the text appears to originate in the middle of the first century BCE. See the discussion of dating Susanna texts in Clanton, pp. 32–41.

5. According to Carol Humphrey, American samplers from this period tend to display more personal information than contemporary English examples. Humphrey atttributes this to the "understandable wish . . . for an immigrant family to be seen as firmly establishing itself in a new land," p. 12.

6. For a sampling of texts in which feminine piety and morality is linked to needlework see Woolley; and A. Walker, p. 34.

7. Previously, I have examined early modern references to biblical women in written/printed texts, looking specifically to ways the Bible

was used to debate, challenge, and confirm female agency and women's linguistic authority. See Osherow, *Biblical Women's Voices*.

8. Taylor extols needlework as a virtuous activity and links that praise to a biblical source in his poem "The Praise of the Needle," unnumbered page. Aylett, too, demonstrates how female virtue is learned through needlework as Susanna embroiders the stories of biblical heroines such as Miriam and Deborah and "The Liues of choisest Dames of Iewish nation." According to Aylett, hands occupied with a needle do not impede the activities of the stitcher's mind: "Her hands with vse so cunning were become, / That though her eyes lookd off, her worke was done," p. 14.

9. In Proverbs 31, a virtuous woman engages with textiles in verses 13, 19 , 22, 24. See *KJV*.

10. I refer, of course, to the cultural prescripts of chastity, silence and obedience, designated by Robert Greene as the "three especial vertues necessary to . . . euery vertuous woman," sig. i.

11. A viewer's complicity with the elders is understood in images like il Guercino's *Susanna and the Elders* (1617) in which one elder "hushes" viewers by looking directly out from the canvas with a finger to his lips. An elder does the same to Susanna in the *Reni Susanna and the Elders* (1620–25); see Figure 10.2.

12. According to Baker and Richardson, the presence of Susanna's maids in paintings is unusual; "on the contrary, Susanna is almost always portrayed in a suggestive manner, flanked by the Elders," p. 299.

13. The most expensive materials in this piece appear in the frame surrounding the Susanna illustration. V&A Clothworkers' Center staff indicate that the frame was likely the work of a professional embroiderer given its similarity to other frames in the collection. There is no evidence that the Susanna illustration was made by the hands responsible for the frame or by any professional needleworker.

14. The Greek verbs of perception translated here are *paratereo* and *horao*.

15. According to Morrall, most of the needlework on biblical themes are based on patterns drawn from de Jode, which suggests that "a very limited number of workshops were engaged in the supply of designs" (p. 225). Geuter also notes that Jean de Tourne's *Quadrins Historiques de la Bible* provided models for embroidered scenes (p. 57).

16. In their discussion of needlework as a vehicle to establish gender, Pristash, Schaechterle and Wood offer up the image of a young woman embroidering sheets for a hope chest and describe the work as a "rhetor-

ical display of readiness for marriage," p. 17.

17. Alter detects a sexual double meaning in Jael's beckoning, and notes that Jael's language is used elsewhere in the Bible to refer to a man's sexual entry, p. 49.

18. The Hebrew word for "foot," רגל (*regel*), also means "leg." The plural (*regaliym*) is a biblical euphemism for both male and female genitalia.

19. A reminder that rape commonly accompanies male military victory in the Bible appears at the close of Deborah's song, several verses after the prophetess praises Jael: "Haue they not diuided the pray to euery man a damosell or two?" See *KJV*, Judges 5:30.

20. The narrative details Judith's regimen designed to allure: she discards her widow's weeds, sweetens herself with ointments, braids her hair, and adorns herself with accessories and "garments of gladness" prior to approaching the enemy's camp. See *KJV*, Judith 10:3.

21. According to Browne, men's eyes were incapable of turning from mermaids. Ch XIX, no pagination.

22. Brooks reads the mermaids as representing uncontrolled female sexuality, concluding "Certainly, the Elders' uncontrolled lust ultimately resulted in their deaths," *Feller Collection*, p. 53.

23. Susanna does instruct her maids to bring her "oile and washing bals" (KJV, Susanna v. 17) which may be taken to demonstrate her vanity; it is worth noting, however, that similar products are used by biblical heroines Judith and Esther. See Judith 10.3 and Esther 2.12.

24. Ballard, too, invites Medusa into his poetic history of Susanna in a warning against lustful indulgences. Med. V, D2[r].

WORKS CITED

Alter, Robert. *The Art of Biblical Poetry*. Basic Books, 1985.

Anderson, Anthony. *A godlie sermon, preached on Newe yeeres day*. Thomas Purfoote, 1576.

Aylett, Robert. *Susanna: or, the arraignment of the two vniust elders*. Iohn Teague, 1622.

Bach, Alice. *Women, Seduction, and Betrayal in Biblical Narrative*. Cambridge UP, 1997.

Baker, Malcolm, and Brenda Richardson. *A Grand Design: Art of the Victoria and Albert Museum*. V&A Publications, 1999.

Bal, Mieke. *A Mieke Bal Reader*. U of Chicago P, 2006.

Ballard, George. *The History of Svsanna Compiled according to the Prophet Daniel.* Thomas Harper, 1638.

Bentley, Thomas. *The Monument of Matrons.* H. Denham, 1582.

Brooks, Mary. *English Embroideries.* John Horne Publications, 2004.

Brooks, Mary M., Elizabeth Feller, and Jacqueline Holdsworth, editors. *Michael and Elizabeth Feller: The Needlework Collection: 1.* Needleprint, 2011.

Browne, Thomas. *Pseudodoxia Epidemica.* T. H., 1646.

Clanton, Dan W. *The Good, the Bold, and the Beautiful: The Story of Susanna and its Renaissance Interpretations.* T&T Clark, 2006.

Elkins, James. "'The End of the Theory of the Gaze': The Visual How it is Studied." *JamesElkins.com.* www.jameselkins.com/index.php/essays/217-end-of-the-theory-of-the-gaze. Accessed 20 October 2017.

Frye, Susan. *Pens and Needles: Women's Textualities in Early Modern England.* U of Pennsylvania P, 2010.

Garrard, Mary D. "Artemesia and Susanna." *Feminism and Art History: Questioning the Litany,* edited by Norma Broude and Mary D. Garrard, Harper & Row, 1982, pp. 146–71.

—. *Artemisia Gentileschi Around 1622: The Shaping and Reshaping of an Artistic Identity.* U of California P, 2001.

Geuter, Ruth. "Embroidered Biblical Narratives and Their Social Context." *English Embroidery from the Metropolitan Museum of Art, 1580–1700,* edited by Andrew Morrall and Melinda Watt, Yale UP, 2009, pp. 57–77.

Glancy, Jennifer A. "The Accused: Susanna and Her Readers." *A Feminist Companion to the Bible: Esther, Judith and Susanna,* edited by Athalya Brenner, Sheiffeld, Academic Press, 1995, pp. 288–302.

Glenn, Cheryl. *Rhetoric Retold: Regendering the Tradition from Antiquity through the Renaissance.* Southern Illinois UP, 1997.

Goggin, Maureen Daly, and Beth Fowkes Tobin, editors. *Women and the Material Culture of Needlework and Textiles, 1750–1950.* Ashgate Publishing, 2009.

—, editors. *Women and Things,1750–1950: Gendered Material Strategies.* Ashgate Publishing, 2009.

Greene, Robert. *Penelope's Web.* London, 1587.

Gries, Laurie E. "Circulation as an Emerging Threshold Concept." *Circulation, Writing, and Rhetoric,* edited by Laurie Gries and Collin Gifford Brooke, Utah State UP, 2018, pp. 3–26.

Hamling, Tara, and Catherine Richardson. *Everyday Objects: Medieval and Early Modern Material Culture and its Meanings.* Ashgate Publishing, 2010.

The Holy Bible, King James Version (1611) 400th Anniversary Edition. Henderson Publishers, 2010.

Humphrey, Carol. *Sampled Lives: Samplers from the Fitzwilliam Museum; Accomplishment, Identity, Education & Employment.* Fitzwilliam Museum Enterprises, 2017.

Jewish Publication Society. *Hebrew-English Tanakh (1917).* JPS, 2001.

Klein, Lisa M. "Your Humble Handmaid: Elizabethan Gifts of Needlework." *Renaissance Quarterly,* vol. 50, no. 2, Summer, 1997, pp. 459–93.

Levine, Amy-Jill. "'Hemmed in on Every Side': Jews and Women in the Book of Susanna." *A Feminist Companion to the Bible: Esther, Judith and Susanna,* edited by Athalya Brenner, Sheiffeld Academic Press, 1995, pp. 303–23.

Morrall, Andrew, and Melinda Watt, editors. *English Embroidery from the Metropolitan Museum of Art, 1580–1700.* Yale UP, 2009.

Newell, Aimee E. "Tattered to Pieces: Amy Fiske's Sampler and the Changing Roles of Women in Antebellum New England." *Women and the Material Culture of Needlework and Textiles, 1750–1950,* edited by Maureen Daly Goggin and Beth Fowkes Tobin, Ashgate Publishing, 2009, pp. 51–68.

Orlin, Lena Cowen. "Three ways to be Invisible in the Renaissance: Sex, Reputation and Stitchery." *Renaissance Culture and the Everyday,* edited by Patricia Fumerton and Simon Hunt, U of Pennsylvania P, 1999, pp. 183–203.

Osherow, Michele. *Biblical Women's Voices in Early Modern England.* Ashgate Publishing, 2009.

Parker, Rozika. *The Subversive Stitch: Embroidery and the Making of the Feminine (1984).* I. B. Tauris, 2010.

Pedersen, Tara E. *Mermaids and the Production of Knowledge in Early Modern England.* Routledge, 2015.

Pietersma, Albert, and Benjamin G. Wright, editors. *A New English Translation of the Septuagint.* Oxford, 2007.

Pristash, Heather, Inez Schaechterle and Sue Carter Wood, "The Needle as the Pen: Intentionality, Needlework and the Production of Alternate Discourses of Power." *Women and the Material Culture of Needle-*

work and Textiles, 1750–1950, edited by Maureen Daly Goggin and Beth Fowkes Tobin, Ashgate Publishing, 2009, pp. 15–27.

Snook, Edith. *Women, Beauty and Power in Early Modern England: A Feminist Literary History.* Palgrave Macmillan, 2011.

Taylor, John. *The Needles Excellency: A New Booke wherin are diuers Admirable Workes wrought with the Needle.* James Baler, 1631.

Tilford, Nicole. "Susanna and Her Interpreters." *Women's Bible Commentary*, edited by Carol Newsom, Sharon Ringe, and Jacqueline Lapsley. 3rd ed., Westminster John Knox, 2012, pp. 432–35.

Ulrich, Laurel Thatcher "Of pens and needles: Sources in Early American History." *The Journal of American History*, vol. 77, June 1990, pp. 200–07.

Waterhouse, Edward. *Fortescutus illustratus, or, A commentary on that nervous treatise, De laudibus legum Angliæ, written by Sir John Fortescue, Knight.* Tho. Roycroft, 1663.

Weardon, Jennifer. "Stitches and Techniques." *Samplers: From the Victoria & Albert Museum*, edited by Clare Browne and Jennifer Weardon, V&A Publications, 1999.

11 Just (Shut Up and) Listen: A Black Feminist Tradition of Teaching Rhetorical Solidarity

Ruth Osorio

At the 2017 Women's March in Philadelphia, prominent Black feminist Feminista Jones, née Michelle Taylor, delivered a fiery indictment of White Feminism, a brand of feminism that caters to the needs of white women at the exclusion of women of color. Speaking to an audience of predominantly white women, Jones reminds her audience that the election of misogynist, white supremacist authoritarian Donald Trump as the forty-fifth president of the United States, "isn't on us. We [Black women] did our part. Ninety-four percent of Black Women made the right choice." She then recounts the history of white women ignoring, silencing, and exploiting the voices of Black women despite the centuries of critical contributions to feminism and human development by Black women:

> We have been speaking our souls and have been silenced. We have given you the blueprint, and we watched you instead build your castles on sand. We sent you to the moon. We have been the model for freedom and liberation and have had labor and grace thrown in our faces. You will listen now. You will listen to Black women.

In her speech, Jones argues to an audience of white women that their repeated failure to listen to Black women has led to catastrophic results, hurting women of all races and colors. Black women have built the foundation of the United States and many of its liberation movements, and if white women want any hope of surviving the Trump administration, Jones insists, they have to begin by finally listening to Black women.

In this speech, Jones draws from the circulation of Black women's rhetorical theory across centuries instructing white women on how to communicate solidarity with Black women. Jones is aware of this genealogy; she concludes her speech by quoting numerous Black women, including Marsha P. Johnson, Coretta Scott King, and Harriet Tubman, who have provided the map for "freedom and liberation." I call this Black feminist rhetorical tradition teaching rhetorical solidarity. Like other chapters in this section, teaching rhetorical solidarity spans across time periods. Echoes of Jones's speech can be traced back to the first known speech delivered by a woman to a mixed-gender and mixed-race audience in the United States. In 1832, Maria W. Stewart directly addressed white women in her lecture at the Franklin Hall: "O, ye fairer sisters, whose hands are never soiled, whose nerves and muscles are never strained, go learn by experience!" (8). Shirley Wilson Logan writes that Stewart's use of apostrophe urged white women in the audience and beyond "to recognize their privileged positions" (38). Stewart's call has been echoed across centuries, with Black women urging white women to acknowledge their privilege as well as their complicity in white supremacy—and further, for white feminists' rhetorical stance to be informed by that acknowledgement.

As a white woman, I have turned to Black feminists for years for guidance on how to practice intersectional feminism. Because Black feminist thought has been integral to teaching me how to communicate—verbally and bodily—I read Black feminist thought as rhetorical theory. In Jane Donawerth's introduction to *Rhetorical Theory by Women before 1900*, Donawerth expands the perimeters of rhetoric and rhetorical theory beyond argument and persuasion; she defines "rhetoric as an 'art of communication' and rhetorical theory as 'an extended treatment teaching an aspect of the art of communication'" (xv). Donawerth argues that an expanded definition of what "counts" as rhetorical theory opens new avenues for researching rhetorical theory, inviting us to approach different genres, such as conversation, letter writing, blogging, activist conduct books, as rhetorical theory. For if rhetorical scholars only study texts that are explicitly focused on how to craft a persuasive argument, our field will miss a wealth of knowledge, debate, and mediation on communication.

I take up Donawerth's call to expand our notions of rhetorical theory by examining the circulation of Black women instructing white women on how to communicate solidarity as a site of rhetorical theory that crosses temporal boundaries. In this chapter, I argue that Black feminists have been teaching rhetorical solidarity to white women for over two centuries in the United States. Their rhetorical instruction has occurred in a variety of genres, from speeches at women's conventions to Twitter hashtags; it has embodied a variety of appeals, styles, and approaches, from praise to condemnation to outright instruction. I begin my exploration of teaching rhetorical solidarity by first defining solidarity through a feminist rhetorical framework and unpacking how whiteness challenges the manifestation of intersectional solidarity. Then, I trace the US Black feminist tradition of teaching rhetorical solidarity in the nineteenth, twentieth, and twenty-first centuries. I highlight significant case studies of teaching rhetorical solidarity (tragically leaving out hundreds more), moving from the nineteenth-century pleading of former enslaved woman Harriet Jacobs to the twenty-first century righteous rage of Black queer blogger Mia McKenzie. These examples illustrate that, though their strategies have changed over time, Black feminists have been teaching rhetorical solidarity to white women for centuries. This study, thus, impresses upon the importance of attending to how race animates the circulation of feminist discourse. In particular, it demonstrates how white supremacy can threaten the circulation of Black feminist rhetoric and how Black women have worked to overcome that silencing by building upon the arguments of their foremothers.

The Challenges of Rhetorical Solidarity

Rhetorical solidarity is the communicative practice of building meaningful, sustained coalitions across difference. In her writing on political solidarity among women, bell hooks provides a rhetorical framework for feminist solidarity:

> When women actively struggle in a truly supportive way to understand our differences, to change misguided, distorted perspectives, we lay the foundation for the experience of political solidarity . . . To experience solidarity, we must have a community of interests, shared beliefs and goals around which to unite, to build Sisterhood. . . . Solidarity requires sustained, ongoing commitment.

hooks' description of solidarity underscores both its transformative nature and its inherent challenges. Solidarity is not a single utterance: it is an ongoing rhetorical project. Solidarity unites people around a common goal, yet as hooks points out, true solidarity cannot erase difference. Rather, acknowledging that women have different identities, experiences, and struggles is the first step in developing coalitions; only after that, can women from different backgrounds get to the hard work of coming together, building communities, and transforming society. Yet, this most crucial first step of building solidarity is often the biggest obstacle.

The history of feminist activism reveals that acknowledging differences can result in discomfort, defensiveness, and withdrawal—especially from white people. To acknowledge difference in a cross-racial coalition, whiteness must be named. When I say whiteness, I follow the lead of whiteness and rhetoric scholars Tammie Kennedy et al., who explain that the study of whiteness "is not about individual white people per se; rather, it is about how whiteness as a cultural and racial category functions within US language use and haunts US people, literature, and institutions" (360). Though whiteness is wide-ranging and influences daily life in the United States, whiteness often goes unseen by white people. It is, as Matthew Jackson argues, the unstated premise in an enthymeme. Jackson illustrates his claim with a common—and fatal—example in popular discourse: news media does not need to outright state that white police officers are more trustworthy than Black victims of police brutality for that unspoken premise to be powerfully understood and acted upon by society. Whiteness's seeming invisibility masks its presence and power and, as whiteness studies scholars have long pointed out, fuels white supremacy (Frankenburg; Morrison; McIntosh; Kennedy, Middleton, and Ratcliffe; Keating; Barnett; DiAngelo). Indeed, identifying whiteness's presence and power can trigger what sociologist Robin DiAngelo calls "white fragility" even in liberal white people, leading to "argumentation, silence, and withdrawal from the stress-inducing situation" (*White Fragility* 2). White fragility, though, is not rooted in weakness: rather, as DiAngelo argues, white fragility works to maintain white supremacy by allowing white people to avoid discussing race. The communicative tropes of white fragility work to minimize discussions of whiteness, thus impeding the political project of building solidarity hooks describes.

Feminism has long grappled with the toxicity of whiteness, white fragility, and white supremacy. Feminist rhetoricians Lisa Ede, Cheryl Glenn, Andrea Lunsford, Susan Jarratt, Helen Tate, and others have noted how whiteness as a rhetorical trope prevents identification among different groups of women. From Susan B. Anthony's vow to get white women the vote before Black people in the nineteenth century to the absence of race in Sheryl Sandberg's advice for women to lean in in their workplaces in the twentieth, concepts of *womanhood* and *sisterhood* have long referred to white women in mainstream feminist discourse. Intersectional feminist activists of the twenty-first century describe this brand of feminism as White Feminism. As Alli Kirkham writes,

> White Feminists™ are people who espouse feminist beliefs but are not aware of the double standards they perpetuate when discussing issues of race . . . The problems of White Feminism™ are grounded in white supremacy and a noxious sort of "color blind" thinking that pretends all issues of race are resolved.

Not all those who subscribe to White Feminism are white, and not all white feminists subscribe to White Feminism. Rather, as Kirkham illustrates, White Feminism is an ideology that promotes the advancement of white women at the expense of women of color. White Feminism stands in contrast to intersectional feminism, which forces attention to the fact that "discrimination or disempowerment often is more complicated for people who are subjected to multiple forms of exclusion," such as women of color (Crenshaw). By ignoring race, and thus by pushing women of color to the sidelines, White Feminism prevents women from building solidarity across difference in the effort to end sexist oppression for all women. White Feminism is then not only an activist obstacle—it is also a rhetorical failure.

TEACHING RHETORICAL SOLIDARITY ACROSS CENTURIES

Even before the concept of *White Feminism* was named in the twenty-first century, Black feminist writers have long noted its existence and harm (hooks; Lorde; Smith; Combahee River Collective). Since the nineteenth century, when Stewart urged white women to go learn about privilege and race, Black women in the United States have devoted labor, time, and expertise to teaching white women rhetorical solidarity. Nabila Hijazi demonstrates how Zainab Al-Ghazali revised her rhetorical methods due to changing politics and technologies in Egypt and beyond in chapter 4 of this collection; similarly, Black women's rhetorical instruction evolved across centuries depending upon the political situation in the United States and the modes of communication available to Black women. As teaching rhetorical solidarity circulated through different times and contexts, the goal changed from asking white women to speak up for Black women to establishing detailed rules for communicating solidarity. In this section, I trace parts of this robust and longstanding history, highlighting the rhetorical wisdom Black women have been imparting to white women since the nineteenth century.

Praising "Saintly" White Women in the Nineteenth Century

Black women in the nineteenth century frequently spoke directly to white women in speeches and writings. In speaking about slavery, discrimination, and injustice, Black women in the nineteenth century did not necessarily provide white women with specific instructions on how to communicate solidarity. Rather, they often attempted to move white women past silence and to speech, especially speech on behalf of Black women. In her 1861 autobiography *Incidents in the Life of a Slave Girl*, formerly enslaved woman Harriet Jacobs pleads with white women to care about the suffering of Black enslaved women. Jacobs understood two truths: that the activism of white women could advance abolition, and that white women had so far been too silent about the treatment of their Black sisters below the Mason Dixon line. Jacobs speaks directly to white women several times in her autobiography, attempting to identify with them while also drawing stark contrasts between the experiences of motherhood for Black and white women. In light of the brutal, inhumane treatment of Black enslaved women, Jacobs chastises white women (and men) for their apathy: "In view of these things, why are ye silent, ye free men and women of the north? Why do your tongues falter in the maintenance of the right? Would that I had more ability!" (28). Here, Jacobs reprimands white women for their silence in the face of grave injustice and urges them to speak up and speak out for enslaved Black women who lack access to a platform. How can white women allow Black enslaved women to suffer the cruelties of slavery, such as sexual violence and forced removal of children? Jacobs' tone throughout the memoir is urgent and desperate: she condemns white women's apathy about slavery while also pleading with them to care and express solidarity with enslaved Black women. Jacobs does not overtly tell white women what to say, but she does urge white women and men to speak out against slavery—an early example of teaching rhetorical solidarity in the United States.

Logan's work on Black women's rhetoric in the nineteenth century illustrates that Jacobs was not alone in her direct appeals to white women. Indeed, Black women were powerful and prolific speakers and writers, developing social groups, publications, and political organizations for the advancement of Black women and Black people generally. At the same time, they continued to reach out to white women, especially at conferences devoted to women's rights. Black women such as Sojourner Truth, Fannie Barrier Williams, and Anna Julia Cooper wanted to ensure that the burgeoning women's movement was devoted to all women—not just white women. At the 1893 World's Congress of Representative Women in Chicago, Williams and Cooper both sought to move white women to express solidarity with Black women. Williams uses this opportunity to move her white women audience to feel care and concern for the plight of Black women, and for white women to allow that care and concern to shape their future rhetorics for the advancement of women:

> Women who are tender enough in heart to be active in humane societies, to be foremost in all charitable activities, who are loving enough to unite Christian womanhood everywhere against the sin of intemperance ought to be instantly concerned in the plea of colored women for justice and treatment. (118)

Williams uses praise to encourage white women to be open to her rhetorical instruction. She speaks to "saintly" white women with "tender" hearts, a move that Logan analyzes as a strategic attempt of identification with her audience of primarily white women. Williams, alongside Cooper, Truth, Jacobs, and many more, provide a roadmap to white women for organizing a feminist movement devoted to equal opportunities for all women—not just white women. Through their instruction, they observe the importance of identification, empathy, and care to crafting rhetorical solidarity, encouraging—and at times pleading—with white women to see Black women as collaborators in the project of women's progress. Yet, despite the urgency expressed by Black women in the nineteenth century, white women often sacrificed the needs of Black women for the sake of political expediency—leading to a fractured feminist movement that perpetuated white supremacist logics in their pursuit of opportunities for white women (Terborg-Penn).

TEACHING THROUGH CRITIQUE IN THE TWENTIETH CENTURY

When white women did not heed the advice of Black women in the nineteenth century, Black women changed their strategy for teaching rhetorical solidarity. Over a hundred years since Jacobs published her autobiography, white feminists in the 1970s and 1980s continued to overlook race; whiteness, again, acted as both a barrier and the exigence to the circulation of teaching rhetorical solidarity within the feminist movement. As Agatha Beins's study of 1970s feminist movements illustrates, "sisterhood" was often evoked as a way to leave white "privilege unquestioned and allow certain women to reproduce their privilege at the expense of others" (296). In response, Black feminists in the 1970s and 80s, such as Audre Lorde, bell hooks, and Barbara Smith, overtly condemned White Feminism's rhetorical failure. Unlike their predecessors in the nineteenth century, who asked white women to speak up for or with them, Black feminist writers in the 1970s and 1980s taught through critique. By identifying the rhetorical failures of white feminism, Black feminist writers instructed white women in what not to do or say when attempting sisterhood with Black women.

By explaining to white women how they were communicating solidarity incorrectly (or not at all), Black feminist writers implicitly taught white women what to avoid in their interactions with Black women— and, thus, how to practice rhetorical solidarity. The Combahee River Collective, a collective of Black feminists, wrote in 1977,

> As Black feminists we are made constantly and painfully aware of how little effort white women have made to understand and combat their racism, which requires among other things that they have a more than superficial comprehension of race, color, and Black history and culture. (273)

The Combahee River Collective decries White Feminism's ignorance about race and Black feminist thought. Embedded in this critique is an implicit rhetorical instruction: in order to practice rhetorical solidarity and build an intersectional feminist movement, white women must begin by understanding and combating their racism. Then, the Combahee River Collective directs white women to demonstrate "more than a superficial comprehension" of Black history, literature, and culture. The Combahee River Collective instructs white women to take it upon themselves to learn more about Black women's history and culture—and hopefully, that knowledge will inform white feminist attempts at rhetorical solidarity. Hence, the Combahee River Collective constructs an inventional heuristic for white women, strategies to prepare white women for practicing rhetorical solidarity.

Black lesbian poet Audre Lorde echoes the Combahee River Collective's call for white women to dismantle white supremacy within themselves and the mainstream feminist movement. Lorde provides instructions-within-critique in her famous 1979 open letter to white feminist Mary Daly, whom Lorde accuses of neglecting the wisdom of Black women by presenting Black women only as victims in Daly's written work. In this letter, Lorde notes the storied history of white women's racism: "The history of white women who are unable to hear Black women's words, or to maintain dialogue with us, is long and discouraging" (66). The history weighs on Lorde and other Black feminists in the late twentieth century, leading to less praise and patience in their rhetorical instruction to white women than their nineteenth-century counterparts. Lorde's letter is written to Daly; however, as an open letter, Lorde addresses white feminists generally as well, teaching them how to thoughtfully and intentionally incorporate Black feminist thought into their own work. To do so, Lorde deploys questions pedagogically:

> So the question arises in my mind, Mary, do you ever really read the work of Black women? Did you ever read my words, or did you merely finger through them for quotations which you thought might valuably support an already conceived idea concerning some old and distorted connection between us? This is not a rhetorical question. (68)

Through these real-not-rhetorical questions, Lorde prompts white readers to consider if and how they listen to Black women—a critical component of rhetorical solidarity. Lorde's point here is that for true solidarity to occur, white women need to seek out and learn from Black women's history. Lorde further calls for a stance of openness, encouraging white women to approach Black women's writing without a self-serving agenda. Rather than ask white women to speak on their behalf, as Jacobs did in the nineteenth century, Lorde and other Black feminists in the late twentieth century demand that white women acknowledge and work to abolish their own racism. Black women, then, continued to provide rhetorical instruction to white women, informing white feminists to invent intersectional feminist arguments by first confronting their own and their community's anti-Black racism.

NETWORKED AND DIRECTIVE IN THE TWENTY-FIRST CENTURY

Teaching rhetorical solidarity, especially in the pursuit of intersectional feminism, continues to be a Black feminist project in the twenty-first century. I observe two major shifts in this time frame: first, Black women leverage networked digital spaces to broadcast multivocal moments of teaching rhetorical solidarity. By offering rhetorical instruction in social media settings, the Black feminist tradition of teaching rhetorical solidarity becomes polyvocal and continues to span both historical and spatial boundaries. Second, unlike many of their predecessors, Black feminists in the twenty-first century instruct white women on specific practices, including lists of steps to take when practicing rhetorical solidarity.

The rhetorical tradition of teaching rhetorical solidarity thrives in online spaces, where Black feminists leverage the aggregating feature of the hashtags to network with each other and widely circulate their rhetorical instruction to white women. One prominent example is the hashtag #SolidarityIsForWhiteWomen, created by Black feminist Mikki Kendall on Twitter in 2013. Kendall wrote the hashtag in response to a high-profile story of White Feminists ignoring the voices of Black women in the US (Kendall). The hashtag caught on quickly, inspiring eighty thousand original tweets with the same hashtag within three days. Though the hashtag began by a Black woman, other non-white women joined in, as well as queer, disabled, and immigrant women of color, to document the harm caused by White Feminism. The conversation circulated beyond borders, as well, with women of color across the globe describing the ways white feminists perpetuate racism through colonialism in countries such as Egypt and Somalia. Similar to the early modern women's petitions Danielle Griffin examines in chapter 9 of this collection, the tweets in the hashtag operated as a rhetorical genre "among a great body of marginalized rhetors."

In the 11,900 tweets I collected from the first twenty-four hours of the hashtag, the tweeters underscore the historical legacy of teaching rhetorical solidarity, citing Black women and other women of color by name. Indeed, hooks, Lorde, Kimberlé Crenshaw, the legal scholar who coined the term intersectionality, and Gloria Anzaldúa are mentioned by name seventy-one times. Their repeated invocation illustrates how, though Lorde and Anzaldúa passed away over a decade before the hashtag emerged, their arguments continue to circulate among feminists of color. Tweets such as @tinymuslimah's refer to and rewrite Truth's famous 1851 speech in terms of her own positionality in 2013: "I'm black. And I'm Muslim. And I'm broke. And ain't I a woman?" These references illustrate that the participants of #SolidarityIsForWhiteWomen recognize that they are a part of a rhetorical tradition that spans centuries—and indeed, the burden of this centuries-old project exhausts the writers. Unlike their nineteenth-century counterparts, Kendall and other women of color on Twitter refuse to offer praise or comfort to their white audiences. Rather, the tweets convey righteous rage, condemning white feminism's apathy toward the high rates of sexual violence, poverty, and murder facing women of color. The stakes are high for the rhetorical failure of White Feminism.

#SolidarityIsForWhiteWomen goes beyond condemning White Feminism; it offers rhetorical instruction to the white women reading the hashtag in real time. The advice is simple: *listen. Listen, listening*, and *learn* are in the top one hundred words mentioned in #Solidarity tweets, with listen appearing 419 times, listening 137 times, and learn 270 times out of 11,990 tweets. In an early assessment of the hashtag, @laviyah tweets, "#solidarityisforwhitewomen is snatching wigs. brilliant perspectives. sisters rise up and speak up! please follow, listen and learn." Here, a Black woman on Twitter encourages Black women to continue speaking and instructs others to "follow, listen and learn." Twitter user @blackxlioness is more direct: "dammit, just shut up and listen. #solidarityisforwhitewomen," echoing the sentiments expressed by other non-white and some white participants of the hashtag. Just like the civil rights song leaders Elizabeth Ellis Miller studies in chapter 7 of this collection, the activists in the hashtag demand active listening, embodied from their audience. In those tweets, listening is described by both women of color and white women as an act of solidarity, alliance, and accountability. The calls for listening in this digital activist context echo rhetoricians Jacqueline Jones Royster's, Krista Ratcliffe's, and Asao Insoe's claims about the transformative power of listening. In her 1995 address to the Conference on College Composition and Communication, Royster highlights the importance of listening in teaching, research, and interpersonal communication:

How do we listen? How do we demonstrate that we honor and respect the person talking and what that person is saying, or what the person might say if we valued someone other than ourselves having a turn to speak? How do we translate listening into language and action, into the creation of an appropriate response? (38)

Listening is an active act, one in which we allow ourselves to learn, grow, and take action informed by other people's stories. Furthermore, in her work on rhetoric and whiteness, Ratcliffe demonstrates that listening can be particularly generative for conversations and coalitions across racial difference. For Royster, Ratcliffe, and the contributors of #SolidarityIsForWhiteWomen, listening, especially to perspectives that threaten our comfort and sense of self, is the first step to building solidarity.

Listening also plays a critical role in Mia Kenzie's rhetorical instruction to white people broadly. In 2013, McKenzie published a widely circulated blog post on her popular website *Black Girl Dangerous* (later published in her book with the same name). The blog post, "No More Allies," provides direct rhetorical instruction to not just white women but all privileged people who want to practice rhetorical solidarity. In "No More Allies," McKenzie, a Black queer woman, outlines several steps privileged people can take to "operate in solidarity with" marginalized communities. Though the piece does not directly name white women as its audience, much of the other content posted on *Black Girl Dangerous* does. Unsurprisingly, the piece has circulated widely in feminist spaces and is assigned in Women's Studies classes.

McKenzie delivers her rhetorical instruction directly to her audience, using the stated and implied second-person to outline a set of rhetorical expectations for practicing rhetorical solidarity. Like hooks, McKenzie envisions solidarity as an ongoing practice and chastises privileged people who identify themselves as allies without cultivating solidarity through their actions. McKenzie explains, allyship is "not supposed to be about you. It's not supposed to be about your feelings. It's not supposed to be a way of glorifying yourself at the expense of the folks you claim to be an ally to. It's not supposed to be a *performance*." Here, McKenzie begins her rhetorical instruction by listing what solidarity doesn't look like. At this point, she introduces the dominant theme in her treatise: the *ethos* of rhetorical solidarity. McKenzie rejects artifice, demanding that rhetorical solidarity requires meaningful engagement, authenticity, and education. To meaningfully communicate solidarity, privileged people should truly, deeply care about the community they seek to align themselves with—and this care should be communicated by listening, sacrifice, and intentional silence.

Unlike the other texts surveyed in this chapter, McKenzie provides detailed steps for communicating solidarity across difference. She provides seven steps, though McKenzie lists "shutting up and listening" twice, underscoring again the importance of listening. McKenzie also instructs privileged people to amplify marginalized voices ("our voices get to be the loudest on the issues that affect us"); to accept feedback without a defensive posture; and to learn from the centuries of wisdom archived by marginalized people. By highlighting the importance of "shutting up," McKenzie's advice also emphasizes the generative potential of silence. As feminist rhetoricians have noted, the white male rhetorical tradition is full of advice on how to command the attention of one's audience and persuade them (Foss and Griffin). But McKenzie's vision of rhetorical solidarity demands that white women and other privileged people instead divert attention away from themselves and onto marginalized people. Like McKenzie, Cheryl Glenn acknowledges that silence is rhetorical: "all silence has a meaning," and it can be used to circulate power (11). McKenzie's description of silence isn't the silence of withdrawal or defensiveness, such as when white women leave community spaces during conversations of whiteness and racism. Rather, McKenzie's model of silence is intentional and transformative: within a rhetorical solidarity framework, white women can use silence to invite, amplify, and learn from Black women.

CONCLUSION

This chapter builds upon the scholarship of so many feminist rhetoricians, but especially Jane Donawerth and Shirley Logan—two scholar-teachers who shaped my own understanding of rhetoric as a graduate student at the University of Maryland, College Park. When Donawerth revised the definition of rhetorical theory to "an extended treatment treating an aspect of the art of communication," she did more than encourage rhetorical scholars to seek out individual rhetorical theorists who have been overlooked by the field. She calls for us to recover entire rhetorical traditions that have been neglected, pushed aside because they do not align with traditional masculine notions of persuasion. Logan provides a model for such critical recovery work in *We Are Coming:*

The Persuasive Discourse of Nineteenth-Century Black Women. Logan traces the recurrences of US Black women's oratorical tradition in the nineteenth century, "common practices across rhetorical acts that were molded and constrained by prevailing conventions and traditions" (xiv). I see teaching rhetorical solidarity as a recurrence in the Black feminist rhetorical tradition: as the case studies illustrate, Black women in the US have been trying to teach white women how to practice solidarity for centuries. Donawerth's and Logan's work, teaching, and mentorship moved me to examine teaching rhetorical solidarity as a site of rhetorical theory. Following their lead, our field can continue deepening our understanding of communicating across time, difference, and power.

Truthfully, I wrote this chapter not only with rhetorical studies scholars in mind: I imagined writing to white women more broadly, especially white women who don't know about or don't care to know about the wisdom embedded in the Black feminist tradition of teaching rhetorical solidarity. In my analysis of the hashtag above, I left out an important element of the #SolidarityIsForWhiteWomen story. As Black and other non-white women joined to offer rhetorical instruction to white women, many white women responded with frustration and condemnation. Martha Plimpton, a white woman actress and feminist activist, responded to the hashtag complaining it gave "women another reason to fight with each other." She followed up by condemning the hashtag for sparking "infighting" among women. Other white women echoed Plimpton's criticism that the hashtag threatened the unity of the feminist movement (Goldberg). For critics of the hashtag, Black women discussing race was the cause of division within the feminist movement—not the white women who perpetuated white supremacy by pushing Black women to the margins. In her writing on white fragility, DiAngelo explains that white people's "continual retreat from the discomfort of authentic racial engagement . . . perpetuates a cycle that keeps racism in place" (111). Plimpton and white critics of the hashtag refused to engage in "authentic racial engagement," thus rejecting hooks' model of building solidarity across difference. Furthermore, by dismissing the concerns of women of color on Twitter, White Feminists™ maintained the centuries-long project of maintaining a racial hierarchy that positions white women's concerns as supreme.

So, I wrote this chapter with white women like Plimpton in mind as well as white women like myself who do *try* to practice solidarity but still fail at times. Too often, white women dismiss Black feminists for sparking "infighting," when in reality, the Black feminist rhetorical tra-dition has worked to build meaningful, transformative, and sustained solidarity across difference. The act of teaching rhetorical solidarity to privileged people is not an attack—it is a gift. Black feminists have sacri-ficed time, labor, and even safety to move white women toward an inter-sectional feminist movement for everyone. In Lorde's letter to Daly, she describes the "emotional cost" of talking to white women about racism, describing it as "wasted energy because of destructive guilt and defen-siveness" (70). Yet, despite the centuries-old rhetorical failure of White Feminism™, Black women have continued to reach out and offer not only their rhetorical wisdom, but also, and as Jones says in her speech at the 2017 Women's March in Philadelphia, their time-tested map to liberation. If we white women can push aside the discomfort, guilt, and defensiveness of white fragility, white women can learn from Black women—from Maria Stewart's speech in 1832 to Jones's in 2017 and everything in between and beyond—how to cultivate solidarity built on trust, shared sacrifice, and hope. From there, white feminists can follow the lead of Black women and other women of color as they map out the journey for liberation *all* women.

Works Cited

@blackxlioness. "dammit, just shut up and listen. #solidarityisforwhite-women." *Twitter*, 12 Aug. 2013, https://twitter.com/LizODTweets/status/367087992827293696 Accessed 15 Oct. 2013.

@marthaplimpton. "It's my opinion that infighting is the perfect tool for keeping us from unifying & having any lasting impact as a culture." *Twitter*, 13 Aug. 2013, crasstalk.com/wp-content/uploads/2013/08/plimpton.jpg/. Accessed 25 Jan. 2019.

@marthaplimpton. "The fun thing about this Schwyzer garbage is it gives women another reason to fight with each other. YAY! #solidar-ityisforwhitewomen." *Twitter*, 13 Aug. 2013. Accessed 25 Jan. 2019.

@tinymuslimah. "I'm black. And I'm Muslim. And I'm broke. And ain't I a woman? #solidarityisforwhitewomen." *Twitter*, 12 Aug. 2013. https://twitter.com/TinyMuslimah/status/367040699910201344 Accessed 15 Oct. 2013.

Barnett, Timothy. "Reading 'Whiteness' in English Studies." *College En-glish*, vol. 63, no. 1, 2000, pp. 9–37.

Beins, Agatha. "Sisterly Solidarity: Politics and Rhetoric of the Direct Address in US Feminism in the 1970s." *Women: A Cultural Review,* vol. 21, no. 3, 2010, pp. 292–308.

Combahee River Collective. "The Combahee River Collective Statement." *Home Girls: A Black Feminist Anthology,* edited by Barbara Smith, Rutgers UP, 2000, pp. 264–72.

Crenshaw, Kimberlé. Speech at Netroots Nation 2017 Panel,twitter.com/PPNYCAction/status/896032277062443009. Accessed 25 Jan. 2019.

DiAngelo, Robin J. *White Fragility: Why It's So Hard for White People to Talk About Racism.* Beacon Press, 2018.

Donawerth, Jane. *Rhetorical Theory by Women before 1900.* Rowman & Littlefield Publishers, Inc., 2002.

Ede, Lisa, Cheryl Glenn, and Andrea Lunsford. "Border Crossings: Intersections of Rhetoric and Feminism." *Rhetorica: A Journal of the History of Rhetoric,* vol. 13, no. 4, 1995, pp. 401–41.

Foss, Sonja K., and Cindy L. Griffin. "Beyond Persuasion: A Proposal for Invitational Rhetoric." *Communication Monographs,* vol. 62, no. 1, 1995, pp. 2–19.

Frankenburg, Ruth. *White Women, Race Matters: The Social Construction of Whiteness.* Routledge, 1993.

Glenn, Cheryl. Unspoken: A Rhetoric of Silence. Southern Illinois Press, 2004.

Goldberg, Michelle. "Feminism's Toxic Twitter Wars." *The Nation,* 29 Jan. 2014, thenation.com/article/feminisms-toxic-twitter-wars/. Accessed 25 Jan. 2019.

hooks, bell. *Feminist Theory: From Margin to Center.* Pluto Press, 2000.

—. "Sisterhood: Political Solidarity between Women." *Feminist Review,* no. 23, 1986, pp. 125–138. *JSTOR,* jstory.org/stable/1394725.

Insoe, Asao. "How Do We Language So People Stop Killing Each Other, Or What Do We Do About White Language Supremacy?" Keynote Address to Conference on College Composition and Communication, Pittsburgh, PA, 14 Mar. 2019, docs.google.com/document/d/11ACklcUmqGvTzCMPlETChBwS-Ic3t2BOLi13u8IUEp4.

Jacobs, Harriet. *Incidents in the Life of a Slave Girl.* Dover Publications, Inc., 2001.

Jackson, Matthew. "The enthymematic hegemony of whiteness: The enthymeme as antiracist rhetorical strategy." *JAC,* 2006, pp. 601–41.

Jarrett, Susan. "Beside Ourselves: The Rhetoric of Postcolonial Feminism. *JAC*, vol. 18, no. 1, 1998, pp. 57–75.

Jones, Feminista. "Women's March Speech." 21 January 2017, pscp. tv/w/1BRJjVQZNnNJw.

Keating, AnnLouise. "Interrogating 'Whiteness,' (De)Constructing 'Race.'" *College English*, vol. 57, no. 8, 1995, pp. 901–18.

Kendall, Mikki. "#SolidarityIsForWhiteWomen: Women of Color's Issue with Digital Feminism." *The Guardian*, 14 Aug. 2013, theguardian.com/commentisfree/2013/aug/14/solidarityisforwhite-women-hashtag-feminism. Accessed 25 Jan. 2019.

Kennedy, Tammie M., Joyce Irene Middleton, and Krista Ratcliffe. *Rhetorics of Whiteness: Postracial Hauntings in Popular Culture, Social Media, and Education.* Southern Illinois UP, 2017.

Kennedy, Tammie M., et al. "Symposium: Whiteness Studies." *Rhetoric Review*, vol. 24, no. 4, 2005, pp. 359–402.

Kirkham, Alli. "When White Feminists Respond to Anti-Racism like Men Respond to Feminism." *Everyday Feminism*, 8 September 2015, everydayfeminism.com/2015/09/white-feminists-anti-racism/. Accessed 25 Jan. 2019.

@laviyah. "#solidarityisforwhitewomenissnatchingwigs. brilliantperspectives. sisters rise up and speak up! please follow, listen and learn." *Twitter*, 12 Aug. 2013, https://twitter.com/laviyah/status/366972397858 996224 Accessed 15 Oct. 2013.

Lemons, Gary. "When White Students Write About Being White: Challenging Whiteness in a Black Feminist Classroom." *Counterpoints*, vol. 273, Peter Lang AG: 2004, pp. 231–32, jstor.org/stable/42978610.

Logan, Shirley Wilson. *"We Are Coming": The Persuasive Discourse of Nineteenth-Century Black Women.* Southern Illinois UP, 1999.

Lorde, Audre. *Sister Outsider*. Ten Speed Press, 1984.

McIntosh, Peggy. "White Privilege: Unpacking the Invisible Knapsack." 1989, nationalseedproject.org/Key-SEED-Texts/white-privilege-unpacking-the-invisible-knapsack. Accessed 25 Jan. 2019.

McMenzie, Mia. "No More 'Allies.'" *Black Girl Dangerous*, BGD Press, 2014, pp. 138–141.

Morrison, Toni. "Playing in the Dark: Whiteness and the Literary Imagination." *Modern Philology*, vol. 92, no. 2, 1994, pp. 267–71.

Ratcliffe, Krista. *Rhetorical Listening: Identification, Gender, Whiteness.* Southern Illinois UP, 2005.

Royster, Jacqueline Jones. "When the First Voice You Hear Is Not Your Own." *College Composition and Communication*, vol. 47, no. 1, 1996, pp. 29–40.

Smith, Barbara. "Racism and Women's Studies." *Frontiers: A Journal of Women Studies*, vol. 5, no. 1, 1980, p. 48. www.jstor.org/stable/3346304.

Stewart, Maria W. "Lecture Delivered at the Franklin Hall." *With Pen and Voice*, edited Shirley Wilson Logan, Southern Illinois UP, 1995, pp. 6–10.

Tate, Helen. "The Ideological Effects of a Failed Constitutive Rhetoric: The Co-option of the Rhetoric of White Lesbian Feminism." *Women's Studies in Communication*, vol. 28, no. 1, 2005, pp. 1–31.

Terborg-Penn, Rosalyn. *African American Women in the Struggle for the Vote, 1850–1920*. Indiana UP, 1998.

Williams, Fannie Barrier. "The Intellectual Progress of the Colored Women of the United States since the Emancipation Proclamation." *With Pen and Voice*, edited Shirley Wilson Logan, Southern Illinois UP, 1995, pp. 106–19.

12 Historiographic Fantasies: Connecting Lady Gaga and Alice Paul across Time (and Music)

Jessica Enoch

> *My fantasy of feminist history is one in which [. . .] the relationship between the past and the present is not taken for granted but considered a problem to be explored.*
>
> —Joan Wallach Scott, *The Fantasy of Feminist History*

One running theme throughout this collection is that of contributors connecting women rhetors across time, space, and circumstance to explore what these connections might say about feminist rhetorical history and women's composing practices. These connections, though, are not unique to this volume. Indeed, feminist historians as well as everyday feminist citizens often identify similarities between themselves and those who came before them. Carol Mattingly, for instance, explains that feminist historians of rhetoric often recover those figures whose agendas and politics most "resemble" our own (101), and Barbara Biesecker observes that feminist scholars often search for those whom "we wish to become" (158).[1] Beyond the academy, feminist citizens also find symbolic ways to connect themselves to their feminist past. As just one example, on Election Day in 2016, many feminists wore purple and white to the voting booth, connecting themselves to the suffrage moment and the National Women's Party by donning the party's colors. The goal for this chapter, however, is not to point out that this phenomenon happens or showcase that these connections exist; the purpose is not, borrowing from Joan Wallach Scott's epigraph, to take these connections "for granted." Rather, the project here is to interrogate these connections and examine them as "problems to be explored."

In this chapter, I explore a surprising and compelling connection forged between two figures from the past and present: Alice Paul, early-twentieth century suffragist and leader of the National Women's Party, and contemporary music star Lady Gaga. Here, I examine a 2012 video titled "Bad Romance: Women's Suffrage" (BRWS) that links Paul with Gaga and conveys to audiences a relationship between the two that suggests a feminist lineage and shared feminist politics. This video was composed by Soomo Learning, a company whose "mission" is to "create next-generation learning resources that cost less and work better than traditional textbooks" ("About Soomo"). In BRWS, Paul's suffrage story is mapped directly onto Gaga's 2009 video "Bad Romance." While Paul is now the lead character of the video instead of Gaga, in BRWS, Paul sings about suffrage to the beat of Gaga's megahit, and each frame of BRWS imitates or, as the directors state, "parodies" Gaga's video ("Behind"). To be sure, the popularity of the Soomo Learning video pales in comparison to Gaga's original, but still, it is important to note that the relationship created between the two figures was by no means ignored: one Soomo source from 2015 states that BRWS had over three million views at that time and, in 2012, the video won an Emmy for Best Informational/Instructional Program ("Save").[2]

The goal of this chapter is to envision the connection between Paul and Gaga in BRWS as a "problem to be explored." To make sense of the BRWS relationship, I adopt the feminist analytic of the fantasy echo that Joan Wallach Scott develops in her 2011 book *The Fantasy of Feminist History*.[3] In agreement with Mattingly and Biesecker, Scott asserts that feminist history is often a series of "retrospective identifications" that enable the historian to connect to and make sense of the past (*Fantasy* 48). Scott writes, "There is no shortage of writing about history in these terms: history is a result of an empathetic identification made possible by either the existence of universal human characteristics in some instances or by a transcendent set of traits and experiences belonging to women or workers or members of religious or ethnic communities" (48). Elaborating on this point, Scott claims that identity—and more particularly "feminist" or "woman's" identity—is *produced* through these identifications made across time. Her insight is that feminist identity and even the identity of "woman" rests not in the subjects themselves. Rather, Scott argues, identity can emerge through *historiographic* practice, through the connections the *historian* makes. Thus, the identity of "feminist" or of "woman" is created the moment the past and present are put in relation and animate one another via historiography, not before. Identity occurs through the process of making such connections: I am like those who came before me; she is like those who came before her; they are like those who came before them.

Scott complicates this identificatory process, however. Acknowledging the impossibility of recovering the past exactly as it was, Scott defines historiography as a fantasy echo. Scott breaks this term into two parts, explaining that the *fantasy* of historiography is the desire to "extrac[t] coherence from confusion" and "reduc[e] multiplicity to singularity" (51). Historians, she writes, compose "fantasized narrative[s] that impos[e] sequential order on otherwise chaotic and contingent occurrences" (51). Scott pairs the fantasy of historiography with the idea of the echo. Echoes are, of course, "delayed returns of sound; they are incomplete reproductions" (52). To Scott, the historian's work is one of "sending forth and picking up sounds" (53). They listen for the echo, and then, through fantasy, "eras[e] the divisions and discontinuities, the absences and differences, that separate subjects in time" (54). It is through the process of hearing the echo (and in turn ignoring what seems like static from the past) that the historian "secure[s] identity" (52). In Scott's words, the fantasy echo assures "that while the particular details may be different, the repetition of the basic narrative and the subject's experience in it mean the actors are known to us. They are us" (51).

Scott's project, though, is not just to acknowledge that these connections exist. Instead, she defines the fantasy echo as both a phenomenon of historiography and a "tool" for historiographic analysis (67). As a tool, the fantasy echo enables scholars to examine relationships that historians (both professional and lay) build between figures by "look[ing] for distortions and diffractions" and "account[ing] for the profound differences that the fantasy attempts to efface" (65). Such an approach ultimately positions scholars to interrogate the parts historians and historiography play in identity formation. For, as Scott suggests, identities are created through the echo, through the historiographic process of "elid[ing] historical difference and creat[ing] apparent continuities" (66).

I find Scott's proposal for analytical work one that should be compelling for feminist historians of rhetoric in particular and for rhetoric scholars more generally. As scholars of rhetoric, one of our key goals is to inspect the creation and consequentiality of rhetorical action: How does a rhetorical intervention work and what does a rhetorical act do? The phenomenon of the fantasy echo is a rhetorical action in which historian-rhetors invent identity through crafting connections across time and space. The work that Scott lays out and that feminist historians of rhetoric should take up is to explore how these connections are crafted and the consequentiality of them. The goal of the chapter then is not to judge whether the Soomo video was right or wrong in pairing Paul with Lady Gaga but instead to meditate on what this pairing does to Paul, to Gaga, and to the feminist identity their relationship suggests. In line with Scott, my purpose is to consider what it means to see figures as part of the same lineage and to contemplate what is erased, effaced, or ignored through the fantasized process of hearing an echo between them. Before engaging the particular problem of BRWS, though, a deeper engagement with Alice Paul and Lady Gaga is necessary.

ALICE PAUL AND LADY GAGA

Born into a Quaker family in 1885 in Morristown, New Jersey, Alice Paul was a graduate of Swarthmore College and earned her Master of Arts degree in political science, economics, and sociology from the University of Pennsylvania. In 1916, at just thirty-one years old, she began the National Women's Party, and as its leader she dedicated herself to gaining a federal amendment for women's suffrage (rather than working state by state as activists like Carrie Chapman Catt were doing at the time). Paul's suffrage advocacy took on a number of inventive forms: she orchestrated parades, boycotts, conferences, automobile and train envoys, and she created the party's newspaper *The Suffragist*. The central focus for BRWS, however, is her leadership in 1917 and 1918 to organize hundreds of women deemed the "Silent Sentinels" to picket the White House. During these years, day after day, in groups of twelve to fifteen, Paul's sentinels stood in silence outside the White House gates with banners of protest that often directly addressed President Wilson. Passersby disturbed by the sentinels' banners and silence regularly accosted the women, and the police routinely arrested them for "obscuring traffic" (qtd. in Southard 97). Paul herself was imprisoned for seven months at Occoquan Jailhouse where she initiated a 22-day hunger strike. In response, she was force-fed and placed in the prison's psychiatric ward. A publicity mastermind throughout her life as an activist for women's

rights, Paul circulated the stories of the sentinels' treatment to news outlets, and historians point to Paul's leadership and rhetorical inventiveness
during this period as major factors in changing public opinion towards
women's suffrage (see Adams and Keen, Zahniser and Fry, Southard).
Just one year after Paul and her sentinels ceased picketing, the Nineteenth Amendment was passed in 1920.

When Soomo Learning released BRWS in 2012, twenty-six-year-
old Lady Gaga (born Stefani Joanne Angelina Germanotta) had already
achieved unprecedented fame as a singer, a brazen public icon, and an
advocate for LGBTQA youth. In 2009, she completed her second album
"The Fame Monster," which included the single "Bad Romance." Gaga
won two Grammy awards related to this hit—one for Best Female Pop
Vocal and another for Best Short Form Music Video. In 2011, she completed the "Born This Way" album, and it was at this time that she pro-
claimed self-acceptance through her "Manifesto of the Mother Monster"
where she celebrates "the beginning of the new race" one that "bears no
prejudice/No judgment/But boundless freedom" ("Manifesto"). As an
extension of the "Manifesto," she defined her fans as monsters and herself as the Mother Monster. At this time, too, Lady Gaga demonstrated
support for the LGBTQA community by initiating anti-bullying campaigns and founding, with her mother, the Born this Way Foundation,
which "support[s] the wellness of young people and empower[s] them to
create a kinder and braver world" ("About the Foundation"). By 2012,
Gaga's public persona had also been distinguished by her audacity and
shock value, especially in terms of her fashion choices. As just one example, at the 2010 MTV Video Music Awards, she donned a dress made of
raw beef. News outlets and fashion magazines to everyday bloggers have
tracked Gaga's "style risks" often concluding that she "stands in a category by herself" (Persad).

Soomo Learning capitalized on Gaga's star appeal and the popularity
of "Bad Romance" when the company decided to parody this song in
2012 for their women's suffrage educational video, which aimed to teach
audiences about Alice Paul and the final, successful efforts of the Silent
Sentinels in the late 1910s. To be sure, "Bad Romance"—the song and
the video—is not about women's suffrage rights. The lyrics of "Bad Romance" suggest a narrator who is frustrated by failed romantic relationships, while the setting for the video is situated in a futuristic moment,
and it tells the story of a woman who is drugged and then sold at auction
for sex slavery. Yet, as Emilia Grant, the writer for BRWS, explains in an

interview about the making of the educational video, there was reason for the pairing. Laying the groundwork for this chapter's investigation of the video as an example of the fantasy echo, Grant states, Gaga's "Bad Romance" is "rebellious"; it is "about empowerment." ("Behind"). Grant, however, admits, "It's completely different kind of empowerment than what we're talking about [regarding Paul's suffrage battle]," but Gaga's song and video have "that same emotion and inspires the same mood."

Certainly, the mood of Gaga's "Bad Romance" video is retained in BRWS through both audio and visual parallels. As noted, the music for both videos is the same. The lyrics, however, are different. Whereas Gaga sings, "I want your ugly/ I want your disease/I want your everything/As long as it's free/I want your love/Love-love-love/I want your love," the Paul character sings, "It is a horror/A cruel design/That makes it criminal/a right that is mine/I want the vote/vote, vote, vote/I want to vote." In terms of visual resonance, the BRWS video mirrors its Gaga counterpart scene-by-scene. Anyone familiar with Gaga's video would see the resemblance immediately. The videos open the same way (see Figures 12.1 and 12.2), and then BRWS follows Gaga's: in "Bad Romance," Gaga and her crew emerge out of futuristic pods; in BRWS, Paul and her sentinels crawl out from under National Women's Party tables.

Figure 12.1: Opening Scene, "Bad Romance: Women's Suffrage." Soomo Learning, © 2012. Used by permission.

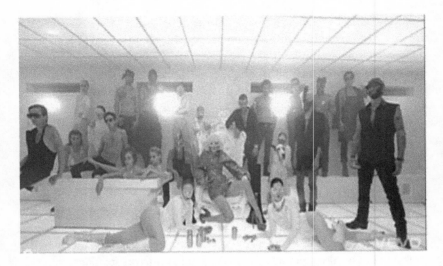

Figure 12.2: Opening Scene, "Bad Romance" © 2009. Used by permission.

Gaga and other sex slaves dance in front of a group of men; Paul and her sentinels dance, using Gaga's exact steps, in front of the White House with President Wilson watching from his window. Gaga is forcibly drugged; Paul, trapped in her straight jacket, is force-fed by jailors at the Occoquan Jailhouse. While the costume and outfit choices in Gaga's video reflect a wild and futuristic moment, BRWS choices stay true to their twentieth-century moment, though there are scenes when the Paul character breaks with temporal dress to resemble Gaga more directly (examples from BRWS are discussed in more detail below).

The connections made between Paul and Gaga suggest the fantasy echo is at work. Viewers are called to see a relationship between Paul and Gaga, identifying one with the other and seeing a lineage between them. The following analysis inspects the rhetorical significance of this echo and pairing to consider not only how the identities of Paul and Gaga take shape but also how the video implicitly forwards an identity of a "feminist" and a definition of "feminism." As Scott notes, taking on the analytical work of the fantasy echo means that scholars must "look for the distortions and diffractions" that the echo creates and discern "the individual variations of detail and figuration in them." In so doing, they "will be able to take into account the profound differences . . . that it is the function of fantasy to efface" ("Fantasy Echo" 303).

In the remainder of this chapter, I move through five reflections on how the fantasy echo created in BRWS crafts identity for both Paul and

Gaga (and for feminism). Before I do, I want to mark one particularly compelling aspect of this echo, and that is how it disrupts the expected temporality of historiographic identification. The expected case for the fantasy echo is one in which the contemporary (or more recent) figure invokes the past: Madonna's invocation of Marilyn Monroe in her "Material Girl" video is just one example. In BRWS, however, it is Paul (albeit the character of Paul in the video) who invokes Gaga: she is the one parodying Gaga's dance moves and singing to her beat. Such a temporal inversion suggests that it is not Gaga who wishes to become Paul but Paul who wishes to become Gaga. Evidence to support this claim is found in the video's final scenes where Paul enters the voting booth, but a Gaga-like figure exits (See Figure 12.3.) For Scott, though, the real question is not to consider if Paul is Gaga or Gaga is Paul. Rather, Scott guides us to consider the identities that emerge from the echo and to interrogate how the echo's *in*exactness works to "conceal and minimize difference through repetition" (*Fantasy* 53).

THE SPECTACLE OF ALICE PAUL

Pairing Alice Paul with Lady Gaga in BRWS accentuates one key aspect of Paul's career: her audaciousness. Though an assessment of Gaga's public and political persona might range from positive to negative to bewildered, one thing that most observers would likely agree on is that she is a provocateur who shocks the public as much through her embodied appearance as with her words. From her meat dress to her Kermit the Frog ensemble, Gaga's visual image and public display rarely disappoint onlookers who expect her to shock and awe. Therefore, when BRWS identifies Paul with Gaga, it calls viewers to understand that, in her day, Paul too was an insurgent rhetorical strategist who leveraged an arsenal of visual and embodied arguments that often astounded and outraged her audiences. Even though Paul's tactics of silent picketing may seem mild from today's standpoint, linking her with Gaga highlights Paul's audacity and helps audiences to the video discern her rhetorical provocations.

Such connections align with much recent recovery work on Paul. Indeed, scholars often define Paul as a charismatic figure who developed and deployed extraordinary protest strategies that were both militant and confrontational. As Adams and Keene write, Paul's "visual campaign" (77) aimed "to shock, to thrill, to shame, to pressure, and to convince" (xviii). Jennifer Borda likewise describes Paul's activism as an "infusion of spectacle, drama, youth, and energy" (359). J.D. Zahniser and Amelia Fry agree, writing that "subtlety was not Alice's strong suit" (176), and they pinpoint how Paul's combined youthful energy and "bold and controversial action . . . made suffrage 'cool,' at least for the young or young at heart" (1). By seeing Paul as Gaga or Gaga as Paul in BRWS, viewers are asked to remember that, like Gaga, Paul welcomed and wanted publicity, and for her it was directed to the cause of suffrage, as early twentieth-century newspapers from the *New York Telegram* to the *Camden Courier* identified how effective Paul's campaigns were in terms of drawing attention. The *Courier*, for instance, reports, Paul's suffragists "have made it their business to stir things up" (qtd. in Adams and Keene xv). Critically, this linkage between Paul and Gaga moves beyond these two figures: viewers are prompted to deduce that provocation, audacity, and publicity are key and repeating strategies of feminists and within the history of feminism.

GAGA'S FEMINISM

Through Gaga, Paul's identity as a provocateur is highlighted in BRWS. Yet seeing Gaga as Paul also suggests an answer to a critical question for audiences about Gaga's feminism. From all corners of the academic and popular universe, people have wondered, in the words of *Ms. Magazine* blogger, N. Williams, "Is Gaga a feminist or isn't she?" Is she, in Curtis Fogel and Andrea Quinlan's words, "a gendered warrior fighting for the advancement of women or a pop-cultural representation of hypersexualized violence against women in the media" (184)? Reading Gaga on her own at the time BRWS was produced, this question was a difficult one to answer. As *New York Times* blogger Nancy Bauer wrote in 2010, Gaga's most consistent characteristic is her inconsistency: "she always keeps us guessing." That same year, *Guardian* writer Kira Cochrane similarly questions, "Who is the 24-year-old pop star formerly known as Stefani Joanne Angelina Germanotta? Is she a brilliant performance artist—or an empty provocateur? Is she driven by ideas, or neediness? Is she a feminist icon, or just a slightly offbeat sex object?" Cochrane goes on to make this assessment: "We never, ever get to see or understand who she really is. Gaga seems to live inside a mass of contradictions."

Such bewilderment has only been compounded by Gaga's own conflicted messages about her feminism. Gaga, at one point, stated, "I'm not a feminist. I hail men, I love men, I celebrate American male culture—beer, bars, and muscle cars" (qtd. in Cochrane); at another, "I'm a "little bit of a feminist" (qtd. in Bauer); and at another, "I'm certainly a feminist." (qtd. in Manders). When asked to offer her definition of feminism, Gaga's inconsistency continued. In one instance, Gaga explained, "A feminist to me is somebody that wishes to protect the integrity of women who are ambitious," yet she has also defined feminism in this way: "This is the type of feminist that I am: that women can be tremendous artists" (qtd. in McLean).

While these comments confirm that Gaga "keeps us guessing," the Gaga identity that emerges through the fantasy echo of BRWS seems to put the guessing to rest. Because Gaga is identified with Paul, Gaga is implicitly forwarded as a feminist figure in line with Paul and her sentinels. For indeed, as discussed in more detail below, there are no doubts about Paul's feminist credentials: she dedicated herself to suffrage and once the vote was won in 1920, she spent the rest of her life fighting for the ratification of the Equal Rights Amendment (ERA). By having Paul invoke Gaga in BRWS and by positioning Gaga as Paul's wished-for descendent at the conclusion of the video, viewers are prompted to understand that Paul would see Gaga as a feminist, and so should we. The echo thus suggests that Lady Gaga is the Alice Paul of the twenty-first century, and here a feminist lineage is drawn.

ALICE PAUL'S FOCUS AND POLITICAL LEADERSHIP

It is important, however, to invert the analytical point just considered. Above, we reflected on how the echo in BRWS works to solidify Gaga's investment in feminism. This connection could also be read as one that "alters" Paul's political dedication and dilutes her focus on women's rights issues throughout her life. Undoubtedly, in BRWS, Paul's investment in suffrage is clear: the refrain of the song ("vote, vote, vote, we want the vote") relays Paul's political intention, as do stanzas such as "We cry for freedom/ Oh, hear our voice/ And see we're equal to all men!/ Oh oh oh oh . . . / We the whole people/ Not just male citizens/ Formed this most perfect Union!" Yet listening to Paul through Gaga's echo creates the potential for audiences to map Gaga's inconsistency onto Paul.

Contemporary viewers of BRWS would likely be familiar with Gaga's contradictions and feminist equivocations (even in light of her LGBTQA advocacy). Furthermore, Gaga's provocations—her dress, her performances, her songs and videos—even if read as feminist, are often understood as intended to discomfort, prompt questions, and elicit confusion. This contemporary knowledge about Gaga could then echo through Paul's story told in BRWS, and, borrowing from Scott, "efface" part of her feminist identity ("Fantasy" 290). Unlike Gaga, Paul's spectacular acts were not aimed to create confusion. They were clear in their purpose and consistent in their service to her political goal during the moment that BRWS recounts: suffrage. This point is made over and again by scholars studying Paul. In their biography, Zahniser and Fry remark on Paul's lifetime dedication to two main political causes, suffrage and the ERA. Belinda Stillion Southard describes Paul as "militant" (400) and "goal oriented" with a "singlemindedness that many admired but few emulated" (126). Adams and Keene similarly note that Paul had "endless determination" (35) with twentieth-century suffragist Mrs. A. D. Ascough commenting, "Paul was a tireless leader. She had given her life to this work, and she has inspired in all of us not only enthusiasm and loyalty but deep personal devotion" (qtd. in Adams and Keene 34). Critical to note too: biographers such as Zahniser and Fry point to a consequence of Paul's dedication to suffrage and the ERA: she did not invest in other important causes during her lifetime such as raced-based civil rights (138).

Scholarship on Paul does not, however, only zero in on her single-minded political investment. It also consistently comments on her personal resistance to and purposeful deflection of public attention. Zahniser and Fry write that Paul "stayed out of the spotlight" (229) and "subsumed her personal life with her political ambition and drove toward her goal relentlessly to the detriment of her health" (126). They continue, Paul's appearance was often "haggard" as she "seemed not to take care of herself" (187), with one of her suffragist colleagues saying that "self-obliteration and self-forgetfulness" marked Paul as a leader (qtd in Zahniser and Fry 187). Thus, while Paul made sure that suffrage spectacles like the Silent Sentinels generated "enormous publicity," she "remained in the background . . . standing in the wings was her usual mien" (241). Unlike Gaga, who no doubt has a real commitment to her personal appearance her identity as an iconic pop star, Paul insisted that public attention turn to suffrage or the ERA, instead of herself.

For viewers of BRWS, these understandings of Paul's self-denial and laser-focused dedication might not be discerned due to the way the video asserts similarities between Gaga and Paul. In BRWS, Paul seems to adopt Gaga's concern with personal appearance and fashion in three especially poignant moments: one in which Paul sings into a mirror bearing her ankle and calf to onlookers—an audacious act in the early twentieth century; another when Paul dances by herself into an empty room in a Gaga-esque outfit and then displays herself on a dais; and in yet another when Paul spins slowly in a room of star crystals while adorning an American flag as a toga-type dress and pearls. In these moments, BRWS is clearly following the visual frames of the "Bad Romance" video. Yet the parody implies that Gaga's interest in personal attention and even outrageous fashion was Paul's. This point is clear in yet another telling moment in the video when one of Paul's sentinel sisters—an overworked mother—identifies the reason she wants suffrage, exclaiming, "I want to wear pants!" Certainly, women's fashion options were constrained in the early twentieth century, and liberation from dresses and corsets were a concern for women's rights activists. But this scene creates a connective tissue between Gaga and Paul through fashion, and Gaga's key interests are seen as Paul's. This moment and the others referenced above imply that personal attention and the option to "wear pants" were foremost in Paul's mind. Furthermore, building on Scott's ideas about the fantasy echo and feminist identity, one might also argue that by extrapolation these scenes suggest that because Gaga and Paul seemingly shared commitments to fashion and personal attention, so too did feminists before and after them.

ALICE PAUL'S NONVIOLENCE

The lineage traced between Paul and Gaga through the BRWS also diffuses a key component of Paul's rhetorical strategy: her nonviolence. Paul was a Quaker whose activism was influenced by the civil disobedience theories of figures such as Mahatma Gandhi, Henry David Thoreau, and Leo Tolstoy. Her suffragist colleague Doris Stevens writes, Paul's activism was based in "passive opposition" and "passive resistance" (qtd. in Adams and Keene 21), and in their study of Paul's rhetorical significance, Adams and Keene equate Paul's deep dedication to nonviolence with Martin Luther King Jr.'s (xviii). When Paul echoes Gaga in BRWS, however, this characteristic could be seen to diminish, especially for those familiar with both Gaga and her "Bad Romance" video.

In assessing Gaga's video oeuvre, scholars have observed that women are not only often victims of extreme violence, they also enact violence. Fogel and Quinlan write that "Lady Gaga fuels a continuing war against women's bodies by a) turning violence against women into a commodity, b) normalizing violence, c) dehumanizing herself" (184). Indeed, in the penultimate scene of the "Bad Romance" video, the main figure played by Gaga, who has been auctioned off as a sex slave, sets a bed on fire with her "buyer" lying atop it. Gaga's character revels in this act, as she joyfully reclines next to the man's charred remains at the video's end. Certainly, this moment could prompt debate regarding who should enact violence, how, and for what purpose. There is an argument here, however, that Gaga normalizes, embraces, or even leverages violence in these cases. We behave violently, Gaga suggests; we need to and we must.

Given Paul's dedication to nonviolence, it seems she would bristle at this assertion and association. Interestingly and importantly, this arson scene is missing from BRWS, its writer Emilia Grant admitting that the penultimate scene in Gaga's "Bad Romance" was not one she could appropriate: "Alice Paul is not going to light a bed on fire with a man in it" ("Behind"). But even though Grant does not have her BRWS version of Alice Paul enact violence on prison guards, the police, or President Wilson, she does contend that Paul is still like Gaga through their shared *passion*. Gaga may show her passion through violence and Paul demonstrate it through her non-violence, yet, Grant explains, "it's that kind of passion; it's that kind of ferocity, you know, is what [Paul] lived for."

One could argue then, with Grant, that passion is a consistent trait shared between Paul and Gaga and, by extension, feminists more generally. Gaga's violence is not mapped onto Paul's; her passion is. However, even though this scene is not included in BRWS, those familiar with Gaga's "Bad Romance" video (of which there are many) would likely remember this scene, and they may connect it to Paul. Though setting a bed aflame might not be something Paul would do, the connection created in BRWS suggests that Paul might accede to and agree with it. The video's identification of Paul with Gaga smooths over the bristling Paul might have experienced, and viewers might not observe the differing positions the two seem(ed) to hold regarding questions of violence as strategy or even as a fact of life.

NORMALIZING GAGA

While the fantasy echo in BRWS may diminish Paul's political dedication and nonviolent activism, it also effaces a characteristic key to Gaga. As noted above, the fantasy echo of the video and especially its final scenes cultivate a feminist identity for Gaga: Paul enters the voting booth and a Gaga-esque figure emerges. The suggestion here is that Gaga is a descendent of Paul's: Lady Gaga is the Alice Paul of the twenty-first century (see Figure 12.3).

Figure 12.3: Exiting the Voting Booth, "Bad Romance: Women's Suffrage." Soomo Learning © 2012. Used by permission.

But a closer look at this scene is telling, especially for Gaga. Three women enter the voting booth: a mother, a woman who seems to be a domestic servant or cook, and the Alice Paul figure. Three women exit: a soccer mom, a twenty-first century working woman in a suit, and the Lady Gaga figure. The exit scene's suggestion is that the 1920 vote has set the course for this 2012 future by enabling these contemporary women's freedoms. However, if this after-the-vote scene reflects the end of or result of Paul's feminism, it is one that offers a pretty limited picture of who feminists of the twenty-first century are or could be: these three women convey their identity as white, middle-class, and heterosexual, or at least they are enacting heteronormativity. (I should note too that they are all wearing pants; that goal has been achieved.) In some ways we could read this scene as an accurate and indeed disheartening vision of Paul's limited feminist vision. As noted, she did not invest heavily in race issues, and throughout her life as a single woman, she was extremely private about her sexuality (Zahniser and Fry 2). As she made her turn to the ERA after suffrage, Paul's singular focus was on women's work options. One could thus argue that Paul did not imagine a capacious vision for feminism—racially, sexually, or culturally.

But while the exit scene in BRWS may seem like an accurate vision of Paul's feminism in the twenty-first century, what do we make of the feminism it suggests for Gaga? When discussing the choice to parody "Bad Romance" and to connect Gaga with Paul, Grant asks and explains, "Who better than Lady Gaga [to pair with Paul]? She's almost the result of women's lib. We've come that far in a way so that we can do and be whatever we want to even if it is outrageous" ("Behind"). However, this final scene that overtly connects the two and creates their lineage does not offer a very outrageous version of Gaga at all. In fact, the post-vote Gaga looks quite tame. Placing her next to the soccer mom and the woman worker in her pant suit distills what could be read as Gaga's most insurgent and radical identity work that, at its root, questions expectations of gender, sexuality, and normalcy.

Celebrating how Gaga challenges norms of gender and sexuality, Sanjana Ray writes, "Gaga's purposefully flamboyant actions of wearing ridiculous meat-plastered outfits, declaring her bisexuality, and her warped presentation of beauty has paved the way for young girls to finally believe that they don't have to conform to the incredibly difficult beauty standards that society has been inflicting on them." Pushing this point further, queer theorist Jack Halberstam argues that Gaga's strength lies in her disruption of femininity, her critique of sexuality, and her varied treatment of gender. Halberstam explains that through her audacious public performances of self, Gaga "call[s] attention to the whimsy of personhood, the ways in which we all need to see each other anew, find new surfaces, name those new surfaces differently, and confuse the relations between surface and depth" (26). Using Gaga as a muse for a new kind of feminism, Halberstam goes so far as to coin the term "Gaga Feminism" and define it as a "hypothetical form of feminism, one that lives in between the 'what' and the 'if': what if we gendered people according to their behavior? What if gender shifted over the course of a lifetime?" (26). This understanding of Gaga as an out-of-the-box, outrageous gender-bender is not what viewers see at the end of BRWS. Instead of celebrating Gaga and her little monsters, playing with ideas of gender and sexuality, BRWS displays Alice Paul's Gaga in tight pants and stilettos on the arms of a soccer mom and a business woman on the go. These women are not in Halberstam's words, "going gaga." The BRWS echo thus normalizes Gaga, and, by extension, we might also argue that the video normalizes present-day feminist politics to concerns of white, middle-class, heteronormative women.

Fantasizing Echoes Between Paul and Gaga

This examination of "Bad Romance: Women's Suffrage" reveals the significant work the fantasy echo can accomplish as a tool for historiographic analysis. The goal here is not to critique the video for misrepresentations or to argue that Soomo Learning could have been more accurate or that the company could have chosen a better song or artist for the parody. As a feminist rhetorical analytic, the fantasy echo prompts examinations of cross-temporal connections and calls us to think deeply and capaciously about what it means to hear one woman's voice through another's (and vice versa). This chapter reveals that in listening to the echo and the static, we can inspect the identities of Alice Paul and Lady Gaga that are produced through BRWS, understanding that by recovering Paul through Gaga (and seeing Gaga through Paul) *both* women's identities are remade, as viewers are called to remember and forget characteristics of each. Additionally, and critically, as Scott has argued, such fantasies that create lineages between feminist figures have much to say about how we make sense of feminist identity itself as well as feminism's past, present, and future. As Scott notes, when the "history of feminism [is] . . . told as a continuous, progressive story of women's quest for emancipation, [it] effaces the discontinuity, conflict, and difference that might undermine the politically desired stability of the categories termed women and feminist." ("Fantasy" 290). Indeed, the fantasy echo invites feminist scholars to hear both consonance and dissonance within the lineages we create and are audience to, listening closely to echoes that define and efface the figure of the feminist and the practice of feminism.

Notes

1. See also Harrison, Hogg, Sinor, and Royster.
2. An accurate count of the number of views for "Bad Romance: Women's Suffrage" is difficult to discern. Due to an issue relating to advertising and a potential suit from Lady Gaga's record label, Sony/ATV Music Publishing, Soomo Learning seems to have removed "Bad Romance: Women's Suffrage" from its site. The video is still available (with advertising) on YouTube, but the number is just under 200,000

views. When I originally conducted this research in 2012, the number of views was over 500,000. For a discussion of this debate, see "Save Bad Romance: Women's Suffrage." Along with "Bad Romance: Women's Suffrage," Soomo created another video about the Declaration of Independence that is set to the tune of Timbaland's remix of the OneRepublic song "Too Late to Apologize."

3. Scott also defines this concept in "Fantasy Echo: History and the Construction of Identity" (2001).

WORKS CITED

Adams, Katherine H. and Michael Keene. *Alice Paul and the American Suffrage Campaign.* U of Illinois P, 2008.

"About Soomo Learning." *Soomo Learning,* www.soomolearning.com/about-us. Accessed 20 Mar. 2019.

"About the Foundation." *Born this Way Foundation,* bornthisway.foundation/about-the-foundation/. Accessed 20 Mar. 2019.

"Bad Romance." *YouTube.* Directed by Francis Lawrence, performance by Lady Gaga, 2009, www.youtube.com/watch?v=qrO4YZeyl0I. Accessed 20 Mar. 2019.

"Bad Romance: Women's Suffrage." *YouTube.* Directed by Tim Grant, Soomo Publishing, 2012, www.youtube.com/watch?v=Gvu3krcs8ec. Accessed 20 Mar. 2019.

Bauer, Nancy. "Lady Power." *The New York Times,* 20 June 2010. opinionator.blogs.nytimes.com/2010/06/20/lady-power/. Accessed 18 Feb. 2018.

"Behind the Scenes of 'Bad Romance: Women's Suffrage." *YouTube.* www.youtube.com/watch?v=MuPCfIM3NWo. Accessed 18 Feb. 2018.

Biesecker, Barbara. "Coming to Terms with Recent Attempts to Write Women into the History of Rhetoric." *Philosophy and Rhetoric,* vol. 25, no. 2, 1992, pp. 140–58.

Borda, Jennifer L. "Woman Suffrage in the Progressive Era: A Coming of Age." *Rhetoric and Reform in the Progressive Era: A Rhetorical History of the United States,* edited by J. Michael Hogan, vol. 6, 2003, pp. 339–86.

Cochrane. Kira. "'Lady Gaga Exposes Femininity as a Sham." *The Guardian.* 17 Sept. 2010. www.theguardian.com/music/2010/sep/17/lady-gaga-feminist-icon. Accessed 18 Feb. 2018.

Halberstam, J. Jack. *Gaga Feminism: Sex, Gender, and the End of Normal*. Beacon, 2012.

Harrison, Kimberly. *The Rhetoric of Rebel Women: Civil War Diaries and Confederate Persuasion*. Southern Illinois UP, 2013.

Hogg, Charlotte. "Including Conservative Women's Rhetorics in an 'Ethics of Hope and Care.'" *Rhetoric Review*, vol. 34, no. 4, 2015, pp. 391–408.

Fogel, Curtis A. and Andrea Quinlan. "Lady Gaga and Feminism: A Critical Debate." *Cross-Cultural Communication*, vol. 7, no. 3, 2011, pp. 184–88.

Manders, Haley. "Lady Gaga Echoes Kesha's Claims of Misogyny in the Music Industry." *Refinery 29*, 17 Oct. 2014, www.refinery29.com/2014/10/76399/lady-gaga-feminism. Accessed 18 Feb. 2018.

McLean, Craig. "Lady Gaga: It's a Very Hard Business. There are Lots of Sharks." *The Sunday Times*. 15 Oct. 2014. www.thetimes.co.uk/article/lady-gaga-its-a-very-hard-business-there-are-lots-of-sharks-thxkjt77dk5. Accessed 18 Feb. 2018.

"Manifesto of the Mother Monster." *Gagapedia*, ladygaga.wikia.com/wiki/Manifesto_of_Mother_Monster. Accessed 18 Feb. 2018.

Mattingly, Carol. "Telling Evidence: Rethinking What Counts as Rhetoric." *Rhetoric Society Quarterly*, vol. 32, no. 1, 2002, pp. 99–108.

Persad, Michelle. "Lady Gaga's Style Evolution Proves There's No Fashion Risk She Isn't Willing to Take." *Huffington Post*, 28 Mar. 2016.www.huffingtonpost.com/entry/lady-gaga_us_56f561fbe4b0143a9b480f8b. Accessed 18 Feb. 2018.

Ray, Sanjana. "Lady Gaga as a Symbol of Contemporary Feminism and an Active Voice Against Body Shaming." *Your Story*, 28 Mar. 2017, yourstory.com/2017/03/lady-gaga-contemporary-feminism/. Accessed 18 Feb. 2018.

Royster, Jacqueline. *Traces of a Stream: Literacy and Social Change Among African American Women*. U of Pittsburgh P, 2000.

"Save Bad Romance." *Soomo Learning*, Nov. 2015, www.soomolearning.com/blogs/posts/save-bad-romance. Accessed 18 Feb. 2018.

Scott, Joan Wallach. *Fantasy of Feminist History*. Duke UP, 2011.

—. "Fantasy Echo: History and the Construction of Identity." *Critical Inquiry*, vol. 27, no. 2, 2001, pp. 284–304.

Sinor, Jennifer. "Reading the Ordinary Diary." *Rhetoric Review*, vol. 21, no. 2, 2002, pp. 123–49.

Southard, Belinda A. "Militancy, Power, and Identity: The Silent Sentinels as Women Fighting for Political Voice." *Rhetoric of Public Affairs*, vol. 10, no. 3, 2007, pp. 399–418.

Williams, N. "Is Lady Gaga a Feminist or Isn't She?" *Ms. Blog.* 11 Mar. 2011. msmagazine.com/blog/2010/03/11/is-lady-gaga-a-feminist-or-isnt-she/. 18 Feb. 2018.

Zahniser, J.D. and Amelia Fry. *Alice Paul: Claiming Power.* Oxford UP, 2014

13 Circulating Letters: Some Afterthoughts

Shirley Logan

> *I washed and cleaned your fountain pen well, Melva, and put it away in the cedar chest. This Lifetime Sheaffer that I found turned out to be better than I figured. It's a glider. I am writing with it now.*
>
> —Azzie Lee Ellis Wilson, *Unpublished Letters*

Background

After over thirty-years of researching the rhetorical histories of women from earlier centuries, I have long wanted to recover the opinions, hopes, dreams, and ideas of one woman in particular. They have been lost to me for many years. My mother died at forty-one as a result of complications following an at-home childbirth in rural western South Carolina. The town was very small, and at that time, without electricity or indoor plumbing. I was four years old and the youngest of five children. My siblings were ten (Mac), twelve (John, Jr.), fourteen (Melva), and sixteen (Thelma). Just a few years ago, several of the letters my mother wrote to my two older sisters became available. I made copies and filed them away, not really sure what I would do with them. The letters were written during the summer of 1947, the summer before she died. Only two included legible dates—June 7 and June 19. The letters were addressed to my sisters jointly as they both were away living on the campus of Harbison Junior College in Irmo, South Carolina, about ninety miles from our home in Due West, in preparation for attendance in the fall and working to help cover the coming year's tuition.[1] My mother wrote some of the letters while she was attending summer school in North Carolina for teacher recertification, and others during her time at home, possibly on the weekends. So, she is addressing an audience of two teenaged daughters, reluctantly away from home and in need of assurance that all is well and that the arrangement is temporary.

CIRCULATIONS, CONNECTIONS, AND DISCONNECTIONS

Most of the chapters in this volume, aptly titled *Feminist Circulations: Rhetorical Explorations across Space and Time*, focus on recovering lost voices and on understanding familiar voices in new spaces and times. Given that there's rarely a straight line between the past and the present, these explorations and circulations help us to recognize many cycles of behavior. In considering an organizational approach, I imagined my mother's letters as a resource for connecting her concerns and rhetorical explorations to those of women across the ages, as represented in *Circulations*. The editors of this volume remind us in the introduction that "just as women's rhetorics have moved and circulated, just as there have been conversations and recurrences, there have also been disconnections, interruptions, divergencies, immobilities, isolations, and silences that have prevented women and their rhetorics to circulate." They encourage readers to mine these constraints as well. To the extent possible, my goal is to listen for traces of my mother's voice in some of these ongoing conversations circulating across time. Enoch's own chapter in this collection cautions against being too quick to make connections between women, for example, Lady Gaga and Alice Paul, who may, in fact, share characteristics but also represent many differences. She argues that such "cross-temporal connections," encourage—citing Joan Wallach Scott—"fantasy echoes," leading feminists to "elide historical differences" and "reduc[e] multiplicity to singularity." Recognizing that there are few straight lines between past and present and that forced connections should be resisted, I will listen for circling echoes:

> *Already Jr. and Mac are showing an interest in the flowers, Mel. They want to keep them up as you asked them.*

We might say then that the circulation of these letters, letters written by a mother to her daughters away in boarding school, was situationally constrained. Although they were not intended for a wider audience, today the letters provide a rich source of cultural information about life in rural mid-twentieth-century South Carolina, chronicling such events, for example, as the turning on of electricity:

> *Dear Girls, Just a minute to say to you that the electric lights were turned on here all over the house about 3 minutes ago so all of us here on the hill are all lights now. . . . The Kelvinator even kicked off nicely but we will have that checked. . . . Papa is going up to get bulbs.*[2]

The letters also reveal something about the family's literacy practices:

> *Mac has read a book this week. She is Thelma all over again in her reading habits. She has read the Arabian Nights. She is really deep.*

The woman in *Feminist Circulations* whose life span was roughly contemporaneous with my mother's is Hallie Quinn Brown. Though Brown lived to be nearly one hundred, the forty-one years of my mother's short life ended two years before Brown's. Of course, there were many differences. Brown had no children and, apparently, never married. As Donawerth points out, Brown traveled a great deal, engaged in the explicit practice of circulating rhetorical principles and might have been considered a member of the African American middle-class. The question of class among Blacks of this period is complicated. My father was a college graduate who taught high school chemistry in North Carolina before moving back to South Carolina and becoming a Sunday school missionary. Mama was a pianist who possibly played for church services and surely for her own pleasure. My mother earned a college degree from Barber-Scotia College in Concord, NC,[3] and was attending school to acquire additional teaching certification. That is why she was away from home while my older siblings were at Harbison for the summer. But we would not have been considered middle-class in the same way that Brown was. Brown traveled extensively and without children was able to maintain independence and meet a variety of people around the country:

> *I can't begin to describe how tired I am. Maybe I'll catch a little rest when I get in school. . . . I am working real hard. Don't know what hard school work in like but I'm trying to stick with it.*

Donawerth demonstrates how Brown's journal entries demonstrate her ongoing quest for self-improvement and for the education of others in the Black community, regardless of perceived class distinctions. Mama's goal was to improve her own employment options and to ensure that her two elder daughters stayed close, focused on their aspirations, and supported each other.

Zimmerelli's essay considers how biographies of exemplary adults served as conduct literature, providing both boys and girls models of proper behavior, focusing on when the adults were young. The letters from my mother could be understood as conduct guidance for teenaged daughters, attending summer school, from a concerned mother, who is also away in school. She constantly reminds them to "be good" and cautions the older daughter to control her temper. She encourages them to get all the rest and sleep they can and not work themselves into "nervous wrecks." She is particularly concerned that as teenaged girls, they should be under her mentoring "to guide them over the rough places in life" when they were becoming interested in boys, but since she is away in school during the week, she felt that this temporary arrangement was best. There are also the reminders about writing other family members and holding out until she can have them come home. There is a recognizable urgency in tone when she assures her daughters that they will not have to be there much longer. Unlike the conduct books written to influence the opinions of others, the letters were designed to bring comfort and support to her daughters.

MIGRATIONS

In 1941, the family moved from Hickory, North Carolina, with a population of approximately fourteen thousand, to Due West, a much smaller town in South Carolina, with a population of a little over one thousand, in an area where my parents grew up. Before the 150-mile move south, my father was a full-time chemistry teacher and a high school coach. He was said to have frequently watched his four-year-old daughter by bringing her to the chemistry lab with him.

During an interview later in life, my sister Melva ponders my mother's situation at the time of the move to South Carolina:

> What did Mama say about the pending move? After all, she held four major positions: (1) a young mom at the beginning of her child-bearing years, already with four children (ages ten, eight, six, and four); (2) the key nurturer of the family; (3) college graduate/certified teacher, fulfilling teaching responsibilities between babies; and (4) keeper of the family, maintaining sanity within the household" (Costen 79).

She doesn't offer any answers to this question, accepting that knowing Mama's thoughts on the matter will remain a mystery.

Reading these chapters broadened and deepened my appreciation for women's rhetorical ingenuity, aside from any indirect links to the circulating rhetorical acts in my mother's 1947 letters to her daughters. The afterword is a difficult genre to develop, but for me the composing process has been a deep source of new knowledge. For example, in their chapters, authors Karen Nelson, Danielle Griffin, and Erin Sadlack all address the important role petitions played as early modern women's first enactment of collective political and personal agency, arguing in support of improved working conditions and retirement benefits, and in support of Queen Elizabeth, using their lower-class status to employ the ostensibly submissive genre of the petition.

> *I wouldn't leave them [the other three children] and home to come here you know if I didn't have to, but you are both old enough to realize that Mama has to work for what she gets and if I don't work I am just like you all or less [and] have nothing and can't ask for anything as you can; it's just a situation I have to face so don't worry I'll be back there soon I trust.*

The plaintive tone of some of my mother's letters suggests that she wants to imply much more than what's on the page about her pressing need to be away in school during the week, perhaps as a form of indirect petition for their understanding.

Miller explains in her chapter how activist Bernice Johnson Reagon memorialized the civil rights movement through sound, image, and words. During a White House performance of the freedom song, "Ain't Gonna Let Nobody Turn Me 'Round," Johnson urges the audience to sing along, observing, "You can never tell when you might need it" (see Chapter 7). I imagine she was referring to the ways in which image, word, and song can serve as sources of inspiration.

Along with urging them to write frequently, my mother encouraged her daughters to send pictures from their summer experience, with the promise that she would have them developed, and she thanked them for the class picture. She tells them that the three siblings at home look at it often, mentioning,

> *had to hang it low enough for Shirley to get a chair and see it good. Sometimes she tells me that she is going up in the hall and spend awhile with Thelma*

Preserving memories through words and pictures was part of family traditions.

From reading Michele Osherow's chapter on embroidered representations of the Biblical narrative of Susanna and the elders, I learned that seventeenth-century women spoke and wrote through their needlework, demonstrating that the needle, too, can serve as a pen. While there is no mention specifically of embroidery in my mother's letters (although she did embroider), she does write a great deal about essential domestic sewing:

> *You all should see the sewing I've done this week. You wouldn't believe I could make our machine go like that—2 dresses for Shirley, 1 for Mac, 2 slips & 2 dresses for myself, PJs for myself, 2 undersuits for Jr., finished your dress, Mel, and many other items I can't think of now.*

This was a household in which the necessary sewing would have left little time for indirect or encoded messages. The sound of the sewing machine did say loudly, "I love you and want you to have plenty to wear while I'm away in summer school."

Reading Adele Seeff's chapter "Staging Gender Politics on a World Stage" brought to mind "Yiimimangaliso: The Mysteries," the 2001 South African interpretation of the medieval Chester plays depicting the medieval English biblical history of the world. The drama, which a former medievalist colleague Theresa Coletti brought to my attention, offers a model for the blending of languages, including English, Latin, Xhosa, Tswana, Afrikaans, and Zulu, along with Latin, throughout the performance. Seeff's work compares differences in representations of female power within a South African retelling of Shakespeare's *Macbeth*. The blending of past and present contexts reminds us of the ever-circulating cycles of political behavior.

Ruth Osorio offers a candid assessment of some of the ways in which Black and white feminists have communicated across difference over the years, in her chapter on a Black feminist tradition of teaching rhetorical solidarity. I suspect that in many instances what may appear to be the superior wisdom of Black women on the subject of rhetorical solidarity is actually borne out of differences in lived experience. Of course, we must be cautious about ascribing Black women with all the wisdom, as did Francis Gage in her description of the effect of Sojourner Truth's "Ar'n't I a Woman" speech: "She had taken us up in her great strong arms and carried us safely over the slough of difficulty, turning the whole tide in our favor" (quoted in Painter, 168). Osorio reminds us that true solidarity enables us all to recognize difference. I have placed the words of my mother alongside those of women over the centuries so that we can better recognize this solidarity among our differences.

Nabila Hijazi highlights some of the ways women have found to work within their own religious beliefs to argue for change. Zainab Al-Ghazali, a Muslim Egyptian, took the action of ultimately rejecting the Egyptian Feminist Union, which emulated the Western secularization of women. Identifying the liberatory nature of Islam, she embraced rather than erased domestic traditional gender roles and worked for change within her own religious tradition (in this volume, see Chapter 4). Self-reliant, my mother seems to have developed her own means of resistance to the pressures of being a returning student, a mother of five, a pregnant wife, and a homemaker, surviving within the traditions of that life.

My father is mentioned in the letters no more than two or three times and primarily in reference to future visits with the girls while they are at Harbison. He is essentially an absent presence due to his travels around a portion of the state where there were few organized churches, as a Sunday school missionary for the Board of National Missions of the Presbyterian Church in the USA.

This exercise in exploring portions of my mother's letters in an attempt to learn more about her through the lives of the women in this collection over the ages has enabled me to think more about her dreams and desires, not from the perspective of a four-year-old but from the viewpoint of a woman taking stock of her own life. Keeping in mind Enoch and Scott's caution not to elide clear differences and reduce multiplicities to singularities, these essays can still enrich our own searches for our foremothers.

EPILOGUE

> *"I speak for the colored women of the South, because it is there that the millions of blacks in this country have watered the soil with blood and tears, and it is there too that the colored woman of America has made her characteristic history, and there her destiny is evolving."*
>
> —Anna Julia Cooper,
> *The Voice of Anna Julia Cooper* (1893), 202

NOTES

1. Harbison was relocated from Abbeville to Irmo, South Carolina, in 1911. It eventually became a coeducational institution, supported by the Presbyterian Church. In 1946, it was renamed Harbison Junior College and served the educational needs of Black men and women until 1958 when it closed.

2. While many cities had electricity by the 1930s, many families in rural areas did not have electricity until the 1940s. Apparently others in nearby areas did, since my grandfather went for bulbs. My brother recently pointed out that we had a Kelvinator in the house, which the family had brought with them from North Carolina, but it was not functional until we got electricity.

3. Barber-Scotia College in Concord, North Carolina, was one of the first Black institutions built after the Civil War. It offered Black women training as social workers and teachers.

WORKS CITED

Cooper, Anna Julia. "Remarks at the 1893 Chicago World's Fair." *The Voice of Anna Julia Cooper*, edited by Charles Lemert and Esme Bhan, Lanham: Rowman & Littlefield, 1998, pp. 201–05.

Costen, Melva Wilson. "From the Baptismal Font into a Life of Service." *Celebrating Our Call: Ordination Stories of Presbyterian Women*, edited by Patricia Lloyd-Sidle. Louisville: Geneva P, 2006, pp. 77–86.

Painter, Nell Irvin. *Sojourner Truth, A Life, A Symbol*. New York: W.W. Norton, 1996.

Wilson, Azzie Lee Ellis. Unpublished Letters. June–July 1941. In the author's possession. I'm mindful that these letters were personal. My two surviving siblings—my brother, John, Jr., and Melva—were helpful in answering questions, to the extent our collective memories allowed, and I am grateful for their insights.

Contributors

Jane Donawerth, Emerita Professor of English and Affiliate in Women's Studies, is a Distinguished Scholar-Teacher and former director of Academic Writing at the University of Maryland. She has published nine books in Rhetoric or Early Modern Studies, including *Conversational Rhetoric: The Rise and Fall of a Women's Tradition, 1600 to 1900* with Southern Illinois University Press, *Rhetorical Theory by Women before 1900: An Anthology, Selected Letters, Orations, and Rhetorical Dialogues* by Madeleine de Scudéry (translated with Julie Strongson), *Women, Writing, and the Reproduction of Culture* (with three of her former graduate students), and *Shakespeare and the Sixteenth-Century Study of Language.* Her most recent book, an edition of Margaret Fell's rhetorical writings, was co-edited with Rebecca Lush. Dr. Donawerth was a founding editor of the award-winning *Early Modern Women: An Interdisciplinary Journal.* She has won seven teaching awards, two NEH fellowships, and career awards for her work on early modern women's writings (from the Society for the Study of Early Modern Women), and for gender and science fiction (from the International Association for the Fantastic in the Arts). She now divides her time between Arizona (grandkids) and Maryland (research and writing).

Jessica Enoch is Professor of English and Director of the Academic Writing Program at the University of Maryland. Her recent publications include *Domestic Occupations: Spatial Rhetorics and Women's Work*; *Mestiza Rhetorics: An Anthology of Mexicana Activism in the Spanish-Language Press, 1887–1922* (co-edited with Cristina Ramírez), *Women at Work: Rhetorics of Gender and Labor* (co-edited with David Gold), and *Retellings: Opportunities for Feminist Research in Rhetoric and Composition Studies* (co-edited with Jordynn Jack).

At the University of Maryland, **Danielle Griffin** is a PhD Candidate. Her research interests include feminist historiography, the history of literacy, and early modern studies. She is currently working on her dissertation, which explores the literacy practices and skills of working women in early modern England.

Nabila Hijazi holds a PhD in Language, Writing, and Rhetoric from the University of Maryland. Her research interests include multilingual writing, intercultural communication, Muslim women's rhetoric, and refugee women's literacy practices.

Professor Emerita **Shirley Wilson Logan** retired from the English department at the University of Maryland. She has published books and essays on the rhetorical performances of nineteenth-century African American speakers and writers and on composition theory. She currently co-edits, with Cheryl Glenn, the SIU Press series Rhetorics and Feminisms.

At Mississippi State University, **Elizabeth Ellis Miller** is assistant professor of English. Her work appears in *Rhetoric Review* and *College English*. She is writing a book about the rhetorics of civil rights mass meetings.

Karen Nelson is Director of Research Initiatives and Co-Director of the Center for Literary & Comparative Studies in the Department of English at the University of Maryland and serves as Editor for the *Sixteenth Century Journal*. Publications include articles on Spenser, Shakespeare, and early modern women writers, and co-edited and edited collections on early modern women's lives and works.

Associate Professor of English and affiliate faculty member and former director of UMBC's Judaic Studies Program, **Michele Osherow**'s publications include several articles on Shakespeare, the Bible, and early modern women, and she is author of *Biblical Women's Voices in Early Modern England* (Ashgate 2009). She also serves as Resident Dramaturg for Folger Theatre, part of the Folger Shakespeare Library in Washington D.C. where she has contributed to over forty productions.

Ruth Osorio is an Assistant Professor of Rhetoric and Women's Studies at Old Dominion University. Her scholarship on feminist, queer, and disability activist rhetoric has appeared in *enculturation*, *Rhetoric Review*, and *Peitho*.

Erin A. Sadlack is Professor of English at Marywood University in Scranton, Pennsylvania. Her book on Mary Tudor, the French queen, and women's letter-writing, titled *The French Queen's Letters: Mary Tu-*

dor Brandon and the Politics of Marriage in Sixteenth-Century Europe, was published by Palgrave Macmillan in 2011 as part of its Queenship and Power series. She is currently editing Shakespeare's *Romeo and Juliet* for *Linked Early Modern Drama Online (LEMDO)* and working on her next project, a study of Elizabethan petition letters.

From 1986 to 2011, **Adele Seeff** served as Director of the Center for Renaissance & Baroque Studies at the University of Maryland. Now an independent scholar, she publishes in the area of Shakespeare in performance and teaches part time. Her latest book, *South Africa's Shakespeare and the Drama of Language and Identity* (Palgrave Macmillan) appeared in 2018.

Lisa Zimmerelli is associate professor and chair in the writing department at Loyola University Maryland. She won the *Rhetoric Society Quarterly* Charles Kneupper Award for best essay in 2013. For her work in community engagement, she won the Loyola University Maryland Faculty Award for Excellence in Engaged Scholarship in 2015. Among her publications are *Nineteenth-Century American Activist Rhetorics* and *The Bedford Guide for Writing Tutors* and essays in *Rhetoric Society Quarterly*, *Rhetoric Review*, *WLN: A Journal of Writing Center Scholarship*, and *Writing Center Journal*.

INDEX